Writers of the 21st Century
PHILIP K. DICK

Edited by

MARTIN HARRY GREENBERG

and

JOSEPH D. OLANDER

philip k.
dick

TAPLINGER PUBLISHING COMPANY / NEW YORK

First Edition

Published in the United States in 1983 by
TAPLINGER PUBLISHING CO., INC.
New York, New York

Library of Congress Cataloging in Publication Data
Main entry under title:

Philip K. Dick.

  (Writers of the 21st century)
  Bibliography: p.
  Includes index.
  1. Dick, Philip K.—Criticism and interpretation
—Addresses, essays, lectures. I. Greenberg,
Martin Harry. II. Olander, Joseph D. III. Series.
PS3554.I3Z79   813.'54   77-76723
ISBN 0-8008-6292-9   AACR2
ISBN 0-8008-6291-0 (pbk.)

CONTENTS

Introduction: Philip K. Dick

BARRY N. MALZBERG

IT IS ALL THERE in the introduction* to *The Golden Man* (1980), written less than three years before he died of a massive stroke at fifty-four:

> In reading the stories included in this volume, you should bear in mind that most were written when SF was so looked down upon that it virtually was not there, in the eyes of all America. This was not funny, the derision felt toward SF writers. It made our lives wretched . . . people would say, "But are you writing anything serious?" We made no money . . . and really cruel abuse was inflicted on us. To select SF writing as a career was an act of self-destruction; in fact, most *writers*, let alone other people, could not even conceive of someone considering it. . . .

> . . . I have a lot of anger in me. I always have had. Last week my doctor told me that my blood pressure is elevated again and there now seems to be a cardiac complication. I got mad. Death makes me mad. Human and animal suffering makes me mad; whenever one of my cats dies I curse God and I mean it; I feel fury at him. I'd like to get him here where I could interrogate him, tell him that I think the world is screwed up, that man didn't sin and fall but was pushed—which is bad enough—but was then sold the lie that he is basically sinful, which I know he is not.

---

*Reprinted in this volume under the title, "Now Wait for This Year."

. . . Wives come and go; girlfriends come and go; we SF writers stay
together until we literally die . . . which I may do at any time (probably
to my own secret relief. . .)

This essay is an introduction to a book of essays, many of them
written by professors—*professors*—about the works and vision
of Philip K. Dick who, if he had stayed a little less mad, might
have lived to see it, might have lived to see this incontrovertible
evidence that he had broken through, that his work was indeed
now taken seriously and that like few writers of his (or any) time
he had survived his losses. Phil Dick would have enjoyed this
book, I think, just as he enjoyed much of his last half-decade: the
works coming back into print, the beautiful uniform editions from
the Gregg Press, the movie production of his novel *Do Androids
Dream of Electric Sheep?* (retitled *Blade Runner* for the film)
which will surely break him into an enormous popular audience,
too. But I think that to leave the issue at that is to miss the point
because Phil Dick enjoyed *all* of it—the Ace Doubles, the serial
sales to *Worlds of Tomorrow*, the cover *Fantasy & Science Fiction* gave him for "Cantata 140," the conventions, the fans, the
slow confirming assurances from the post-assassination era that
his vision was not merely predictive, it was confluent. "He loved
being Phil Dick, the great science fiction writer," a colleague
wrote to me; "the rest of his life might have been squalor but he
loved his career and the field kept him alive." I take that to be
true. Philip K. Dick who died too young in too much pain was not
a victim of science fiction but, in a way, its great beneficiary. The
field sustained him, endured him, accepted his work when his
literary novels would not sell, paid him and gave him an audience
while the literary novels languished. "When are you going to
write something serious?" He *was* writing something serious and
if only science fiction at that time could see it, that was not the
fault of the field but to its enormous credit.

One has to talk about context: it is not likely that a writer as
individual, as idiosyncratic, as *driven* as Phil Dick could have
succeeded within the context of the non-genre markets during the
Fifties, certainly not at the level of haste of composition which led
him, as he sought to live upon his writing, to turn out six to eight
first-draft novels a year. It was not so much the crudity and un-

polished nature of the writing (which could, when there were editors, have been worked over) that mattered as the insistence of the vision, the strange, rending, off-center visions which probed at the borders of reality and finally ruptured reality itself. This was difficult work and even if it had been carefully done, there is some question as to whether it would have been received outside of science fiction. Perhaps the only American literary writers of this period who could even be compared to Dick were William Burroughs and Hubert Selby, Jr., and both were regarded as marginal figures; certainly neither of them was prolific.

Much has been written of the material and vision of Philip K. Dick for this volume and little insight need be added to the professorial, but perhaps a word might be said about the context in which this work appeared and why Phil Dick and science fiction were so amiable to one another. Science fiction has always accommodated the off-center, the extrapolative or the technologically abstruse. Phil Dick, a classic third-generation Fifties writer, came to this body of speculation in a fashion of commentary which perhaps made time travel, alien visitation, and the confluence of alternate worlds metaphoric rather than simply speculative, but the field in which his work was appearing had a readership so accustomed to taking those ideas for granted that for a long time his work, for the bulk of that audience, appeared to be almost indistinguishable from the stories and novels by which it was surrounded. Although a few aficionados were alive to Dick's implication, most of the science fiction audience was not; it took many years, perhaps twenty, for Dick's work to be perceived as surrealistic rather than technological in its essential intent. In the pulp markets' ability to absorb for their audience work of this ambition without causing a ripple can be seen both science fiction's magnificence and its plight: it remains a great open field for experimentation of a certain kind and the advancement of a body of work; on the other hand, it prints and distributes that material in a fashion indistinguishable from most of what is published within the genre for an audience which cannot really tell the difference. The outcome—and Dick was perhaps the paradigm of the modern American science fiction writer in this regard—is a certain relative ease of publication and an initial sense of appreciation which can lead quickly to prolificacy and a career, followed by a subsequent, leaching despair as the writer begins to perceive how indistinguishably extinct superior work can become, in a relatively short period of time, in a genre largely perceived as being indistinguishable not only outside but within its own audience.

Dick lived through all of this. As Robert Silverberg has commented, there is a certain kind of heroism in the way that he went on, writing his novels under great pressure for small advances, inching forward his body of work regardless of the difficulties of the market, the indifference of all but his core audience; he persisted for almost two decades until overwhelming medical and political problems did him under; but he returned in the mid-Seventies with a new novel and several short stories and never thereafter did his output cease. There is no question but that the damages of the science fiction field for this writer were less than the damages inflicted by other areas of his life, and there is no question either that his talent remained essentially intact or that toward the very end of his life he was moving, in the mystical, elegiac short stories, toward an entirely different kind of work. There is no saying what he might have done over the next decade, and the fact that he might well have done it removes any sting of indictment from science fiction: science fiction might have kept Philip K. Dick poor but it did not, ultimately, do him in.

Or at least, that is one way of looking at the matter . . . that but for the terrible cerebral accidents which took his life, Dick might have gone on and on and, in the wake of the audience and publisher support which awaited him after *Blade Runner*, have gone on to do work which in its resonance and more careful craft would have transcended the body of work he left with us. There is another way to consider the matter, however, and I have believed it to be this way for a long time: first-rate writers, composers, artists or performers give us exactly what is in themselves to give and their creative lives are not truncated but complete—Mozart's sensibility and his mad output were framed by the fact that somewhere, possibly in the cells, he knew he would die at thirty-six; F. Scott Fitzgerald had (as he wrote) functioned under the "authority of failure" all his life; from Nijinsky's madness the fervor of his dance was struck. Dick functioned from the outset under the assumption that he would die before the years that his

generation had been allotted. The work is filled with the same
rage that roiled his blood and cooked the brain; the mad, unreel-
ing visions of all of the $1500 paperback original novels originated
from a man who deep within himself knew that he was not going
to last long. All the characters in the novels and short stories are
doomed: some of them meet that doom with the kind of gaiety
which informs "Oh, to Be a Blobel!" or "The War with the
Fnools"; others, of course, like the man in the high castle, go to
the condition of common oblivion solemnly or broken. But
nowhere in any of the collected works is there other than a poised
acceptance of the truncated nature of human existence and the
folly of rational plans, long-range ambitions; these works are so
informed by the condition of abysmal forces yanking at the parti-
tions which define existence that, retrospectively, it is almost
impossible to imagine them written by a man who did not for most
of his life work within the tight confines of the pulp markets for an
uncomprehending audience and miniscule advances and who did
not die at fifty-four when seemingly on the brink of his Payoff
Years.

The difference between writers of the first rank and those who
are not, I thought in the wake of Phil Dick's death, is that the
first-raters always—*always*—make their lives part of their Collected Works, they manage to bring their "reality fix" into such
order that it becomes inextricably bound with their vision. The
second-raters (or worse) plug along, filling up the pages, doing
what they can, now and then making a strike or two; but the
first-raters *are* their work, their condition and their end not
merely prophesied in their fiction but bound to it. Phil Dick's life
and death stand on the shelf with *Ubik*, *Solar Lottery*, and *The
Man Who Japed*, and all the others, as part of the oeuvre.

So, ultimately, what is there to say? In early 1981, Dick wrote
his agent at Scott Meredith, Russell Galen, a long, frightened
letter. Dick had had a blackout while driving on the freeway—a
blackout which the doctors put down to exhaustion but which for
Dick clearly prefigured the end which was to come just a year
later. Dick wrote at length and movingly about what he felt to be
the accumulated damages of functioning for three decades at the
center of American science fiction, of the penalty he was paying
for having asked too much of himself for too little, too long; he

sensed that the damages were irreparable and for him nothing would be the same again. He talked of getting away from writing, even getting away from the field, taking a long rest, trying to do something else. But even as all of this was happening, he struggled to complete the manuscript for *The Transmigration of Timothy Archer* (his last book, then titled *Bishop Timothy Archer*) for Timescape/Pocket Books, he worked on the galleys of *The Divine Invasion*, and he accepted an invitation to return as guest of honor to the Metz convention in France which he so loved. It is very doubtful that for Phil Dick there was any way out at all; his persona was inseparable from his career and if he was not an American science fiction writer, he came to realize, then he was nothing at all.

So he is gone and *Blade Runner* has been released and this book honors him and it is all over for him, for a while anyway. The field sustained him—at a certain cost—but the act of life itself is exposition to that which we select to kill us; even the most routine of science fiction writers know *that*. Because he was accepted by science fiction he chose to write within it; because science fiction honored him, Phil Dick was able, in his way, to honor the field. So it will go, on and on, the inspiriting and the destructive fused as, in this most ambivalent of all fields, the memory and impress of its most ambivalent writer remains to tell us certain small finalities.

BARRY N. MALZBERG
NEW JERSEY
1982

1. Toward the Transcendent: An Introduction to *Solar Lottery* and Other Works*

THOMAS M. DISCH

THERE ARE, by now, many "science fictions," but for myself (and for any reader) there is really only one science fiction—the kind I like. When I want to find out if someone else's idea of science fiction corresponds significantly with mine (and whether, therefore, we're liable to enjoy talking about the stuff), I have a simple rule-of-thumb: to wit, do they know—and admire—the work of Philip K. Dick?

An active dislike, as against mere ignorance, would suggest either of two possibilities to me. If it is expressed by an otherwise voracious consumer of the genre, one who doesn't balk at the prose of Roger Zelazny, van Vogt, or Robert Moore Williams, I am inclined to think him essentially unserious, a "fan" who is into science fiction entirely for escapist reasons. If, on the other hand, he is provably a person of enlightenment and good taste and he nevertheless doesn't like Dick, then I know that *my* kind of science fiction will always remain inaccessible. For those readers who require the genre always to aspire to the condition of art,

---

*This chapter originally appeared, in slightly different form, as the "Introduction" to the hardcover reprint edition of *Solar Lottery* (Boston: Gregg Press, 1976). "Introduction" © 1976 by Thomas M. Disch.

Philip Dick is just too nakedly a hack, capable of whole chapters of turgid prose and of bloopers so grandiose you may wonder, momentarily, whether they're not just his little way of winking at his fellow laborers in the pulps. Even his most well-realized characters have their moments of wood, while in his bad novels (which are few), there are no characters, only names capable of dialogue. His plots may limp or they may soar, but they don't hang together. In short, he is not a bard in fealty to Apollo, not a "literary" writer.

What sets Philip Dick apart and lets him transcend the ordinary categories of criticism is simply: genius. A genius, what's more, that smells scarcely at all of perspiration despite a published output, over the last twenty years, of thirty-one novels and four collections of stories. Perhaps I'm being unfair to an art that conceals art, but the effect of his best books is of the purest eye-to-hand first-draft mastery. He tells it as he *sees* it, and it is the quality and clarity of his Vision that makes him great. He takes in the world with the cleansed, uncanny sight of another Blake walking about London and being dumbfounded by the whole awful unalterable human mess in all its raddled glory. Not always an enviable knack. Vision, if you're not well trained in its use, is what bad trips are made of; and most of us, given the choice, will avoid the roads that tend in that direction. So, possibly, it is the very excellence of Dick's books that has kept readers away.

Not all readers, of course. There is a fair-sized and growing cult that faithfully buys each new book before it passes from the paperback racks into oblivion. But by comparison to the science fiction writers who have made a name for themselves in the Real World, who can be bought at the SuperValu and are taught in the trendier tenth-grade classrooms, by comparison to the likes of Asimov, Bradbury, Clarke, or Vonnegut, Dick might as well be an avant-garde poet or a composer of electronic music. The public hasn't heard of him.

It isn't fair. If he were guilty of metaphors or some such elitist practice that makes books hard to read, you could understand people being leery of him, but Dick is as democratic as Whitman, as demotic as Spillane. When at his best he is—even by "literary" standards—terrific. His prose is as plain and as sturdy as Shaker furniture, his characters as plausible as your next-door neighbors, his dialogue as authentic as a Watergate transcript, and his plots go rattling along with more ideas per paragraph than the College Outline Series' *Introduction to Western Philosophy*. He makes you laugh, he makes you cry, he makes you think, and think again: who could ask for more?

So what went wrong? Why have so many sf writers who are clearly his inferiors (naming no names) been so much more successful in the marketplace—and even in attracting the attention of academics, who, after all, are supposed to be able to recognize Quality? The simplest theory is "that's the breaks." A careless agent sold his first books to what was then the worst of all paperback houses, and for years he was stuck on a treadmill of speedwriting to meet deadline after deadline, world without end. The wondrous thing is that instead of being broken by this system and declining into a stumblebum twilight of hackwork, drunk on the Gallo burgundy of fannish adulation (many the bright young writer who has vanished into that Sargasso!), Dick moved steadily from strength to strength with no other reward (excepting a single Hugo Award for *The Man in the High Castle* in 1963) than the consciousness of having racked up yet another Triple-Star Bonanza score on the great literary pinball machine in the sky.

That's one theory. The theory I prefer is that Dick's books have failed to win a mass audience precisely because of their central excellence—their truth to life. Not that Dick (or *any* other science fiction writer, for that matter) is in the Prediction Sweepstakes. Forecasting the future is best left to Jeanne Dixon and the Rand Corporation; science fiction has better things to do. The truths of science fiction (in its platonic form) and of Philip K. Dick are prophetic truths in the Old Testament sense, home truths about here, now, and forever.

Also, they're dark truths. Any reader with the least proclivity toward positive thinking, anyone whose lapel button shows a sappy grin, anyone, in short, who still believes in the essential decency, or even feasibility, of the System is liable to experience one of Dick's novels as a direct assault on his sanity. Indeed, that, in a nutshell, is the plot of what many hold to be his most mindbending novel, *The Three Stigmata of Palmer Eldritch*.

For all that, Dick isn't really one of that infamous Brotherhood of Blackness that includes Swift, Beckett, William Burroughs, and the suicide brigades of modern poetry. There is too much of the sunlight and wine of California in him to let Dick qualify for the deepest abysm of Literature.

Perhaps the problem is his evasiveness, the way his worlds refuse, iridescently, to stay in any kind of unequivocal moral focus. (As against the clear blacks and whites of Heinlein's homilies, or even the subtly graduated grays of Ursula LeGuin's.) Guys you thought were on Our Side end up acting like monsters—even, or especially, such guys as God. Dick is slippery, a game-player whose rules (what is possible, and what isn't, within the world of his invention) change from book to book, and sometimes from chapter to chapter. His adversary in these games is—who else?—the reader, which means that as fun as his books are, as smooth as they are, they are also surprisingly strenuous.

There is a form of the board game Monopoly called Rat in which the Banker, instead of just sitting there and watching, gets to be the Rat. The Rat can alter all the rules of the game at his discretion, like Idi Amin. The players elect the person they consider the slyest and nastiest among them to be the Rat. The trick in being a good Rat is in graduating the torment of the players, in moving away from the usual experience of Monopoly, by the minutest calibrations, into, finally, an utter delirium of lawlessness. If you think you might enjoy Rat a bit more than a standard game of Monopoly then you should probably try reading Philip Dick.

Where to begin?

Not, in fact, with the book in hand, *Solar Lottery*. While it is far from being one of his downright losers (by all accounts, *Our Friends from Frolix 8* takes the cake in that category), neither is it a book by which converts may be won. In this respect, it is like the early work of many titans-to-be.

Few readers approaching Shakespeare by way of *Titus Andronicus* and *Henry VI* would feel awfully impelled to plunge on. Similarly, Henry James' first novel, *Watch and Ward*, does not represent the Master at his most enticing. First novels are interesting, usually, as grindstones for the sharpening of hindsight. They show us the size and shape of the still unfaceted diamond, but to appreciate them properly one must first have some notion of the diamond in its polished state.

So: if there are readers of this introduction who are as yet unacquainted with Dick's masterpieces, I'd advise them to begin with two or three of those and then return to *Solar Lottery*. (An alternative course, and not necessarily a worse one, if you possess unbounded faith, is to begin with *Solar Lottery* and read all the rest in sequence.) Having read *The Man in the High Castle*, *Martian Time-Slip*, *The Three Stigmata of Palmer Eldritch*, and *Do Androids Dream of Electric Sheep?*, and the novella "Faith of Our Fathers," which are my nominations for Dick's quintessential and all-time classics, one may then return to *Solar Lottery* with an eye for all the excellences that exist here in, as it were, an embryonic state.

Solar Lottery is also illuminating with regard to all that Dick had in common with his predecessors and his peers in that long-ago year of 1955 when *Solar Lottery* was published. Even the highest and loneliest artists are engaged in a communal endeavor. Art is a vineyard in which all contemporaries—Kyd and Shakespeare, James and the myriad manufacturers of penny-dreadfuls, Dick and . . . whoever—work side by side, in a perpetual condition of reciprocal influence and aid. Dick's influence on later writers is clear enough. It seems highly unlikely that Ursula Le-Guin would have written *The Lathe of Heaven* without an example of such earlier adventures in solipsism as Dick's *Eye in the Sky* and *The Three Stigmata of Palmer Eldritch*. What *his* inspiration may have been is less readily evident, especially if one's acquaintance is limited to the works of his maturity, in which early influences have either been assimilated or eliminated. In *Solar Lottery* this is not the case, and it offers us an ideal middle ground from which to view both the heights of what is to come and the common grounds from which these were to spring.

Solar Lottery first appeared in 1955 as half of an Ace Double Novel. (A badly edited edition of the book appeared the next year in England from Rich & Cowan, under the title *World of Chance*. Its copy editor showed unerring literary tact in eliminating, wherever possible, all the book's more inspired passages. Truly, a monument of what may be achieved by patient mediocrity!) Unlike the novel on the flipside of the American edition, Leigh Brackett's *The Big Jump, Solar Lottery* was not first published serially. A yellow blurb above the red-and-white title declares: "FIRST PRIZE WAS THE EARTH ITSELF!" (This, if inaccurate, does try to make sense of the title, a task that the novel itself never fully undertakes—probably because the title was not of the author's choosing.) The cover art shows a man in a spacesuit hurling a red boulder at a speck of a man (unsuited) below him on a cratered plain of celadon green. For a wonder, this scene does derive from the novel (the close of Chapter 12), right down to the paradoxical detail of the person walking about on the moon without so much as a snorkel. There is this further oddity—that the threatened figure is the villain, his threatener one of the minor heroes, and it is he who is actually in danger at this moment. Even in this early novel, things aren't what they seem.

What is being promised by such a cover, and what Dick in fact delivers (if somewhat grudgingly) is an action-adventure set in the future world of 2203 (and in outer space), a story with heroes and villains, with a beginning, a middle, and an end. By comparison to almost any of his later books, *Solar Lottery* seems conservative in dramatic conception and (except for the rare flare-up) restrained, even perfunctory, in execution. A journeyman space opera. It is, after all, the first published book of a young man who could not know, at that point in his career, the degree to which he might be permitted to depart from the established ceremonies of an Ace Double.

The nature of that ceremony and the requirements it places on its celebrants are very much at issue here. As with other rigid dramatic forms, such as the Western or the requiem mass, the artist must find how to be sincere within the narrow bounds of the form given him. Most pulp science fiction never gets off the ground because most hack writers write cynically, parroting the early, genuine successes of the genre without tracing them back to their emotional, intellectual, and aesthetic sources. (Ditto for Westerns and requiem masses.) But it is always possible. Witness the Westerns of Bud Boetticher and Sergio Leone. Witthe requiems of Mozart (a Freemason) and Verdi (an atheist). Witness the science fiction of Philip Dick.

I've written at length elsewhere (in "The Embarrassments of Science Fiction," which appears in Peter Nicholls' 1976 critical anthology *Science Fiction at Large)* concerning the emotional dynamics of pulp science fiction, the ways in which the needs of its audience dictated the form and content of classic space opera. In that essay I maintain that through most of its history science fiction has been a lower-class literature that purveyed compensatory power fantasies specially aimed at readers sensitive to their social and educational shortcomings. At its most intense and obsessive, in science fiction fandom, this purpose becomes so overriding that fans may well be likened to Jehovah's Witnesses, whose millennialist theology is likewise calculated to feed the insatiable hungers and nurse the unhealing wounds of those among the oppressed who would still resist their despair. If this is so, one may better understand why ordinary literary criteria are not only a matter of indifference to readers of science fiction but are actually a matter of alarm: the sheer urgency of their need is so great that so long as the need is satisfied nothing else matters. The clarity that Art brings represents an unwanted degree of illumination. Some actions are best performed in the dark.

The writers who most perfectly fit the above description are L. Ron Hubbard and A. E. van Vogt. Hubbard left the genre relatively early in his career to found his own religion (one which precisely delineates the interface of fandom and millennial religion). Van Vogt simply wrote. And wrote simply: his books make the productions of such other founding fathers of proletarian pulp as Dashiel Hammett and Raymond Chandler look like mandarin poetry. His prose rises above the laws of rhetoric and approaches the condition of phatic noise, the direct communication of emotional states by means of grunts and groans.

Now, if there is a single writer who may be said to have exerted a forming influence on the author of *Solar Lottery,* it is A. E. van Vogt. It is possible, as well, to hear echoes of more sophisticated voices, specifically those of Bester and Kornbluth/Pohl. Like *The Demolished Man, Solar Lottery* is about a crime that must be carried out despite a corps of telepathic guards. Like *The Space Merchants,* it presents a world of systematic and ironic reversals, as in the contrast between the random choice of a world president and the very orderly convention called to elect that leader's assassin. (This Erewhonian procedure would reach its apotheosis in the geopolitical ingenuities of *The Man in the High Castle*.) Yet it would be several years before Dick could be said to have rivaled or beaten Bester and Kornbluth/Pohl at their own game. In the case of van Vogt, Dick has certainly done just that even at this early point in his career. In a sense, *Solar Lottery* is van Vogt's best novel.

The opening of *Solar Lottery* is substantially identical to that of van Vogt's most characteristic work, *The World of Null-A*. In both books a down-and-out hero is on his way to what seems a cross between a final exam and a job interview. Though suffering momentary doubts as to his ability to succeed, it is suggested that each hero's apparent lack of success so far has been due to bad luck and, possibly, lack of effort. But this time, the story promises, the hero *will* try, and he does, and as a result he ends up in the last chapter as President of the Universe. It is the plot skeleton of the Brave Little Tailor and a hundred fairy tales besides. But with this difference, that the readers of science fiction may be presumed to be older and to have a somewhat solider grasp on reality (where fantasies of infantile omnipotence don't stand much of a chance). Some reason, however spurious, must be offered for the hero's success. He is surrounded not only with rockets and blasters to tickle the readers' sense of wonder but also with such plausibilities as coffee cups and contemporary (to 1955) urban landscapes, like this one: "Across the street a looming hotel shielded a motley family of parasitic stores and dilapidated business establishments: loan shops, cigar stores, girl houses, bars" (*SL*, 2). Further, pseudoscience is called on to explain the hero's specialness. In van Vogt's *The World of Null-A*, the hero, Gilbert Gosseyn, by his mysterious command of the non-Aristotelian logic of the title (an elusive discipline borrowed from a once-faddish movement called General Semantics), is destined to triumph over those ignorant sods and highbrow Establishment Scientists still mired in the old-fashioned Aristotelian logic of either/or. In fact, not much is ever really made of null-A logic, for the sufficient reason, I would think, that not much can be.

The *real* reason a van Vogt hero wins through is that his innate genetic superiority (and the author's predestining hand) has thrust greatness on him. *Slan* is the supreme example in his corpus of paranoid racism, while the Null-A books offer his most full-blown Superman. The political implications of these traditional "sci-fi" themes have been exhaustively and hilariously dealt with in Norman Spinrad's 1972 satire, *The Iron Dream,* a novel written as if it were the work of Adolph Hitler. Dick, in 1955, could not be so audacious as Spinrad in the 1970s. He was committed to producing a novel of van Vogtian intrigue that would provide its readers with their traditional vicarious satisfactions. That he has found a way to do so that no longer need offend a liberal sensibility is no mean achievement.

Consider Dick's use of Game Theory. Though not so questionable a discipline as van Vogt's General Semantics, it was being used in the 1950s as a kind of intellectual smokescreen for U.S. foreign-policy decisions that would have appeared much more unseemly without such scholastic trappings. In an author's note in the front matter of the Ace edition of *Solar Lottery,* Dick writes: "I became interested in the Theory of Games, first in an intellectual manner (like chess) and then with a growing uneasy conviction that Minimax was playing an expanding role in our national life. . . . Both the U.S. and the Soviet Union employ Minimax strategy as I sit here. While I was writing *Solar Lottery,* Van Neumann, the co-inventor of the Games Theory, was named to the Atomic Energy Commission, bearing out my belief that Minimax is gaining on us all the time." This is certainly alarming, but then no more is made of Game Theory until well into the penultimate chapter of the book, when there is a flurry of Minimax terminology followed by some hugger-mugger between the leading ladies. There *is* a lottery by which the Quizmaster (President of the Universe) is selected, but it is the simplest kind of lottery, and in no way requires Game Theory to be understood. Game Theory, in short, has about as much to do with Dick's story as the logic of Aristotle, or its refutation, has to do with *The World of Null-A.* It is a bit of legerdemain calculated to give the guileless reader a sense that the book is about Something Important, a name to drop if not a whole idea. The difference is that in van Vogt such hocus-pocus is associated with the Good Guys; in

Dick (as in real life) it is associated primarily with the Bad Guys.

Consider the social landscape of *Solar Lottery*. Like van Vogt, Dick is writing for the proverbial "little man," for readers who will feel an instant bond of kinship for the elderly Cartwright when he is challenged by the villain, Herb Moore, in these terms:

> "You can't operate this [the post of Quizmaster/President]. This isn't your line. What are you? I examined the records. . . . You had ten years of nominal school in the charity department of the Imperial Hill. You never excelled in anything. From high school on you dropped courses that dealt with symbolization and took manual shop courses. You took welding and electronic repair, that sort of thing." (*SL*, 3)

And here is Dick's epic catalogue of the "unks" (people who lack "classified" ratings—i.e., proletarians) who set off in a rickety ore freighter on a quixotic quest for the Flame Disc (the utopian planet promised to them by their prophet John Preston):

> A bewildering variety of people crowded anxiously around [Cartwright]: Mexican laborers mute and frightened, clutching their belongings, a hard-faced urban couple, a jet stoker, Japanese optical workmen, a red-lipped bed girl, the middle-aged owner of a retail dry goods store that had gone quack, an agronomy student, a patent medicine salesman, a cook, a nurse, a carpenter. . . . These were people with skill in their hands—not their heads. Their abilities had come from years of practice and work, from direct contact with objects. They could grow plants, sink foundations, repair leaking pipes, maintain machinery, weave clothing, cook meals. According to the Classification system, they were failures. (*SL,* 2)

These are the Good Guys clearly. There are two Bad Guys, the super-rich multinational corporation director, Reese Verrick, whom Dick allows to glow with the glamor of power, a glamor entirely denied to the subvillain, Herb Moore, who is obliged to represent so many of the things that Dick dislikes (the servility of the Organization Man, the desexed rationality of a behavioral scientist, etc.) that he never coheres as a character. Moore creates a kind of golem for Verrick, the purpose of which is to assassinate the usurping (but benevolent) Cartwright. Which is to say: Money rules the world and shores up its power, whenever threatened, by its control of Science (a Science that is, for that reason, dehumanizing). That is far from being the sole or even a primary "meaning" of *Solar Lottery*, but it is surely one of the book's underlying assumptions. The chief difference between then (1955) and now is the degree to which, then, left-wing sympathies of any consistency had to be disguised and "translated" into politically neutral language. (Cf., in Pohl/Kornbluth's *The Space Merchants* of 1953, one of the models for *Solar Lottery*, the authors' clever substitution of the imaginary "Consies" [Conservationists] for the dreaded "Commies." An uncannily correct extrapolation.) Again, Dick's use of the Pellig/superman figure may be contrasted to the work of van Vogt, in which the golem/superman is there precisely to afford his readers an unequivocal vicarious delight: *If only It were me!*

Solar Lottery, along with most of its successors, may be read as self-consistent social allegories of a more-or-less Marxist bent. As such they are unique in the annals of American science fiction, whose brightest lights have either been outspokenly right-wing, like Heinlein, or blandly liberal in the manner of Asimov or Bradbury, or else they've back-pedaled after a fire-eating youth, like the post-Kornbluth Pohl. Doubtless this is what has enabled Dick to be excepted from the anathemas of Stanislaw Lem, the Polish writer and critic. But Dick's political imagination, though powerful, is not, I believe, his central strength.

Dick's major theme, the one that consistently calls forth his finest and most forceful work, is transcendence—whether it's possible, what it feels like, and whether that feeling ultimately represents wishful thinking or some larger reality. He is constantly torn between a rationalistic denial of the ultimate reality of transcendent experience and a (still ironic) celebration of the brute fact of it.

Viewed in the light of this concern, many of his themes take on shades of meaning that sort oddly with strict dialectical orthodoxy, or even with any known variety of revisionism. Why, for instance, does he celebrate "people with skill in their hands—not their heads"? Not just because they're underdogs who perform vital work and are denied adequate recompense or recognition. Handicraft, for Dick, is a spiritual discipline, somewhat in the way it was for the Shakers, whose motto, "Hands to work and hearts to God," might well be his own. The most fully developed of Dick's craftsmen/heroes is Frank Frink in *The Man in the High Castle*, a maker of modern silver jewelry. Much of that novel's plot centers around the specifically spiritual quality of Frank's jewelry, a spirituality that in one instance allows another character, Mr. Tagomi, to transcend the terrifying Nazi-dominated world of that novel by, ironically, escaping into our own.

The Prestonites' voyage in quest of the Flame Disc and their discovery, en route, of the seemingly resurrected John Preston represent *Solar Lottery*'s initial sounding of this typical theme. It is not one of the stronger elements in the book, in part simply because it is slighted in Dick's pell-mell rush to get the second half of his advance. But it may also be that the Flame Disc sequences fail because they haven't been sufficiently transformed from orthodox Christian eschatology. Dick is not about to make a declaration for Christ, though he always seems to be flirting symbolically with the possibility. However, his confessional impulse is invariably contradicted by dramatic events of much greater emotional suasion. In *Solar Lottery* the exhumed body of John Preston proves not to be alive, as expected, but a simulacrum. Through all his novels, Dick entertains the possibility that creatures of flesh and blood are all essentially robots, mechanical monads obeying laws of a mechanistic creation. *Do Androids Dream of Electric Sheep?* is his single most compelling vision of man's unredeemably material nature, but there is one moment in *Solar Lottery*, about two-thirds of the way through the book, when the later book's dark paradoxes are powerfully prefigured. To say more would spoil *Solar Lottery*'s finest *coup de theatre*.

This chapter cannot begin to enumerate all Dick's characteristic motifs, much less to analyze their complex interactions. The best I can do is to suggest a context in which Dick's work may be viewed more fruitfully than that of other science fiction stories, and that is the context of romantic poetry, especially the poetry of Blake and Shelley. Both were political radicals whose circumstances prevented them from translating their convictions into political action. Both demonstrated a profound and prophetic understanding of those realms that lay beyond the Age of Reason.

Both were artists of process, prevented by the very urgency of their apprehensions from creating works of classic amplitude and concinnity of form.

This is not to say that readers will find no formal pleasure in Dick's novels, that it is all a matter of snuffling about for truffles of Meaning, as I've been doing here. But his commitment to an aesthetic of process means that, by and large, whatever he writes is what we read. There is no turning back to rethink, revise, or erase. He improvises rather than composes, thereby making his experience of the creative process the focus of his art. This is not a novelty, of course. It is the wager of Scheherazade, too, that she can be interesting and authentic absolutely *all the time,* and this tradition of the novel is as old and as honorable as the more Flaubertian idea of the novel-as-prose-poem that presently holds sway in academia. Within this tradition Dick is one of the immortals by virtue of the sheer fecundity of his invention. Inevitably there are dull patches, days when his typewriter refuses to wake up, but on the whole these are few, and the stretches of song, when they come, are all the more remarkable for being, so visibly, the overflow of a spirit that from Heaven, or near it, pours its full heart in profuse strains of unpremeditated art.

2. The Encounter of Taoism and Fascism in *The Man in the High Castle*

PATRICIA S. WARRICK

PHILIP K. DICK's *The Man in the High Castle,* published seven years after his first novel *Solar Lottery* appeared in 1955, is his only novel to receive a Hugo Award. It is generally regarded as the work introducing his most creative period—that of between 1962 and 1965, when he wrote such acknowledged masterpieces as *Martian Time-Slip, Dr. Bloodmoney,* and *The Three Stigmata of Palmer Eldritch.* Critical opinion regarding *The Man in the High Castle* is mixed, however. Critics commending it have noted that it is well written, presents an imaginative alternative history, maintains narrative suspense, and artfully uses a complex narrative technique. But the novel has also received a substantial number of derogatory comments. It has been noted that: no character has a viewpoint wide enough to see the whole picture;[1] Dick is guilty of a political blunder in assuming a victorious Japanese fascism would be radically better than a German one;[2] the complex narrative structure and variety of characters are dismaying;[3] the ending, in which the novelist Hawthorne Abendsen admits to Juliana Frink that Germany and Japan really lost the war, vitiates the novel as science fiction.

High Castle is generally read as a political novel exploring the topic of fascism. Strangely enough, the central role of Oriental philosophy in the novel has largely been ignored by critics. While allusions in the novel to the *I Ching,* or *Book of Changes,* have been noted, no one except Dick himself has emphasized the major function of not only the *I Ching* but also the overall Taoist philosophy and world view in *High Castle.* In an interview published in *Vertex* in 1974, Dick says he used the *I Ching* as a plotting device for *High Castle.* Indicating that he personally has been using the *I Ching* since 1961 "to show me a way of conduct in a puzzling or unclear situation," he concludes: "If you use the *I Ching* long enough and continually enough, it will begin to change and shape you as a person. It will make you into a Taoist, whether or not you have ever heard the word, whether or not you want to be."[4]

The theme of the horrors of fascism in *High Castle* is obvious and has received considerable critical attention. But until the reader understands that fascism in the novel involves more than Nazi Germany under Hitler, until the reader sees Nazism as a symbol for *all* fascist drives to overpower and control—be they German, Japanese, American, or Russian—he has not explored the fullness of Dick's fictional history. *High Castle* is a work condemning every totalitarian drive—economic, political, and military. At the same time as it condemns fascism, *High Castle* proposes another way by which the ethical man should travel. Opposed to the fascist Western world in *High Castle* is the Oriental way of the Taoist, a view centered in but not limited to the view of the Japanese Trade Mission official, Mr. Tagomi. The central tension of the novel, and the source of much of the narrative suspense, is the encounter of fascism and Taoism. Each of the four major characters—Frank Frink, Juliana Frink, Nobusuke Tagomi, and Robert Childan—dramatizes this encounter; each faces a moment when he or she must choose a way through the chaos of political and economic violence, fraud, change, and intrigue in an alternate world that is technologically of the near future. The complex meanings of the novel are embodied in the four choices. Such a reading of the novel reveals *High Castle* as Dick's most finely wrought novel, one in which all the parts, intricately interlocked, are essential to create a fictional world mirroring reality as Dick envisions it. Because Dick sees much of that reality as mysterious and incomprehensible, the artifice he creates to reflect it must encompass those same elements of mystery and incomprehensibility. The difficulty the reader encounters in readily understanding the novel is to be regarded as a necessary mark of Dick's artistic success—not as an indication of his failure to master novelistic techniques, as some critics charge.[5]

Dick's fascination with the Nazi mentality[6] is apparent in other novels—*The Unteleported Man* (1966) and *The World Jones Made* (1956), for example—but none explores this theme as fully as *High Castle*. *High Castle* describes the German mind as having "an unbalanced quality," "a psychotic streak." Dick suggests that this characteristic is not limited to the Germans alone, however: we all live in a psychotic world where the madmen are in power.[7]

In the alternative history of *High Castle*, Germany and Japan have won World War II and occupy the United States. When the novel begins, Hitler, now allegedly insane, is confined to a mental institution, and Martin Bormann is the Chancellor. This much is science fiction. But all the details of the German political and military factions are accurate extrapolations. One needs only to consult works like William Shirer's *The Rise and Fall of the Third Reich* and *The Goebbels Diary*—texts Dick acknowledges he used in writing the novel—to verify his accuracy.

The Germanic temperament, as Dick dramatizes it, contains elements of romantic idealism; and when these are coupled with a powerful urge to dominate, as they are under Nazism, the imminent destruction or twilight of civilization is at hand. Nietzsche's "splendid blond beast" becomes a giant cannibal, devouring the world.[8] In the novel a group of Nazi officials—Goering, Goebbels, Heydrich, and von Schirach—embody these fascist totalitarian drives, and while the reader almost never directly encounters the high officials in the Partei, he hears commentary from a variety of characters about the ideas and actions of the group of Nazi leaders. Robert Childan, a dealer in American antiques, reviews their post-war accomplishments. They have virtually eliminated "Jews and Gypsies and Bible Students." They have drained the Mediterranean and turned it into tillable farmland. They have almost disposed of the African "aborigines" in just fifteen years. They have taken the lead in space exploration and made the first flights to the moon and Mars. The Germans' ability to create a grandiose "dream that stirs one" (*MHC*, 2), plus their fabulous talent for hard work and efficiency coupled with science and technology, have plunged the whole globe into chaos. And yet, Childan muses, they are unaware of "what they do to others, and the destruction they are causing" (*MHC*, 3).

Juliana Frink, the estranged wife of Frank Frink, muses about the ideas that came from Hitler's diseased brain and developed "first [into] a political party, then a nation, then half the world" (*MHC*, 3). Like evil spores, the blond Germans spread the contamination through the world. After first meeting Joe Cinnadella, she soon identifies the element of death emanating from this fanatical assassin who is urged on by a powerful destructive drive. The problem lies in the fascination of the German mind with the ideal and the abstract, and its divorce from the reality of the social world around it. Rudolph Wegener, himself a German though masquerading as the Swede Baynes, provides the deepest insight into their destructive urge:

> Their view; it is cosmic. Not of a man here, a child there, but an abstraction: race, land. *Volk. Land. Blut. Ehre.* Not of honorable men but of *Ehre* itself, honor; the abstract is real, the actual is invisible to them. *Die Güte,* but not good men, this good man. It is their sense of space and time. They see through the here, the now, into the vast black deep beyond, the unchanging. And that is fatal to life. Because eventually there will be no life; there was once only the dust particles in space, the hot hydrogen gases, nothing more, and it will come again. This is an interval, *ein Augenblick.* The cosmic process is hurrying on, crushing life back into the granite and methane; the wheel turns for all life. It is all temporary. And they—these madmen—respond to the granite, the dust, the longing of inanimate; they want to aid *Natur.*
>
> And, he thought, I know why. They want to be the agents, not the victims, of history. They identify with God's power and believe they are godlike. That is their basic madness. They are overcome by some archetype; their egos have expanded psychotically so that they cannot tell where they begin and the godhead leaves off. It is not hubris, not pride; it is inflation of the ego to its ultimate—confusion between him who worships and that which is worshiped. Man has not eaten God; God has eaten man. (*MHC*, 3)

Jean-Michel Angebert's *The Occult and the Third Reich* (1971) is an extensive nonfictional study of this religious fanaticism described by Dick. Angebert suggests the Nazi cosmology saw Hitler as an apocalyptic prophet and the rise of the Third Reich as the arrival of the Millennium.⁹ The new age could arrive only after the destruction of the old.

The Nazi horror depicted in *High Castle* is brought to a climax when Chancellor Bormann dies and the various fanatical factions in Germany begin a power struggle to claim the chancellorship. Mr. Tagomi, the little Japanese trade official who becomes involved in the intrigue, finds it difficult to comprehend the fascist temperament because it is so foreign to his Taoist mentality. He concludes that the Nazis seem determined to exalt and immolate themselves (*MHC*, 6) and later that German totalitarian society resembles some faulty form of life (*MHC*, 12). Frank Frink, also trying to comprehend the German mind, decides that it is atavistic, that it represents a kind of "prehistoric man in a sterile white lab coat . . . experimenting with uses to which other people's skull, skin, ears, fat could be put" (*MHC*, 1). It horrifies him that this ancient, gigantic cannibal near-man should reappear to rule the world once more after mankind has spent a million years escaping him.

Except for one phone conversation between Goebbels and Consul Hugo Reiss (*MHC*, 11), the reader hears only by indirection about the ideas and actions of the top officials in the Nazi hierarchy who represent fascism in the novel. In contrast, one encounters the Taoist philosophy directly. Tagomi, Frank Frink, Childan, Juliana Frink, and the Japanese couple Betty and Paul Kasoura all serve to define aspects of the Taoist view, and each uses the *I Ching* as an aid in deciding the right action in uncertain situations.

At least a rudimentary understanding of Taoism and the *I Ching* is essential to appreciate the complexity and depth of meaning in *High Castle*. Taoism is a Chinese philosophy containing concepts also found in Hinduism, Buddhism, and Confucianism. The two texts of Taoism are the *Chuang-tzu*, written about 300 B.C., and the *Tao-te Ching* of Lao-tzu, probably written at a slightly later date.¹⁰ These texts are collections of sayings and stories, involving allegories, often ambiguous, that point to some aspect of the meaning of Taoism. Because the Taoist perception of the real world differs essentially from our usual Western one, an easy grasp of its view is not possible. Nor is there a single school of Taoism. There have been many cults with a variety of doctrines which have produced a large body of literature. Consequently, no comprehensive definition of Taoism will be attempted here; we can do no more than note those important elements differentiating it from the ontology of Western rationalism.

The concept of the Tao lies at the heart of Chinese philosophy. In its narrowest sense, *Tao* means a way or a road, and beyond that, the proper way to go or the way of nature. In the broader view of Tao given by Lao-tzu in the *Tao-te Ching*, Tao is the all-controlling principle of the universe. The natural world and all its creatures are created by and are part of the Tao. Because man is "in" the Tao, he cannot separate himself from it to define it. The first three lines of the *Tao-te Ching* say:

> The Tao that can be told is not the eternal Tao
> The name that can be named is not the eternal name
> The nameless is the beginning of Heaven and Earth.[11]

The cosmology of Taoism does not see matter as consisting of discrete building blocks in empty space which can be studied by an observer. Taoism eschews this static, discrete view of reality, holding instead a view of a mobile reality which is a continuum in which movement and matter cannot be differentiated. Reality is a web of time and change, a seamless net of unbroken movement filled with undulations, waves, and patterns or ripples. Motion is ceaseless; consequently nothing is permanent. Because every observer is an integral function of the reality network, it is impossible for anyone to define it. All the separations the observer claims to decipher in the web are no more than fabrications, useful though they may be, and must be understood as merely fictions in the observer's mental stream.[12] The constant flux and incessant transformation of nature is a universal process binding all things into the Great One, and equalizing all things and all opinions.[13] Heaven, earth, and man constitute a single, indivisible unity governed by cosmic law.

Reading this Taoist description of reality, one is struck by the parallels with the nature of reality as defined by modern physics. Joseph Needham notes this similarity in the second volume of *Science and Civilization in China* (1956). More recently and in more detail, *The Tao of Physics* (1975) by Fritjof Capra provides a detailed study of the relationships and parallels between the concepts of modern physics and the basic ideas in the philosophical and religious tradition of the Eastern world. Capra concludes that Western science, proceeding in the rational mode, and Eastern mysticism, working by intuition, have arrived at a similar view of reality:

> We . . . see how the two foundations of twentieth-century physics—quantum theory and relativity theory—both force us to see the world very much in the way a Hindu, Buddhist or Taoist sees it, and how this similarity strengthens when we look at the recent attempts to combine these two theories in order to describe the phenomena of the submicroscopic world: the properties and interactions of the subatomic particles of which all matter is made. Here the parallel between modern physics and Eastern mysticism are most striking, and we . . . often encounter statements where it is almost impossible to say whether they have been made by physicists or by Eastern mystics.[14]

Fundamental to the Taoist philosophy is the concept of *yin* and *yang*. This doctrine holds that all things and events are constituted by the interplay of these two forces. *Yin* is the negative principle: passive, yielding, destructive, cold, wet, dark, mysterious. It is the shade on the north side of a hill, and the south bank of a river, the essence of shadow and water. *Yang* is the positive principle: active, hard, creative, warm, dry, bright. It is the south side of a hill, the north bank of a river, the essence of sunlight and fire.

Taoism describes reality as a pair of opposites incessantly in the process of interacting; the outlook is dynamic, not static. The "end is an ordered nature rather than chaos. In point of process, there is contradiction as well as harmony, and in point of reality, there is unity in multiplicity. The apparent dualism and pluralism are, in each case, a dynamic monism through the dialectic."[15] The complementary view of reality encompassed in the *yin-yang* doctrine reminds one of the notion of complementarity essential to the way modern physicists talk about nature. Niels Bohr, who introduced the notion of complementarity, was aware of its parallels with Chinese thought.[16]

Joseph Needham comments on the similarity of the *yin-yang*

concept to the Hegelian dialectic, noting that the dialectical reconciliation of contradiction into a higher synthesis appears in the Taoist writings.[17] Hegel himself was acquainted with Chinese philosophy; and in his lectures on the history of philosophy given at the University of Heidelberg in 1816, he refers to the Tao and to Lao-tzu.[18]

The dualism of *yin* and *yang* is essentially different from Western philosophical dualism in that no conflict between the two elements is involved. There is no struggle between light and dark, or good and evil. They are complementary aspects of the Great One, and both are necessary to the order of the universe. The path of virtue is the way embracing harmony between the two opposites, and the Tao, the origin of all things, is the source of that order. The aim and task of every man, then, is to find the Tao or way of harmony balancing opposites. Action contrary to nature (known as *wei*) is to be avoided, and its opposite *(wu wei)* to be desired. But one does not strive for *wu wei;* quite the opposite, it is attained by inaction or nonattainment. Spontaneity—an effortless flowing with the moment—achieves harmony. All the major elements of the Taoist view are shared by Dick except the attitude regarding the subject of the existence of evil. Here Dick varies from the Oriental view, because he holds that evil is real, not merely an imbalance of opposites. "Regarding evil," he says, "I am basically Zoroastrian in my theology. I believe in the Gnostic dualism, that this world was created by an evil or false deity who is being overthrown by the Wise Mind."[19]

The *I Ching (Book of Changes)* is a classic text of Confucianism cherished by the Taoists. It considers the incessant movement of the cosmos not as random and chaotic, but as arranged in orderly patterns and cycles. The *I Ching* outlines a rationalistic approach to a well-ordered and dynamic universe.[20] It represents these patterns of change with a series of sixty-four hexagrams. Each hexagram is made up of combinations of six horizontal *yin* and *yang* lines (*yin* is represented by a broken line and *yang* by a solid line.) Each hexagram in turn is divided into two trigrams. There are eight basic trigrams, consisting of all the patterns possible when combining three units of two kinds of lines. The trigrams—the basis of the sixty-four hexagrams—are represented by a triangle, which is a key symbol in *High Castle.*

The triangle is the form Frank Frink uses when he makes the silvery jewelry containing *wu*.

The *I Ching* discusses the sixty-four hexagrams, each of which is given a title and represents a cosmic archetype or pattern of the Tao in nature and in human situations. The *I Ching* is made up of several texts. One, called the Judgment, indicates the course of action appropriate to the cosmic pattern in question. Another text, the Image, elaborates the overall meaning of the hexagram, and this meaning is often expressed in poetic lines. A third text interprets each of the six lines of the hexagram.[21] The user of the *I Ching* brings a question to the book. To determine which hexagram contains the appropriate answer, he constructs the hexagram, using either yarrow stalks or coins to sequentially define each of the six lines as either *yin* or *yang* (broken or solid). Once the pattern of the prevailing hexagram is ascertained, he consults the *I Ching* to discover the disposition of the present situation so he will be able to take the proper action. The *I Ching* for the Taoist is not primarily an aid in knowing the future; more important, it is a book of profound wisdom, pointing to the way of harmony between men, and between men and nature. All the characters in *High Castle* who serve as focal centers for their part of the narrative network consult the *I Ching* regularly.

Returning now to the subject of *High Castle* as an encounter of fascist and Taoist world views, we find that Dick's narrative form, characters, symbols, and themes all combine to describe a world in which the harmony of complementary process has been forced to the precarious edge of an abyss by the fanatical quest of the Nazi fascists. Dick draws on the Taoist philosophy, but—we will discover—he seems to suggest that a revision of this world view is required. The introduction into the contemporary world of a new technological element, the nuclear bomb, makes nuclear holocaust a possibility. This is a development so radical and so unanticipated by the seers of earlier ages that the Taoist world view denying evil as a reality in the universe must be revised. According to Dick's view in *High Castle,* German technological expertise and the work ethic have produced the atomic bomb. Further, romantic idealism and fascist fanatical action have combined in an overwhelming drive to dominate the world—by nuclear war, if that is the requisite price. This is a unique development in the history of mankind; consequently, *High Castle* suggests, the ancient Chinese cosmological views must be revised. The narrative traces the process of Mr. Tagomi's consciousness, which is the central focus for the Taoist view, as he encounters, grapples with, and is changed by the Nazi drive for national, world, and finally cosmic domination.

Darko Suvin, in an analysis of Dick's technique of story telling contained elsewhere in this volume, points out that Dick uses neither an old-fashioned omniscient narrator nor a first-person narration by a central character.[22] Instead, he constructs a narrative network supporting a large number of characters, with selected characters who serve as narrative foci.[23] Bothersome and difficult as this narrative method is to some readers and critics, it is essential to the Dickian and Taoist world view which holds that everything in the universe is connected to everything else and that no part is fundamental or superior to any other. Dick's fictional universe is parallel to the real universe as he understands it. Frank Frink, maneuvering his yellow stalks to determine the proper action in his situation, is aware that he is:

> rooted in the moment in which he lived, in which his life was bound up with all other lives and particles in the universe. . . . He, Juliana, the factory on Gough Street, the Trade Missions that ruled, the exploration of the planets, the billion chemical heaps in Africa that were now not even corpses, the aspirations of the thousands around him in the shanty warrens of San Francisco, the mad creatures in Berlin with their calm faces and manic plans—all connected in this moment of casting the yarrow stalks to select the exact wisdom appropriate in a book begun in the thirtieth century B.C. A book created by the sages of China over a period of five thousand years, winnowed, perfected, that superb cosmology—and science—codified before Europe had even learned to do long division. (*MHC,* 1)

Thus in this passage very early in the novel, Dick describes for his reader the characters and events of his narrative network. They are set in motion when Frank, a little man in a little job, does nothing more than speak out of line at work and as a result loses his job. As he later grimly notes: "You can't fart without changing the balance of the universe. It makes a funny joke with no-body around to laugh" (*MHC*, 4).

The characters of *High Castle,* despite the interlocking narra-tive network which asks us to see them as in a continuum, can be classified for purposes of discussion into several groups. Suvin diagrams these groups, categorizing them according to an upper, middle, and lower level.[24] I would like to suggest instead an *outer* and an *inner* grouping. The Taoist interpretation of *High Castle* I am undertaking here asks us to refrain from the judgmental group-ing implied by the terms *higher* and *lower.* The San Francisco plot, the outer level, is concerned with the social reality of exist-ence; the Rocky Mountain plot, the inner level, proceeds without having an impact on the events of the San Francisco plot, and can most meaningfully be understood as a commentary on the San Francisco text, offering illuminations into the inner meaning of the San Francisco events. We will find that the *inner* meaning of the *outer* events of reality is the primary concern of this novel. With this pattern of a text with commentary, Dick parallels further the structure of the *I Ching.*

There are three kinds of events in the San Francisco plot. The *political events* have Mr. Tagomi as their primary narrative center. Tagomi indirectly encounters the Nazi power elite in a moment of crisis when Chancellor Bormann has died and the Nazi factions are struggling for control; Baynes-Wegener mediates between the Oriental and the fascist positions. Sec-ondly, the economic events have Robert Childan as their focal center. He represents the businessman who sells the products manufactured by society. This productivity takes two forms—mass production and individual creativity. Finally there are the events of artifice, which use Frank Frink as the narrative focus and which describe the creation of artifices by the individual. Frink first produces destructive artifices, Colt .44s, but then turns to creating jewelry, his most interesting artifice being the silver triangle that plays such a key role in Tagomi's moment of crisis. Each of the three characters who function as narrative foci in the San Francisco narrative—Tagomi, Childan, and Frank—regularly questions the *I Ching* and uses its answers for guidance in situations where a choice must be made.

In the inner or Rocky Mountain narrative, Juliana is the focal character, and she also uses the *I Ching*. She is "a daemon, a little chthonic spirit" (*MHC*, 15) a mysterious creature who Frank believes is a "direct, literal invention of God's, dropped into his life for reasons he would never know" (*MHC*, 1). These allusions ask us to understand her symbolically, beyond the literal level. Literally she is Frank's former wife who now teaches judo in Canon City, Colorado; she unwittingly forms a liaison with the Nazi assassin, Joe Cinnadella, who has been sent to kill the creative artist, Hawthorne Abendsen. After she destroys Joe, she thinks she may return to Frank, who now creates artifacts in metal, though she remains unaware of his new role or of his narrow escape from death. It is she alone, among the readers of Abendsen's science-fiction novel, *The Grasshopper Lies Heavy*, who intuits the inner or true meaning of the book. She mediates between the reader and the universe of *High Castle* and provides the key to the inner or true meaning of Dick's novel.

Several symbols function to carry the insights Dick wishes to suggest in *High Castle*. Two are artifices created by Frank Frink: the Colt .44 and the silver triangle of jewelry. Although Frink never encounters Tagomi directly, his jewelry comes into Tagomi's hands and serves Tagomi creatively in a moment of emotional crisis, while earlier a Colt .44 (whether it is authentic or a facsimile possibly made by Frink is never spelled out) saves him in a moment of physical crisis. Two books are also important symbols in *High Castle*—the *I Ching* and *The Grasshopper Lies Heavy*, the science-fiction novel written by Abendsen that describes an alternate world in which Japan and Germany lost the war. The characters who read *The Grasshopper Lies Heavy* are generally different from those who consult the *I Ching*, the major exception being Juliana, who reads both. On the surface, the two books, one very old and one very recent, seem to have little resemblance. On a deeper level, however, similarities exist. Both science fiction and the *I Ching* are concerned with transformations and changes; in the view of neither is reality or matter fixed, defined, and static. The *I Ching* suggests a cyclic pattern of ebb and flow, a shifting between the *yin* and the *yang*. The connotations of the title, *The Grasshopper Lies Heavy*, propose a similar pattern. (The title is a phrase taken from Ecclesiastes, Chapter

12, a biblical text describing a universe where time passes and change comes to all men alike, reversing high and low, light and dark, good and evil; a text admonishing its readers to recognize the vanity of taking themselves too seriously.) All three works of literature—the two just mentioned and Dick's novel, *High Castle*—suggest a view of a universe incessantly transforming itself, a world in which defining statements are outdated almost as soon as they are uttered because reversals negate meanings.

Narrative events, characters, and symbols work together to assert several themes significant not only in *High Castle* but in Dick's other major novels. The themes are closely related and defy tidy definitions, just as they refuse to provide pat answers. Dick describes how for him there is a "mysterious chaotic quality in the universe which is not to be feared."[25] *High Castle* embodies this inexplicable quality and thus defies analysis. Its meaning, finally, can only be intuited, as Juliana achieves insight about the meaning of *The Grasshopper Lies Heavy* in the last chapter of Dick's novel. As we list the themes, we come to recognize that the analysis is tidier than what is actually to be found in *High Castle*. One theme explores the web of illusions masking reality. Mr. Tagomi realizes that reality can only be "seen through glass darkly . . . our space and our time [are] creations of our own psyche" (*MHC*, 14). The territory of sanity cannot, therefore, be clearly differentiated from the world of madness since the reality with which the sane man is supposedly in touch is unknowable. In his later novel, *Martian Time-Slip*, Dick explores this theme in greater depth. In *High Castle*, the theme is present, if not overpowering. Throughout the novel, persons and events give a first impression which turns out to be only an illusion masking another reality. The Wyndam-Matson Corporation officially is in the business of manufacturing wrought-iron staircases, railings, and fireplaces, but its illegal and real business is making forgeries of prewar artifacts. Baynes, apparently the representative for a Swedish firm manufacturing new injection molds, is in reality a member of the Abwehr, a political faction in Nazi Germany. Mr. Shinjiro Yatabe, first seen as an elderly retired Japanese man coming to the West Coast for health purposes, turns out to be

General Tedeki, a contact person from the Japanese government sent to meet the Abwehr representative. Joe Cinnadella is not a dark-haired Italian truck driver but a blond Nazi assassin. Nothing is as it first seems.

A second theme closely aligned to the theme of the illusionary nature of reality, is the one exploring the relationship of the artificial and the authentic. Man is an artificer, a maker of artifacts, both creative (the Edfrank jewelry and Abendsen's science-fiction novel *The Grasshopper Lies Heavy*) and destructive (the gun and the atomic bomb). How are these artifacts to be regarded? As with every question raised in Dick's novel, the answer is ambiguous. But the discussion about the difference between historicity and authenticity points toward the Way of the answer. The discussion focuses on the authenticity of a Civil War Army Model Colt .44 (*MHC*, 4). The gun in question turns out to be a forgery made by Frank Frink, and yet it is authentically a revolver in that it can perform its function of killing, and an apparently fake Colt .44 does just that in Mr. Tagomi's hands, when Baynes and Yatabe are threatened by the Nazi thugs. The "real" Zippo lighter in Roosevelt's pocket the day he was assassinated cannot be differentiated from a fake, *"unless you know."* Its authenticity can only be proved with a document, a paper. But, as Wyndam-Matson remarks, "the paper proves its worth, not the object itself" (*MHC*, 5). We can never get closer to reality than the words on paper by which we define it.

What, then, is the *function of the artist, the maker of artifices?* This is another important theme for Dick, a theme explored at length by Darko Suvin elsewhere in this volume. Two works of art play a creative role in *High Castle*: the silver triangle made by Frank Frink and the science fiction novel written by Hawthorne Abendsen. The silver triangle contains *wu*. It is a "blob" possessing no particular shape or form. It is the *Clod*, a fundamental form in Taoism. Herrlee G. Creel, discussing this concept in "The Great Clod," says of the Taoist view:

> If one could win through to the very center of the universe, and enter the holy of holies, he would find there only a simple clod: utterly simple, because it is essentially like the clod that lies here at my feet; and utterly mysterious because, like everything else, it can never be

understood in an absolute sense at all. Nothing can be understood absolutely. Man's mind is not a machine constructed for the purpose of understanding everything; neither is it a bit of the special essence of the universe implanted by special grace in human beings. What we call man's mind is rather a complex of functions, akin to the complex we call "man's digestion." All digestion is good, because insofar as there is digestion at all it solves a human problem. Some digestion is better than other digestion, but there is no perfect digestion and no absolute standard by which to measure it. Similarly, all thought is good insofar as it solves a human problem. Some thought may be better than other thought, but there is no perfect thought and no standard of absolute truth. Thus the opinion of every man is worthy of consideration, and no one is entitled to suppose that his own view must be accepted without question.[26]

Reality for the Taoist does not lie in an ideal world elsewhere; it lies in the world of things—of clods. One is reminded of William Blake, who could "see the world in a grain of sand . . ."

The silver triangle of jewelry has authenticity, in contrast to historicity. It is alive in the now, and as Paul Kasoura explains, "It somehow partakes of Tao . . . . It is balanced. The forces within this piece are stabilized. At rest. So to speak, this object has made its peace with the universe" (*MHC,* 11). The *wu* contained in the jewelry is another complex Taoist concept. Joseph Needham summarizes *wu* as "letting things work out their destinies in accord with their intrinsic principles." Opposing *wu* is the concept of *wei*, ". . . forcing things in the interests of private gain, without regard to their intrinsic principles and relying on the authority of others."[27]

Dick gives to the young Japanese, Paul Kasoura, the task of explaining how true art functions:

To have no historicity, and also no artistic, esthetic worth, and yet to partake of some ethereal value—that is a marvel. Just precisely because this is a miserable, small, worthless-looking blob; that . . . contributes to its possesing wu. For it is a fact that wu is customarily found in least imposing places, as in the Christian aphorism, "stones rejected by the builder." One experiences awareness of wu in such trash as an old stick, or a rusty beer can by the side of the road. However, in those cases, the wu is within the viewer. It is a religious experience. Here, an artificer has put wu into the object, rather than merely witnessed the wu inherent in it.

In other words, an entire new world is pointed to, by this. The name of it is neither art, for it has no form nor religion. What is it? I have pondered this pin unceasingly, yet cannot fathom it. We evidently lack the word for an object like this. . . . It is authentically a new thing on the face of the world. (*MHC*, 11)

The imaginary science-fiction novel, *The Grasshopper Lies Heavy*, accomplishes something similar to the jewelry. Clodlike, it still contains *wu*. One of its readers comments: "Amazing the power of fiction, even cheap fiction, to evoke" (*MHC*, 8). Taking one step backward in the hall of mirrors Dick builds for us, we can understand the science-fiction novels of the real world—*High Castle*, for example—as having the possibility also of being a new form, a blob possessing *wu* and pointing to "an entire new world."

A fourth theme, and perhaps the most important one in *High Castle*, is *the necessity of faith*. Mr. Tagomi, in his individual moment of crisis, defines the situation of all the characters caught in the network of world crises when he cries out, "I have no faith, but I am currently grasping at straws" (*MHC*, 14). He is temporarily vitiated by his dilemma because, while he has lost his faith, he knows "we must all have faith in something. We cannot know the answers. We cannot see ahead, on our own" (*MHC*, 5). Each of the characters in the novel is looking for some kind of transcendent meaning in the face of the entropy and chaos threatening them as Germany through Operation Dandelion plans to destroy Japan with nuclear warfare. Dick, in a 1970 letter to *Commentary*, discusses this search for faith: "What I write about, I think, is belief, faith, trust . . . and the lack of all three. . . . For me, in each successive novel, the doubt—or rather lack of trust or faith—grows deeper. The split widens, that yawning gap in the earth, into which everything that matters can fall."[28] In his afterword to "Faith of Our Fathers" (1967), Dick suggests that despite the long-standing taboo, God might well be an appropriate topic for science fiction. "I myself," he says, "have no real beliefs about God; only my experience that He is present . . . subjectively, of course; but the inner realm is real too. And in a science fiction story one projects what has been a personal inner experience into a milieu; it becomes socially shared, hence discussable."[29]

The narrative movement or transformational process of the novel climaxes in a moment of choice for each character who is a narrative focus. In the San Francisco plot these characters are Childan, Tagomi, and Frank Frink; in the Rocky Mountain plot the focus is Juliana Frink. In Dick's novels, as he has commented, "there is no plot, but only a great many characters in search of a plot."[30] Dick is to be admired for succeeding in this demanding narrative form; either to write it or read it is not a simple task.[31] Perhaps no better visual images catch the essence of a Dickian narrative structure than Chinese calligraphy, where a configuration of curved and straight lines forms a network. All parts are connected to all other parts, but not directly. By linear threads or veins, one can zigzag a way through the plot, but one is not given the hub of a central narrative view, with other characters circling in a wheel connected by the direct spokes of the protagonist's vision. Difficult as Dick's narrative technique may be, it is essential if his fictional universe is to be a mirror, catching and reflecting the essence of his vision of the real universe in all its forms—individual, economic, political, and cosmological.

In talking about the narrative movement, it is helpful to see the fifteen chapters as a trigram, with each of its sides comprised of five chapters. As we enter the novel, in the first five chapters, the transient balance of each central character is disturbed. All movements are connected, often not directly, but the vibrations of an event occurring in one part of the narrative network will be felt by the whole. The movement of the novel is set in motion with a minor event: Frank Frink "spouts the wrong kind of talk" to his boss, Wyndam-Matson, at work and loses his job. Childan subsequently is unbalanced when Frank, masking his identity, appears at the shop and exposes the Colt .44 as a fake. Mr. Tagomi's work as the head of the Pacific Coast Trade Mission is unsettled when the Nazi, Baynes-Wegener, contacts him and informs him of the intended arrival of the Japanese gentleman, Mr. Yatabe.

This turn of events plunges the little Japanese official into the center of an international political intrigue. Juliana Frink, in Canon City, meets Joe Cinnadella, who "breathes death" and leads her from her role as a karate instructor into his world of fanaticism, violence, and destruction.

In the central third of the novel, representing the second side of the trigram, all the narratives move forward to a moment when each central character must make a choice as to which way he or she will go. The event pushing the moment to its crisis is the death of the Reichs Chancellor, Martin Bormann, an event unleashing a power struggle by several contending political factions in Germany for the vacant position.

The last third of the novel, Chapters 11 through 15, dramatizes a situation in which each focal character is required to make a decision and take some action, but in which the proper direction of that action is not clear. The crisis of Mr. Tagomi is the most dramatic, and the action he must take is the most extreme. His resolution of the mental crisis precipitated by the necessity of his killing two men is dramatized in Chapter 14—surely the most brilliant single chapter Dick has ever written. Chapter 15, Juliana Frink's chapter, elucidates the inner meaning of Abendsen's novel, and by reflection—if the reader can grasp the fleeting truth—the inner meaning of Dick's novel, *High Castle*.

Robert Childan faces his moment of choice first, and his is an economic choice. Paul Kasoura verbalizes the alternatives Childan faces: He has a chance to become extremely wealthy by mass-producing the Edfrank jewelry. To do this, he must bastardize authentic art and turn it into trinkets sold as good-luck charms for the natives in South America and Asia. The *wu*, the authenticity, will be lost. The choice facing Childan is not simple; *ambiguity* is the key word in all the situations—in the economic situation, the political situation, and the situation of the artist. The ambiguity is almost more than Mr. Tagomi can bear when he has to make his choice. "I cannot face this dilemma," he thinks to himself. "That man should have to act in such moral ambiguity. There is no Way in this; all is muddled. All chaos of Light and Dark, shadow and substance" (*MHC*, 12). How will the "inferior man" behave? Which way will the "superior man" go?[32]

Robert Childan, grappling with the temptation to prostitute art for profit, has a brief moment of insight when he rises "to the surface," sees unencumbered, "splits the ambiguity of the moment," and sees the way. He decides against prostituting art: "I am proud of this work. There can be no consideration of trashy good-luck charms. I reject" (*MHC*, 11).

Frank Frink the artist and craftsman, is discouraged by the lack of sales of his handcrafted jewelry. His moment of decision as to whether he should continue his work as a metal artist is less dramatic than Childan's and more deeply tied to the political situation. The network of events leading Childan to complain to his dealer, Calvin, about the fake Colt .44s in turn leads Calvin to report Frank as a Jew to the authorities. His arrest interrupts his deliberation about the direction of his career. Subsequently he is released from jail because of an action Mr. Tagomi unwittingly takes—a refusal to sign a paper allowing Frank's extradition to the eastern German zone for prosecution. Frank can understand neither his arrest nor his release. He concludes that he never will understand anything, that the way is just to "keep moving." He must go back to making jewelry: "Working and not thinking, not looking up or trying to understand" (*MHC*, 14). Frank represents the intuitive artist who works out of the unconscious and cannot analyze or understand through logic.

In contrast, Mr. Tagomi is a man of reason. His moment of choice is the most dramatic, and his decision the most difficult to make, because none of the alternatives open to him is an acceptable one for the "superior man." Dick has described his method of plot development in his letter to *Commentary,* and we can see it at work here. "In my novel the protagonist's comfortable private world is disintegrating and an awful, mystical, puzzling, enormous world is expanding—from elements already there—to fill the void."[33] Tagomi's values as the novel opens are clear, and they are directly opposed to those of Nazism: "No man should be an instrument for another's needs . . . philosophical involvement and fanaticism must not blind us to authentic human fact" (*MHC*, 5). He has faith in the heart of the good man, sometimes locked within two yin lines of passion, but yet flickering with the light of yang at the center (*MHC*, 6). But each of his five encounters with the Nazis pushes him further from the calm balance he has displayed in the early part of the novel as he consulted the *I Ching*. Tagomi has explained to Baynes that it may seem absurd to live by a five-thousand-year-old book, but it *is* alive, animated by spirits, and can answer the questions put to it.

Finally, the situation in which Tagomi finds himself becomes so extreme that he is driven to revise his Taoist view of evil in the universe. He is pushed from his confidence in the balanced harmony of opposites in the universe when he hears the roster of Nazis being considered for the vacant chancellorship: Göring, Goebbels, Heydrich, von Schirach, Seyss-Inquart. Each is almost as monstrous as the others. He thinks: "I am going mad. . . . There is evil! It's actual, like cement. I can't believe it. I can't stand it. Evil is not a view." That the world will be ruled by one among these evil men is beyond his comprehension. "We're blind moles. Creeping through the soil, feeling with our snoots. We know nothing," he concludes (*MHC*, 6). When he consults the *I Ching*, it gives him no help, revealing only that the moment is one of static oppression.

In Mr. Tagomi's final meeting with Baynes, they are joined by Mr. Yatabe, now revealed to be General Tedeki. The Japanese are asked by Baynes to intervene in the German power struggle by supporting Heydrich, the head of the Nazi SS, the most malignant of all the political factions, solely because the SS group are opposed to Operation Dandelion, the sneak nuclear attack supported by Goebbels. Mr. Tagomi cannot face "the dilemma of being forced to assist evil in gaining power in order to save our lives" (*MHC*, 12), of becoming involved in the monstrous schizophrenic morass of internecine Nazi intrigue. Raised as a Buddhist for whom all life is sacred, his moral chaos is total when he is forced to kill two men to protect Baynes. He has only one word for it: "Sickening."

The progress of Mr. Tagomi's moral confusion and despair is worth examining closely, as we have just done, because it is a paradigm for the Dickian view that appears again and again in his novels. The hexagram, The Abyss, prevails in the contemporary world, and the sensitive heart is sick with horror at the bloodbath approaching. None can hide or escape, even the little man, because we all exist together in the network of reality. Later novels such as *Dr. Bloodmoney* picture the world after the nuclear holocaust; *High Castle* stands at the moment just before the climax of horror.

For Dick, entropy is at work in the world; it is the force destroying his protagonists' private worlds. Dick says: "I personally conceive the form destroyer as personified, as an active evil—the evil—force. I also conceive of it winning, at least in the short run, although perhaps not ultimately. Yes, it is an anti-God if by 'God' you mean the 'form creator,' which is how I view him. I am with Luther in his belief of an active Satan who is at work all the time."[34] The terrible dilemma of our lives, as Dick expresses it in *High Castle,* is that "whatever happens, it is evil beyond compare. Why struggle, then? Why choose? If all alternatives are the same . . ." (*MHC*, 15).

Yet Dick is not a total nihilist. As he explains, in each of his novels at least one human has faith; the redeemer exists:

He lives; he can be found—usually—in the novel somewhere, at the center of the stage or at the very edge. In some novels he merely lurks. He is implicit. But I believe in him completely. He is the friend who ultimately comes . . . and in time.

Basically, he is found at the heart of human life itself. He is, in fact, the heart of human life. He is the most alive of all. Where the chattering, bickering, sweating, planning, worrying, scheming center of life holds sway—well, I have faith that he is there and will show himself, countering the process of entropy, of decay, that more and more undermines the universe itself. Stars are snuffed out; planets die into darkness and cold; but there in the marketplace of some small moon, he is busy formulating a plan for action—action against the black counterforce, the Palmer Eldritch figure in all his horrid manifestations.[35]

In *High Castle* the redeemer is Mr. Tagomi, but disoriented by the Nazi evil he cannot continue to act until his faith is restored. That healing process comes to him through the silver triangle, an art object crafted by Frank Frink. It is made from metal, from the dark *yin*-world below. "And yet," Mr. Tagomi observes, "in the sunlight, the silver triangle glittered. It reflected light. Fire . . . Not dank or dark object at all. Not heavy, weary, but pulsing with life. The high realm, aspect of yang: empyrean, ethereal. As befits work of art. Yes, that is artist's job: takes mineral rock from dark, silent earth, transforms it into shining light-reflecting form from sky. . . . Body of yin, soul of yang. Metal and fire unified. The outer and inner; microcosmos in my palm" (*MHC,* 14).

Experiencing a transformation in his heart as he holds the shimmering triangle in his palm in the sunlight, Mr. Tagomi suddenly finds his source of light cut off and looks up to see a policeman standing over him. Pained, Tagomi moans: "My chance at nirvana . . . interrupted by that white barbarian Neanderthal *yank*," (*MHC*, 14). The image Dick creates here is very powerful, catching as it does the essence of the conflict his novel dramatizes: Western authoritarianism opposing the way of art and Taoism.

But Mr. Tagomi does not give in to despair; he now knows what he must do—return to the world even though the route is on "that malignant construction, the Embarcadero Freeway." He is aided in finding a pedecab by a group of children. (Children also act as harbingers of hope in *Dr. Bloodmoney,* and Dick has elsewhere expressed his faith in children as saviors.[36] Restored by the artifice of a man (Frank Frink) who is unknown to him, Mr. Tagomi upon returning to his office refuses to allow that very same man to be extradited to the German zone, and so unwittingly saves Frank's physical life, just as Frank's art has saved Tagomi's inner life.

Juliana Frink's moment of choice is so different from those of Frank, Childan, and Tagomi that it can hardly be called a decision. She kills Joe Cinnadella almost without awareness, once she realizes the act is necessary to save Abendsen. Her scene parallels the Tagomi killing scene, but he acts analytically and logically while she acts intuitively. Her intuitive awareness is one of the clues guiding us to understand the Rocky Mountain plot as a dramatization of the inner truth, a truth that Mr. Tagomi cannot fully understand even when he is directed to it by hexagram sixty-one. Juliana *is* inner truth, intuitive, beyond logic; she symbolizes the Tao, the animating spirit or reality of the universe, embodying both the yin and the yang, the light and the dark, the creative and the destructive. In her dialectical movement, she has lived with Frank, who creates (*yang*); she joins Joe, who destroys (*yin*); at the novel's end, she says she may return to Frank. She is last seen walking "into the patches of *light* from the living room and then into the shadows beyond the lawn of the house, onto the *black* sidewalk" (*MHC*, 15, italics mine).

She is the only one who understands the meaning of Abendsen's book, and it shows her that there is a way out: "There's nothing to be afraid of, nothing to want or hate or avoid, here, or run from. Or pursue" (*MHC*, 15). Her understanding is confirmed when she asks the *I Ching:* What are we supposed to learn from *The Grasshopper Lies Heavy?* The answer: Inner Truth (the same hexagram as Mr. Tagomi's). And what is the Inner Truth? That Germany and Japan lost the war, just as Abendsen's book describes. The winner of the war is really the loser. Dick here asks the reader to follow him through a series of reflections in the artifices mirroring reality. In the world of *High Castle,* the Nazis really won the war, but in the science-fiction world of *The Grasshopper Lies Heavy* (representing Inner Truth), they really lost it. If the reader moves back a step, he realizes that in the real world of human construct, the United States and its allies won the war, so the inner truth, contained in Dick's science fiction, is that they really lost it. An equation is established in which Dick's novel is to the real world as Abendsen's novel is to Dick's fictional reality. The winner of any war is locked into the necessity of continuing to fight to maintain his superior power position. This effort eventually destroys him. On a moral level, he has already been destroyed because of the horrendous acts he committed to win. The winner paradoxically is the loser. The reader's eyes meet Dick's in the hall of mirrors the fiction builds when he understands this meaning.

What is the function of literary art for Dick? According to the parallelism of the San Francisco and Rocky Mountain plots, it offers the same creative salvation as Frank's silver triangle. Abendsen is the artist in one plot, Frank in the other. Abendsen's name—a combination of *evening* and *sun*—suggests the same elements of light and dark as the yin and yang in the silver triangle. Further, according to the structure of the novel, science fiction can function as a kind of contemporary *Book of Changes,* pointing the way into the future. Juliana, who relies on the *I Ching,* says to Abendsen of his book: "You showed me there's a way." Granted science fiction is only "cheap popular fiction" as one character in *High Castle* describes it, but it still has an amazing "power to evoke."

Books are alive, animated by spirit, Mr. Tagomi explains in *High Castle*. They offer wisdom for those who have vision, who can catch the truth as it emerges in a fleeting moment of light and then disappears into the dark. Mr. Tagomi finds meaning in the *I Ching*, Juliana in *The Grasshopper Lies Heavy*; Dick asks the reader to find meaning in his book, to grasp the relationship between the outer events and the inner truth. The title of the novel—*The Man in the High Castle,* embodies the best clue. The array of ideas Dick associates with the name *High Castle* are worth noting. He says the particular castle he had in mind when he chose the name was Vysêhrad, a fortress near Prague revered by Bohemians because of the role it played in the Thirty Years War. He continues:

> The Bohemian composer Bedrich Smetana wrote a musical portrait of this castle in his orchestral cycle *Má Vlast*. When the Protestant Elector Palatine, Frederick, revolted against Ferdinand, Emperor of the Holy Roman Empire, the High Castle came to symbolize the center of religious and political freedom against the autocratic Catholic Hapsburgs. I used the mention of it in the title of my novel as a symbol of Abendsen's "revolt" against the tyranny of the Nazis, suggesting a similarity between the monolithic rule of the Catholics in Europe before the Thirty Years War and the Nazi rule in my novel.[37]

Dick says that in his research on the Third Reich in preparation for writing his novel, he found mention of reference to the Nazi castle system in several sources.[38] He further explains:

> Various lofty and beautiful castles from the old days of the kings and emperors were taken over by the SS and used as places to train young SS men into an elite body cut off from the "ordinary" world. These were to be bases from which the Übermenschen would emerge to rule the Third Reich. They became notorious, since not only were the men being trained into hideous inhuman behavior mods, but there was also the rumor that, like the Catherists of the 13th century Southern France, on whom the structure was modeled, they were either asexual or downright homosexual. You can see, then, that the two castles are bipolarized in the book: the legendary High Castle of Protestant freedom and resistance in the Thirty Years War versus the evil castle system of the elite youth corps of the SS.[39]

Dick concludes his discussion of the sources for his title by point-ing out that it is rumored in *High Castle* that Abendsen lives in a high castle, but that actually "he does not live in this paranoid fashion but in fact lives like anyone else—with a tricycle in the driveway, suggesting not only a wife but a child, and no defenses. Thus there is an irony in the title, inasmuch as Abendsen does *not* live in a high castle or any sort of castle at all."[40]

Abendsen has learned that there really is no high castle where man can safely withdraw, no abstract or ideal realm lying above the real world. As Abendsen has found that truth, so Dick asks his reader to discover it, too. Man is not *above* but *in* the uni-verse, part of the network of existence which connects all things.

This much of the Dickian view—this belief in an imminent universe—is Taoist. But Dick goes beyond to a revisionist view of the nature of evil, a view he seems to suggest was spawned by the evolution of the mechanical in the modern acquisitive world. Evil is real. The totalitarian spirit, implemented by techniques and machines, creates this evil, according to Dick. It is evil be-cause it destroys the authentically human spirit.[41] In its most destructive form—warring with nuclear bombs—it threatens to destroy the physical world.

The Dickian view, although dark, is not nihilistic because Dick trusts: not God, not a man in a high castle, but a little man, gnat-sized but somehow great, who lives in the middle of mun-dane reality. In *High Castle* the little man is Mr. Tagomi. Dick's own commentary on the significance of the actions of the Mr. Tagomis in the world is the most insightful one. He explains it in a 1970 letter to Bruce Gillespie, an Australian critic, excerpts from which follow:

> Mr. Tagomi, in a moment of irritation and awareness of suffocation, refuses to sign a form which will transfer a certain Jew from Japanese authority to German authority—one life is saved, a small life and saved by a small life. But the enormous process of decline is pushed back slightly. Enough so that it matters. What Mr. Tagomi has done matters. In a sense, there is nothing more important on all Earth than Mr. Tagomi's irritable action.
>
> I know only one thing about my novels. In them again and again, this minor man asserts himself in all his hasty, sweaty strength. . . . I

believe . . . in him, and I love him. He will prevail. There is nothing else. At least nothing else that matters. That we should be concerned about. Because if he is there like a tiny father-figure, everything is all right.

Some reviewers have found "bitterness" in my writing. I am surprised, because my mood is one of trust. Perhaps they are bothered by the fact that what I trust is so very small. They want something vaster. I have news for them; there is nothing vaster. Nothing *more*, I should say. But, really, how much do we have to have? Isn't Mr. Tagomi enough? Isn't what he does enough? I know it counts. I am satisfied.[42]

3. Metaphysics and Metafiction in *The Man in the High Castle*

N. B. HAYLES

CALL IT PERVERSITY, poor writing, or simple confusion; the perfect Philip K. Dick novel does not exist. The more closely Dick's work is examined, the more obvious it is that there simply is no scheme under which all of a given novel's details will fit without contradiction.[1] As the reader struggles to make sense of a fictive world whose rules seem to metamorphose even as he reads he can sympathize with the characters inside the fiction who also must struggle to make sense of the bizarre reality in which they are placed. Paradoxically, Dick's work derives much of its power from its irrationality; a comparison with Franz Kafka is inevitable.

In *The Man in the High Castle*, the sense that Dick, like the Queen of Hearts, is changing the rules halfway through the game is more muted, perhaps, than in the later fiction; but it is nevertheless present. There are logical elisions in the work which no amount of critical exegesis can fully explain. Perhaps the most disturbing of these elisions arises from Dick's failure to resolve the conflict he sets up between two contradictory metaphysical systems. These systems are embodied in the two presences that brood over *High Castle*. One is the spirit of the *I Ching, The Book of Changes*, the living intelligence that according to Mr. Tagomi animates the oracle. The other, as yet faceless, later takes form in Dick's fiction as the metallic visage of Palmer Eldritch: it is the face of Absolute Evil. For the moment, it lies disguised behind Joe Cinnadella's Italian persona or appears briefly, indistinctly, in the biographies of those Nazi leaders who are potential successors to the deceased Martin Bormann. As a presence, it may be understood as the underlying archetype entering the world through Nazi Germany, an archetype that Captain Wegener (alias "Baynes") believes the Nazis are driven to reify through an unconcious death wish. At the moment of the events in *High Castle* it is still nascent, trembling on the brink of existence. Its traditional emblem is the sign of the devil.

These two presences imply mutually exclusive metaphysical outlooks. According to the *I Ching,* evil is relative, merely another aspect of a whole that also includes goodness. But if the diabolic archetype—the sign of the devil—is the governing personage, another view emerges, articulated historically by the Doctrine of Original Sin. According to this doctrine, evil is real, actual, and internal—an inescapable consequence of the human condition—not merely another aspect of good.

Although these two presences are both capable of serving as what Dick calls "external points of reference," their different views of evil generate an ambiguity. Depending on which reference point prevails, we can see developing complexities as evidence either of a malignant or a benign universe. This ambiguity is crucial to understanding *High Castle* and central to Dick's work as a whole. In *High Castle*, Dick does not so much resolve the uncertainty as transcend it through the metafictional aspects of his text. Finding the initial dichotomy unresolvable, Dick takes the conflict through a transformation positing it finally not as a problem of whether *evil* is real, but of whether *anything* is real. From this vantage point he is then able to return to the moral problem and suggest a solution. It is at the point of transformation that the logical elision occurs. There is no linear path through the transformation, only a leap from morality to ontology.

In this chapter I shall trace out the assumptions implied by Dick's external frames of reference, locate the points in the text at which the elisions occur, and show how the final resolution emerges as a result of a shift to metafiction. In a sense I am conceding at the outset that *High Castle* is flawed; but like so many of Dick's critics, I will conclude by arguing that the power of the final, overall vision renders the mediating inconsistencies unimportant.

When Dick uses the *I Ching* as one frame of reference, he is invoking a metaphysical system of beliefs that has evolved in Chinese culture over thousands of years. The *I Ching* teaches that change is the essence of reality and that the forms of everyday life are temporary expressions of fundamental underlying patterns. The forms that make up our everyday world, according to the *I Ching*, are created from the dynamic tension between two opposing principles, the *yin* and the *yang*. Without this tension, there could be no world as we know it. The two principles are neither good nor evil; they simply are. Both are required for the world to exist.

While the opposing principles have no moral connotations, they nevertheless do have opposite values. *Yang* is associated with the light of reason; it is firm, masculine, rational. *Yin* is dark, yielding, feminine, intuitive. From the interplay between them, called the *Tao* or "the Way," comes the heavens, the earth, and the human society existing between heaven and earth. Since change is inevitable, the attempt to embrace one polarity is the surest way to initiate a movement toward its opposite. "Returning is the motion of the *Tao*," Lao-tzu says, and "Going far means returning."[2]

The *I Ching* further supposes that there is a fundamental connection between everything that happens at a given moment. The *I Ching* suggests that all things existing at a given moment partake of the same essence, and that this essence is revealed by the pattern of the hexagram derived when the oracle is consulted. The forty-nine yarrow stalks or the three coins that one throws to determine the hexagram can reveal the Tenor of the Moment because they are rooted in the moment, as is everything else that is happening synchronously. The *I Ching* thus supposes that the essential principle connecting events is not, as Western culture traditionally holds, causality, but an acausal, temporal association that C. G. Jung would later define as "synchronicity."[3] Frank Frink meditates on this temporal connection as he consults the oracle:

> Here came the hexagram, brought forth by the passive chance work-ings of the vegetable stalks. Random, and yet rooted in the moment in which he lived, in which his life was bound up with all other lives and particles in the universe. He, Juliana, the factory on Gough Street, the Trade Missions that ruled, the exploration of the planets, the billion chemical heaps in Africa that were now not even corpses, the aspira-tions of the thousands around him in the shanty warrens of San Fran-cisco, the mad creatures in Berlin with their calm faces and manic plans—all connected in this moment of casting the yarrow stalks to select the exact wisdom appropriate in the book begun in the thir-teenth century B.C.[4]

In addition to relying on the *I Ching*'s authority in the classical Chinese tradition, Dick suggests that it may be *scientifically* valid. Frank thinks of it as a "book created by the sages of China over a period of five thousand years, winnowed, perfected, that superb cosmology—*and science*—codified before Europe had even learned to do long division" (*MHC*, 1, my italics). Dick may have taken his hint for the claim that the *I Ching* is consistent with scientific models from C. G. Jung's "Foreword" to the Richard Wilhelm translation. In this edition (the one Dick used to write *High Castle*) Jung writes, "It is a curious fact that such a gifted and intelligent people as the Chinese has never developed what we call science. Our science, however, is based upon the princi-ple of causality, and causality is considered to be an axiomatic truth. But a great change in our standpoint is setting in. What Kant's *Critique of Pure Reason* failed to do, is being accom-plished by modern physics."[5] Jung goes on to contrast the West-ern idea of causality with the principle of synchronicity, suggest-ing that it is synchronicity rather than causality that is consistent with modern physics. "Since [causality] is merely statistical truth and not absolute," Jung concludes, "it is a sort of working hypothesis of how events evolve one out of another, whereas synchronicity takes the coincidence of events in space and time as meaning something more than mere chance, namely, a peculiar interdependence of objective events among themselves as well as with the subjective (psychic) states of the observer or observers."[6] Jung then explicitly draws a parallel between modern physics and the *I Ching*: "The ancient Chinese mind contemplates the cosmos in a way comparable to that of the modern physicist, who cannot deny that his model of the world is a decidedly psychophysical structure. The microphysical event includes the observer just as much as the reality underlying the *I Ching* comprises subjective—i.e., psychic—conditions in the totality of the momentary situation."[7] Frank makes a similar point when he consults the oracle and receives a hexagram that seems to foretell World War III. He wonders, "What's happening? Did I start it in motion? Or is someone else tinkering, someone I don't even know? Or—the whole lot of us. It's the fault of those physicists and that synchronicity theory, every particle connected with every other; you can't fart without changing the balance in the universe" (*MHC*, 4).

The parallel between the *I Ching* and modern physics is not unique with Jung, though Jung was the first to introduce and define "synchronicity." More recently the parallel has been drawn by the physicist Fritjof Capra in *The Tao of Physics* (1975). Capra argues that the world view implicit in particle physics is strikingly similar to that of Eastern mysticism. Among other texts he discusses the *I Ching*, comparing its "synchronicity" model with physicist Geoffrey Chew's "bootstrap" model of reality.[8] Chew's theory holds that the search for a "fundamental structure" of matter is misguided; instead, Chew proposes a kind of synchronicity model for matter, in which every particle brings every other particle into being simultaneously. In this view no one particle can be more "fundamental" than any other, because they all mutually determine each other. In Chew's phrase, reality thus "bootstraps" its way into being.

In believing the *I Ching* to be a work of science as well as cosmology, the Dickian character is thus in good company, joining hands with C. G. Jung and a least some particle physicists. In Jung's "Foreword," Dick found the claim that science and synchronicity were compatible; meanwhile, the Wilhelm edition itself made the *I Ching* accessible to the West in a way it had not been before. These events may explain in part why Dick chose to make the *I Ching* the key to *High Castle*, and further, why he constructed the narrative as he did.

Consider, for example, his use of multiple narrative foci. The narrative switches between various characters, revealing each consciousness it probes as partial, biased, confused, and often simply wrong. With no single focussing consciousness at the novel's center, the stress falls on the interconnections that tie all the fragments to each other. Moreover, the connections are not primarily causal in nature. For example, Mr. Tagomi shoots the German thugs with a Colt .44 that he had bought from Robert Childan, an antique dealer trading in real artifacts and in the fake artifacts manufactured by the Wyndam-Matson corporation, the firm that employs Frank Frink. Unsettled by the shooting, Mr. Tagomi refuses the German consul's request for Frank's extradition, although Mr. Tagomi has never met Frank and has no idea who he is. The line of connection here is so tenuous and convoluted that "causality" is clearly not the appropriate term, even though just as clearly there *is* a connection. The reader who can see the obscure interconnections that link Frank with Mr. Tagomi (through an artifact that is also not what *it* appears to be) must feel the events are not merely chance, and not cause-and-effect either. Similar strands of convoluted connection tie together the other characters. None lies wholly outside the connecting network of events that is, I propose, a literary analogue to Jung's synchronicity model.

I do not, however, wish to overstate the case for synchronicity as a narrative model. Multiple narrative foci and interwoven plot lines are also characteristic of much of Dick's other work, as Darko Suvin points out.[9] It is inappropriate to suppose, therefore, that Dick uses them in *High Castle* to embody the *I Ching*'s metaphysic. More probably Dick found in the *I Ching*, especially as interpreted by Jung, a ready analogue to the characteristic way he chooses to tell a story—that is to say, an analogue to his own metaphysical assumptions. Having found a book, traditionally viewed as imbued with oracular power, that reinforced or crystallized his own assumptions, Dick takes advantage of his creative freedom as a writer of fiction to increase further the weight the oracle carries. He arranges matters so that the *I Ching*'s predictions are substantially correct. He relies on its authority—partly taken from tradition, partly created anew in the course of the novel—to bring off the surprise ending. Finally, he hints at a correlation that the canny reader has perhaps already guessed. Dick apparently used the *I Ching* to write *The Man in the High Castle,* just as Hawthorne Abendsen uses it in *High Castle* to write *The Grasshopper Lies Heavy,* the novel-within-the novel.[10] What *High Castle* presents us with, both in itself and in its writing, is an acausal web of connection in which fact can be transmuted into fiction, and fiction into fact, because it is based on a metaphysical idea that holds everyday "reality" to be illusion, causality a chimera, and the only eternal truth to be that everything changes.

Given the evidence pointing to the *I Ching* as the novel's resident demiurge, what are we then to make of the powerful counterview that surfaces with nearly as much authority? Its chief proponent is Captain Rudolf Wegener, alias "Mr. Baynes." When Tagomi first brings up the *I Ching* to Baynes, Baynes' reaction is revealing:

> "We are absurd," Mr. Tagomi said, "because we live by a five-thousand-year-old book. We ask it questions as if it were alive. It is alive. As is the Christian Bible; many books are actually alive. Not in metaphoric fashion. Spirit animates it. Do you see?" He inspected Mr. Baynes' face for his reaction.
> Carefully phrasing his words, Baynes said, "I—just don't know enough about religion. It's out of my field. I prefer to stick to subjects I have some competence in." As a matter of fact, he was not certain what Mr. Tagomi was talking about. (*MHC,* 5)

Mr. Baynes' puzzlement sets the stage for a rival explanation. Rather than Mr. Tagomi's mystical faith in the *I Ching,* Mr. Baynes prefers a psychological explanation. Meditating on the Nazis, Baynes tries to fathom the essence of their thought, the peculiar way in which it is a form of insanity:

> Their view; it is cosmic. Not of a man here, a child there, but an abstraction: race, land . . . the abstract is real, the actual is invisible to them . . . . They see through the here, the now, into the vast black deep beyond, the unchanging. And that is fatal to life. Because eventually there will be no life . . . This is [only] an interval . . . the wheel turns for all life. It is all temporary. And they—these madmen—respond to the granite, the dust, the longing of the inanimate; they want to aid *Natur.* (*MHC,* 3)

Like the *I Ching*, the Nazis look beneath the surface for an underlying pattern. But whereas the *I Ching* sees constant change, the Nazis see the sterility of a heat-death universe and seek to align themselves with this death-principle. Baynes thinks he understands the appeal of this view:

> They want to be the agents, not the victims, of history. They identify with God's power and believe they are godlike. That is their basic madness. They are overcome by some archetype; their egos have expanded psychotically so that they cannot tell where they begin and the godhead leaves off . . . it is inflation of the ego to its ultimate. (*MHC*, 3)

Baynes believes that under the influence of this archetype, the Nazis aspire to godhood and so follow the banner of Lucifer, the prototype of those who worship death under the guise of becoming God.

It is possible, of course, for Dick to set forth these two different views on the real nature of the universe—forever changing, according to the *I Ching*, or driving towards changelessness, as the Nazis subconsciously believe—and allow them to remain at rest in the text as two alternate explanations, one associated with Eastern mysticism and the other with Western psychology. There is no particular reason why East and West should meet, or if they do (as with Japan and Germany's encounter in America) why they should be of one mind. But through Mr. Tagomi, Dick deliberately brings the two into confrontation.

The possibility that the madness of the Nazis is not merely an interpretation of reality, but reality itself, occurs to Mr. Tagomi when he attends the Japanese government's briefing on the Nazi leaders. As Mr. Tagomi hears the potential Nazi leaders described in devastatingly objective language, he experiences a physical nausea and vertigo which convince him that evil is here manifesting itself as something real, palpable, and concrete. Mr. Tagomi tries desperately to calm himself:

> Think along reassuring lines. Recall order of world. What to draw on? Religion? . . .
> There is evil! It's actual, like cement.
> I can't believe it. I can't stand it. Evil is not view. He wandered about the lobby, hearing the traffic on Sutter Street, the Foreign Office

spokesman addressing the meeting. All our religion is wrong. . . .
It's an ingredient in us. In the world. Poured over us, filtering into
our bodies, minds, hearts, into the pavement itself. (*MHC*, 6)

Mr. Tagomi's epiphany both articulates and exacerbates the conflict. It throws into sharp relief the fact that the *I Ching* and the
archetypal explanation of Nazi evil cannot both be true at
once—for if the *I Ching* is correct, then evil is relative; whereas if
the Nazis prevail, evil will enter the world as an actual, living
presence.

Having set up this conflict and sharply limned its moral implications, Dick draws back from resolving it, again using the figure of
Mr. Tagomi. Mr. Tagomi is forced to violate his Buddist principles of respect for all life when he kills the two men attempting to
kidnap Baynes. In a desperate search for guidance, Mr. Tagomi
turns to the *I Ching*. General Tedeki, watching him abstractedly
manipulating the yarrow stalks, reassures Baynes that

"He will recover his equilibrium. . . . In time. Right now he has no
standpoint by which he can view and comprehend his act. That book
will help him, for it provides an external frame of reference."
"I see," Mr. Baynes said. He thought, another frame of reference
which might help him would be the Doctrine of Original Sin. I wonder
if he has ever heard of it. (*MHC*, 2)

Later Mr. Tagomi announces that he intends to read Goodman
Mather, presumably to learn about the Doctrine of Original Sin
from one of its more emphatic spokesmen.

Since Dick does not acknowledge that the *I Ching* and the
Doctrine of Original Sin are in conflict, much less attempt to
resolve the conflict, the effect is confusing. But his point seems to
be that under neither system does the world make sense. The *I
Ching* is fine as far as it goes, but it fails to account for the
actuality of evil; the Doctrine of Original Sin accounts for evil,
but fails to make the world morally palatable. Mr. Baynes thinks,

To save one life, Mr. Tagomi had to take two. The logical, balanced
mind cannot make sense of that. A kindly man like Mr. Tagomi could
be driven insane by the implications of such reality. . . .And we are
not really different from him . . . . We are faced with the same confusions. (*MHC*, 12)

To resolve the "confusions" would be either to deny the actuality of evil, or to deny that the universe makes moral sense. Dick is unwilling to do either. This is for Dick the ultimate dilemma. It goes to the heart of his work, appearing in various forms in virtually all of his fiction, and in much of his nonfiction as well.

Dick was still struggling with the same problem in 1976. "Man, Android and Machine," an essay published in that year, inevitably circles around the same question of how to make moral sense of a universe that undeniably contains evil elements, if indeed it is not essentially evil.[11] Dick brings to bear on the question the same configuration of eclectic disciplines that he used in *High Castle:* Eastern mysticism, Jungian psychology, and Western science. Explaining how the problem of evil became personally real for him, Dick says that "at noon one day back in 1963" he actually saw a grim metallic face with stainless steel teeth, hollow eye-slots, and a mechanical hand and arm looming at him from the sky.[12] The vision lasted, Dick says, for a month, and was the direct stimulus for *The Three Stigmata of Palmer Eldritch* (1964).

Thirteen years later Dick is obviously still shaken by that vision. In the essay he attempts to neutralize its impact by imagining that the face was a mask, reasoning that the "true face is the reverse of the mask. Of course it would be. You do not place fierce cold metal over fierce cold metal."[13] Dick goes on to apologize for the "deception" he perpetrated on his readers under the influence of that vision—that is, for his representations of evil as absolute and real. But he does not make this renunciation without an important qualification. "I do not intend to abandon my dichotomy between what I call 'human' and what I call 'android,' " Dick says (he uses the term *human* to represent the potential for good in the world, *android* to represent evil.[14] "But I had been going on surface appearances; to distinguish the categories more cunning is required. For if a gentle, harmless life conceals itself behind a frightening war-mask, then it is likely that behind gentle and loving masks there can conceal itself a vicious slayer of men's souls. In neither case can we go on surface appearance; we must penetrate to the heart of each, to the heart of the subject."[15]

Even in this essay affirming that "probably everything in the universe serves a good end," an essay in which Dick tries more or less desperately to argue that the universe is essentially benign, the strong streak of paranoia characteristic of his work keeps breaking through. For if the terrible death-mask is converted to a benign entity by the realization that it is a mask and therefore opposite to the face it covers, the same realization converts all the apparently kind faces into *their* opposites. The only certainty for Dick, and finally the most important one, is the realization that the surface does not correspond to the essence, that what we see is in some sense not reality but a mask.

In *High Castle* Dick seeks a resolution to this continuing dilemma by subtly shifting its terms. He gradually modulates from an opposition between relative evil versus absolute evil, to an opposition between the surface and the essence of things. Whereas the earlier terms emphasized how the *I Ching* and the archetypal view differed, the new terms point to what they have in common. Essential in effecting this shift is the contrast Dick sets up between historicity and *wu*. As we shall see, the distinction between historicity and *wu* enables Dick to restate the problem in terms more amenable to resolution, and leads directly into the powerful closing chapters of the novel.

Historicity, the property an artifact is reputed to possess because it has played some role in a historic event, is a surface characteristic only. It illustrates how slippery reality can become when one fails to "penetrate to the heart of the subject." Wyndam-Matson can prove that one of his two cigarette lighters has historicity only because he has a certificate from the Smithsonian Institution attesting that it was in FDR's pocket when he was assassinated. Should Wyndam-Matson lose the certificate, or should the second lighter become scratched like the first, the historicity would, if not vanish, at least become undetectable. Even Robert Childan, a dealer specializing in objects alleged to possess historicity cannot distinguish fake Colt .44s from real ones. When Childan learns from the laboratory that a gun he had thought to be authentic is really a fake, he compares the realization to a "primal childhood awakening. . . . As if . . . question might arise as to authenticity of our birth certificates. Or our impression of Dad" (*MHC*, 9).

As Mr. Childan contemplates the significance of his new knowledge, he teeters on the edge of vertigo as everything previously unquestioned becomes suspect, susceptible to the suspicion that it may be unreal.

> *Maybe* I don't actually recall F.D.R. as example. Synthetic image distilled from hearing assorted talk. Myth implanted subtly in tissue of brain. Like, he thought, myth of Hepplewhite. Myth of Chippendale. Or rather more on lines of Abraham Lincoln ate here. Used this old silver knife, fork, spoon. You can't see it, but the fact remains. (*MHC*, 9)

What Mr. Childan realizes is how very tenuous "facts" that are tied to surface appearances become once one begins to question them. In the book's climax the entire world of Childan's Axis-dominated America is revealed as a fiction, corroborating Mr. Childan's intuition that a "bit of knowledge like that goes a long way."

Although it is clear that Dick intends the property of *wu* to be the opposite of historicity, it is not clear exactly what the term means. It remains almost without definite shape, like the abstract forms of the Edfrank jewelry. It can inhere, we are told by Paul Kasoura, either in the object or in the perceiver; it is unpretentious but very powerful; it can derive either from the holiness of a relic or from the unconscious oneness of a craftsman with his material. Characteristically it cannot be discerned at first glance (Paul Kasoura confesses that he laughed behind his hand when he first saw the piece of Edfrank jewelry), yielding its meaning only after long contemplation.

Paul comes to feel that the *wu*-laden Edfrank jewelry can serve as an external reference point at least as potent as the *I Ching* or the Jungian archetype. Speaking of the jewelry, Paul insists

> "I do not even now project into this blob, as in psychological German tests, my own psyche. I still see no shapes or forms. But it somehow partakes of Tao. You see?" He motioned Childan over. "It is balanced. The forces within this piece are established. At rest. So to

speak, this object has made its peace with the universe. It has separated from it and hence has managed to come to homeostasis." (*MHC*, 11)

An object centered in the Tao, participating in the essence of the universe and yet separated from it, is almost by definition an independent reference point. The lack of a definable shape in these "blobs" is significant. These are objects pointing beyond themselves to something else—though not merely, Paul insists, to the solipsistic mirroring of one's own psyche. Freeing itself from the limits of surface, the *wu*-object is a conduit to the interior, to the "heart of the subject." Thus in Chapter 14, when Mr. Tagomi meditates on the Edfrank silver triangle, he penetrates through the surface of his world to another world beyond. He appears momentarily to have broken through, in fact, to the world as we know it: modern-day San Francisco, complete with the Embarcadero Freeway.

But is this reality? Mr. Tagomi understandably regards it as a frightening illusion, a "dreadful gliding among shadows." He regards his experience as the "world seen merely in symbolic, archetypal aspect, totally confused with unconscious material." We, of course, would disagree; for us this is the real world. But within the fictional construct of *High Castle*, the answer comes out differently. For at the end, we learn that the "real" world, according to the *I Ching*, is that depicted in Hawthorne Abendsen's alternate-history novel, *The Grasshopper Lies Heavy*. And the world of *Grasshopper* is *not* our world.

Abendsen takes as his initial premise that the Allies were victorious in World War II. From this we might infer that this fiction-within-a-fiction is a representation of history as we know it, reality turned upside down twice, so that the second inversion again brings it (from our viewpoint) right side up again. But from the brief excerpts of *Grasshopper* given in *High Castle*, it is apparent that there are significant differences between the world it depicts and our own. For example, in *Grasshopper*'s world Rexford Tugwell succeeds FDR as President; there is no color problem in the United States after 1950; Russia, divided between the United States and Britain, ceases to exist as an independent state; there is no revolution in China, which instead remains loyal to the

United States; and, in the decade following World War II, the United States and Britain begin a period of intense economic competition from which Britain emerges the victor to become the single most powerful nation in the world.

It is possible, of course, to interpret these hardly insignificant discrepancies between our world and *Grasshopper*'s as "slippage" in the divination process. As anyone who has ever consulted it knows, the *I Ching* is nothing if not ambiguous. It is therefore possible—indeed, almost inevitable—that Abendsen would have misinterpreted at least a few of the thousands of divinations he received. It is also possible that the *I Ching*, like us, can only see through a glass darkly, and that it has only dimly glimpsed the shape of the "real" universe.

But a more interesting possibility is that *Grasshopper*'s world is not merely a distorted mirror of our own, but a genuine other world, a *third* alternative history. If, as the *I Ching* asserts, *Grasshopper*'s world is the "true" one, then we—like Childan, Tagomi, and all the other inhabitants of *High Castle*—are also living in a world that is in some sense a fiction. Thus Mr. Tagomi's interpretation of his visit to our world as a "hypnosis-induced somnambulism" is not altogether inaccurate. His meditation on the significance of his brief vision of another world applies as much to the readers of *High Castle* as to him:

> Now one appreciates Saint Paul's incisive word choice . . . seen through glass darkly not a metaphor, but astute reference to optical distortion. We really do see astigmatically, in fundamental sense; our space and our time creations of our own psyche . . . . (*MHC*, 14)

When we allow ourselves to entertain this possibility, the concluding chapters acquire a depth of meaning that is remarkably and aesthetically compelling.

The richness of these last sections begins to emerge almost immediately after the section in Chapter 14 devoted to Mr. Tagomi's vision of our world. After his visitation to another world, Mr. Tagomi looks at his own world and his role in it differently. He had previously come to think of Mr. Baynes and Mr. Yatabe as wearing masks, and himself as the true face in the group. Knowing that the others are incognito, Mr. Tagomi had initially thought, "And I am Tagomi. That part is so" (*MHC*, 12).

But later he realizes that "I am a mask, concealing the real. Behind me, hidden, actuality goes on, safe from prying eyes" (*MHC*, 14). For a moment, Mr. Tagomi seems almost to grasp that he is a fiction, a character who acts as a façade behind (or through) which something else is manifesting itself.

Consider the situation that Tagomi's realization creates. *The Man in the High Castle* presents an alternative history that we readily recognize as a fiction. Within this fictive world is a character (Hawthorne Abendsen) writing a book as recognizably fictional to those around him as *High Castle* is to us. When the *I Ching* points to the world of *The Grasshopper Lies Heavy* as the real one, however, the characters within *High Castle* are forced to confront their fictionality, a fact that eludes their rational comprehension but which is plain enough to the readers of *High Castle*. But then, when we realize that the world of *Grasshopper* is not ours either, we are forced to recognize that we too may be fictions. Like the characters in *High Castle*, we cannot fully grasp how or why; but the fact remains. Dick uses his fiction-within-a-fiction-become-real-world to set up an equation: as we think the characters of *High Castle* are to us, so we are to reality.

With this novel, Dick joins the ranks of those modernists and post-modernists in mainstream fiction, such as John Barth and Julio Cortazar, who have attempted to expand the boundaries of fiction to include a consideration of the premises that make fiction possible. But Dick puts his own peculiar stamp on the technique. For he imbues a character's realization of his own fictionality with something that few others have seen: the chance for human dignity. The affirmation is all the more extraordinary for the unlikely circumstances in which it is made. Morality is mired in contradictory requirements; the world itself is blurring into unreality; but in the midst of this, the best of Dick's characters manage to break through to a vision of hope and serenity.

The solution Dick arrives at in *High Castle* seems unlikely to occur again. In later novels the protagonists, like Joe Chip in *Ubik* (1969), never stop trying to make sense of a reality that grows progressively harder to grasp, but their efforts are doomed to failure. In *High Castle* that effort is almost successful. "Almost," because the insights the characters receive must still be taken on faith. But somehow the faith is there to answer the need—and this, not the doubts that remain, is what allows Dick to achieve closure in this fractured work.

The beginnings of the transforming vision occur in Mr. Tagomi after he realizes that he too is a mask, a *persona*. This intuition both disquiets and reassures him. In a way that he cannot quite grasp, Mr. Tagomi senses that his fictionality serves a larger purpose. The intuition that his fictionality is somehow useful gives Mr. Tagomi a glimpse of *satori*, the ecstatic state in which the self is at one with reality.

> Odd, he thought. Vital sometimes to be merely cardboard front, like carton. Bit of satori there, if I could lay hold of it. Purpose in overall scheme of illusion, could we but fathom. Law of economy: nothing is waste. Even the unreal. What a sublimity in the process. (*MHC*, 14)

Though we, like Mr. Tagomi, may be unable to "lay hold of " just what purpose our fictionality serves, his example reassures us that the role need not be ignoble. For Mr. Tagomi that purpose has been defined by his part in *High Castle*. Beyond his act of heroism, his role in that fiction has been to help the readers of the novel to realize their fictionality. If his role can have this worthwhile end—to lead us to deeper insight about our condition—might not our roles as personae in a larger fiction have an equally valid purpose?

In "Man, Android and Machine," Dick gives some indication of what that purpose might be. He proposes that the world as we know it is an illusion, a veil of *maya* woven collectively by the right hemisphere of our brains that, in Robert Ornstein's view, are not merely separate parts of the brain but entirely separate minds.[16] The "benign purpose" that this occlusion of reality serves is to protect us from our own potential evil. By hiding from our vision some essential part of ourselves and the cosmos, the occlusion protects the "hidden seeds" of reality until it is safe for them to come to light. Dick envisions that, when we have become *wise* enough or *good* enough or *real* enough (these three terms are more or less synonymous for him), the veil will lift and then, he believes, we will for the first time see not our self-created fiction, but reality.

These speculations are present in *High Castle*—but only in embryo. Mr. Tagomi can sense that there is a purpose in his fictionality, but fails to grasp what it might be. The conception of that purpose, as Dick was later to define it, nearly surfaces again in Rudolf Wegener's (Baynes') belief that there must be other realities so that if we destroy ourselves, not everything would be annihilated. Foreseeing World War III, Wegener believes that the Nazis are driving "toward that Götterdämmerung. They may well crave it, be actively seeking it, a final holocaust for everyone." But if the holocaust is to come, Wegener consoles himself with the belief that it "is impossible that ours is the only world; there must be world after world unseen by us, in some region or dimension that we simply do not perceive" (*MHC*, 15). That we fail to perceive them is chiefly why we cannot despoil them. Seen clearly, Dick hints through these characters, our unreality is evidence of an ultimately benign spirit manifesting itself through us.

But Dick does not allow this final accommodation to blind him to the evils in the here and now. Until the veil of *maya* is lifted, Dick says, the best we can hope for is what the characters of *High Castle* sometimes achieve: a moment of seeing unencumbered. Such a moment comes to Robert Childan when he demands an apology from Paul Kasoura for suggesting that the Edfrank jewelry be mass-produced as good-luck charms:

> Calmness descended in Childan's heart. I have lived through and out, he knew. All over. Grace of God; it existed at the exact moment for me. Another time—otherwise. Could I ever dare once more, press my luck? Probably not.
> He felt melancholy. Brief instant, as if I rose to the surface and saw unencumbered. (*MHC*, 11)

But these moments, Dick reminds us, are brief. For the most part, we live in the same kind of world Mr. Tagomi perceives when he hears of Operation Dandelion, a world in which evil and good are so inextricably mixed that it is impossible to act cleanly and unambiguously.

> Evil, Mr. Tagomi thought. Yes, it is. Are we to assist it in gaining power, in order to save our lives? Is that the paradox of our earthly situation?
> I cannot face this dilemma, Mr. Tagomi said to himself. That man should have to act in such moral ambiguity. There is no Way in this; all

is muddled. All chaos is light and dark, shadow and substance. (*MHC*,
12)

To Dick, moral ambiguity is inevitable in a world that is ontologi-
cally ambiguous.

Though he insists on the complexity of moral choices in a world
that we cannot be sure is real, Dick also makes clear that it is
necessary to choose, and that some choices are better than
others. Wegener, on his way back to an uncertain fate in Germany, struggles with just this problem:

> No wonder Mr. Tagomi could not go on, he thought. The terrible
> dilemma of our lives. Whatever happens, it is evil beyond compare.
> Why struggle, then? Why choose? If all alternatives are the same
> . . . (*MHC*, 15)

But it is clear they are not all the same, as Wegener continues:

> Evidently we go on, as we always have. From day to day. At this
> moment we work against Operation Dandelion. Later on, at another
> moment, we work to defeat the police. But we cannot do it all at once;
> it is a sequence. An unfolding process. We can only control the end by
> making a choice at each step.
> He thought, We can only hope. And try.
> On some other world, possibly it is different. Better. There are clear
> good and evil alternatives. Not these obscure admixtures, these
> blends, with no proper tool by which to untangle the components.
> We do not have the ideal world, such as we would like, where
> morality is easy because cognition is easy. Where one can do right
> with no effort because he can detect the obvious. (*MHC*, 15)

If such a world exists, it is not ours. In our world too, Dick
believes, we have these "obscure admixtures" that are ultimately
the result of a flawed perception. In reality—whatever that might
be and however we are to come to it—morality is easy because
we perceive correctly. If that is not so, Dick implies, then what
we see is not reality but illusion.

With this formulation, Dick is able to resolve his dilemma. Evil
is ultimately unreal, Dick reasons, because a world where evil is
real is itself unreal. Moreover, we cannot see the real world be-

cause we see through a veil that we have created to protect us from the very evil that we believe to be real. When we cease to believe in evil, the veil will lift—and we will see clearly a world which is both good and real.

The danger in this formulation is its neatness. Were it not a vision won at considerable cost, its circular argument could become an easy way to rationalize an uneasy world. To his credit, Dick does not succumb to facile solutions. The pressure of incipient paranoia in the Dickian world is so strong that the real temptation for Dick is not the easy solution, but the impossible one. Increasingly in his later fiction, Dick turns to problems of false realities that admit of no moral or ontological resolution.

With its delicate balance between reality and unreality, metafiction and metaphysics, *The Man in the High Castle* stands at a cusp in the Dickian canon. The resolution it achieves is so fragile that it is unlikely to be repeated. It represents a moment in Dick's evolving perspective in which it is possible for him to reach affirmation while still recognizing the deeper problems that will dominate his later work. If at times Dick, blinded by his own occlusions, has fallen short of attaining the standard he set with *The Man in the High Castle,* he gives witness to his testimony that the moments of seeing clearly and unencumbered are all too brief.

4. Artifice as Refuge and World View: Philip K. Dick's Foci*

DARKO SUVIN

I WOULD divide Dick's writing into three main periods: 1952–62, 1962–65, and 1966–74.[1] The first period is one of apprenticeship and limning of his themes and devices, first in short or longer stories (1952–56) and then in his early novels from *Solar Lottery* to *Vulcan's Hammer* (1955–60), and it culminates in the mature polyphony of *The Man in the High Castle* (1962). Dick's second, central period stands out to my mind as a high plateau in his opus. Following on his creative breakthrough in *High Castle*, it comprises (together with some less successful tries) the masterpieces of *Martian Time-Slip* and *Dr. Bloodmoney*, as well as that flawed but powerful near-masterpiece *The Three Stigmata of Palmer Eldritch*. The latest phase of Dick's writing, beginning in 1966, is in many ways a falling off. It is characterized by a turning from a fruitful tension between public and private concerns toward a simplified narration increasingly preoccupied with solitary anxieties and by a corresponding concern with unexplainable ontological puzzles; and it has clearly led to the creative sterility of 1970–74 (*We Can Build You*, though published in 1972, had appeared in magazine version by 1970). However, *Ubik* (1969), the

---

*This chapter appeared originally in slightly different form in *Science-Fiction Studies* 5 (March 1975).

richest and most provocative novel of this phase, testifies to the necessity for a closer analysis of even this downbeat period of Dick's. Thus an overview of his opus can, I trust, find a certain logic in its development, but it is not a mechanical or linear logic.

Dick's work intimately influenced by and participating in the great processes of the American collective or social psychology in these last twenty years, shares the hesitations, the often irrational though always understandable leaps backwards, forwards, and sideways of that psychology. It is perhaps most understandable as the work of a prose poet whose basic tools are not verse lines and poetic figures but (1) relationships within the narrative; (2) various alternate worlds, the specific political and ontological relationships in each of which are analogous to the United States (or simply to California) in the 1950s and 60s; and (3) —last but not least—the vivid characters on whom his narration and his worlds finally repose. In this chapter I propose to deal with just these three specific areas of Dick's creativity: some basic relationships in Dick's story-telling—a notion richer than, though connected with, the plotting—will be explored by an analysis of narrative foci and power levels; Dick's alternate worlds will be explored in function of his increasing shift from mostly political to mostly ontological horizons; finally, Dick's allegorically exaggerated characters will be explored in their own right as fundaments for the morality and cognition in his novels.

1. PILGRIMAGE WITHOUT PROGRESS: NARRATIVE FOCI AND POWER LEVELS

> Amazing the power of fiction, even cheap popular fiction, to evoke. (*MHC*, 8)

In order to illuminate the development of Dick's story-telling, I shall follow his use of characters as *narrative foci* and as indicators of *upper and lower social classes or power statuses*. The concept of narrative focus seems necessary because Dick as a rule uses a narration which is neither that of the old-fashioned all-knowing, neutral and superior, narrator, nor a narration in the first person by the central characters. The narration proceeds instead somewhere in between those two extreme possibilities, simultaneously in the third person and from the vantage point of the central or focal character in a given segment. This is always clearly delimited from other segments with other focal characters—first, by means of chapter endings or at least by section breaks within a chapter, and second, by the focal character's being named at the beginning of each such narrative segment, usually after an introductory sentence or clause which sets up the time and place of the new section. The focal character is also used as a visual, auditive, and psychological focus whose vantage point in fact colors and limits the subsequent narration. This allows the reader to empathize into—usually to sympathize with but always at least to understand—all the focal characters, be they villains or heroes in the underlying plot conflict, for Dick has no black or white villains and heroes in the sense of van Vogt (from whom the abstracted plot conflicts are often borrowed). In the collective, nonindividualist world of Dick, everybody, high and low, destroyer and sufferer, is in an existential situation which largely determines his/her actions; even the arch-destroyer Palmer Eldritch is a sufferer.

The novels before 1962 are approximations to such a technique of multifocal narrative. This technique's primitive seed, the one-hero-at-the-center narrative, is to be found in *Eye in the Sky*, and together with a half-hearted try at two subsidiary foci in *The Man Who Japed*. *Solar Lottery* has two clear foci, Benteley and Cartwright, with insufficiently sustained strivings toward a polyphonic structure (Verrick, Wakeman, Groves). Similarly, though there are half a dozen narrative foci in *Time Out of Joint*, Ragle is clearly their privileged center; in fact, the whole universe of the book has been constructed only to impinge upon him, just as all universes impinged upon the protagonist of *Eye in the Sky*. *Vulcan's Hammer* is focussed around the two bureaucrats Barris and Dill, with Marion coming a poor third; the important character of Father Fields does not become a narrative focus, as he logically should have, nor does the intelligent computer though he is similar, say, to the equally destructive and destroyed Arnie Kott in *Martian Time-Slip*. However, in *High Castle* there is to be found for the first time the full Dickian narrative articulation, surpassed only in *Martian Time-Slip* and *Dr. Bloodmoney*. With some simplifying of secondary characters and subplots, and taking into account the levels of social—here explicitly political—power, *High Castle* divides into two parallel plots with these narrative foci (marked by caps, while other important characters are named in lower case):

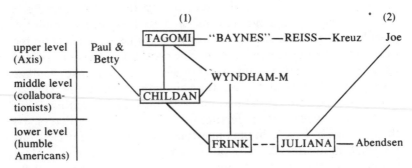

The upper level is one of politico-ethical conflict between murderous Nazi fanaticism and Japanese tolerance (the assumption that a victorious Japanese fascism would be radically better than the German one is the major political blunder of Dick's novel). In (1), the San Francisco plot, the two sympathetic focal characters are Frank Frink, the suffering refugee Jew and creative little man, and Mr. Tagomi, the ethical Japanese official. In (2), the locomotive plot, the sole focal character is Juliana. Tagomi helps "Baynes" in trying to foil the global political scheme of Nazi universal domination, and incidentally also foils the extradition of Frink to the Nazis, while Juliana foils the Nazis' (Joe's) plot to assassinate Abendsen, the science-fiction writer of a book postulating Axis defeat in World War II; Tagomi and Juliana both turn out to be, more by instinct than by design, antagonists of the fascist politico-psychological evil. But the passive link between them is Frink, Juliana's ex-husband, and his artistic creation, the silvery pin mediating between earth and sky, life and death, past and future, the *High Castle* universe and the alternate universe of our empirical reality. Tagomi's reality-change vision (Chapter 14), induced by contemplating Frink's pin, is a Dickian set scene which recreates, through an admittedly partial narrative viewpoint, the great utopian tradition that treats a return to the reader's freeways, smog, and jukebox civilization as a vision of hell—exactly as at the end of *Gulliver's Travels, Looking Backward,* or *News From Nowhere.* But it is also an analogue of the vision of Abendsen's book: the book and the pin come from chthonic depths but become mediators only after being shaped by the intellect, albeit an oracular and largely instinctive one. For Dick, a writer (especially a science-fiction writer) is always first and foremost an "artificer," both in the sense of artful craftsman and in the sense of creator of new, "artificial" but nonetheless possible worlds. Frink and Abendsen, the two artificers—the former the broodingly passive but (see diagram above) centrally situated narrative focus of the book, the other a shadowy but haunting figure appearing at its close—constitute, with Tagomi and Juliana, the two instinctive ethical activists, the four pillars of hope opposed to the dominant political madness of fascism. Though most clearly institutionalized in German Nazism, it can also be found in middle-class Americans such as Childan, the racist small shopkeeper who oscillates between being a helper and a deceitful exploiter of creative artificers such as Frink.

The second or plateau period of Dick's opus retains and deepens the narrative polyphony found in *High Castle.* It does both by increasing the number of the narrative foci and by stressing some relationships among the focal characters as privileged, thereby providing an easier overview with less redundancy and a stronger impact. The two culminations of such proceeding are *Martian Time-Slip* and *Dr. Bloodmoney.* In *Martian Time-Slip,* three of the focal characters stand out (underlined):

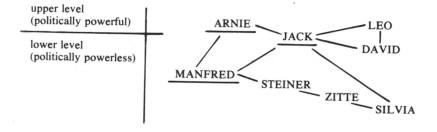

Of the three privileged characters, the labor boss Arnie is powerful and sociable, the autistic boy Manfred politically powerless and asocial, while the central character, Jack Bohlen, mediates between the two not only in his sociopolitical status but also in his fits of and struggle against psychosis. However, Jack, the manual craftsman, and Manfred, the time-binding precog, are allied against the tycoon Arnie. This is the first clear expression in Dick's opus of the alliance and yet also the split between Rousseauist personal freedom, realized in Manfred's final symbiosis with the totally asocial, noble-savage Bleekmen, and an ethical communal order, implied in Jack. The politically powerless turn the tables on the powerful—as did Juliana in *High Castle*—by means of their greater sensitivity. This allows them a much deeper understanding of people and things, inner and outer nature (which they pay for by greater suffering). Therefore, the set-piece or obligatory situation in *Martian Time-Slip* is again a visionary scene involving Manfred, Jack, and Arnie in several interdependent versions of nightmarish reality-change (Chapters 10 and 11).

The oppositions are aggravated and therefore explored more fully in Dick's narratively most sophisticated work. Nine personal narrative foci are here, astoundingly, joined by two choral focal groups—the secondary characters who get killed during the narrative but help decisively in Hoppy's defeat, such as Fergesson, and the post-Bomb-community secondary characters, such as June. The double division in *Martian Time-Slip* (powerful/powerless plus personal freedom/ethical order) is here richly articulated into (1) the destructive dangers which are opposed to the new prospects of life and vitality, and further subdivided into (2) the search for a balanced community, and (3) the search for personal happiness (see below). Very interestingly, Dangerfield, the mediator of practical tips and past culture, provides the link between all those who oppose the destroyers. In this most optimistic of Dick's novels, Bloodmoney's Bomb was a Happy Fall: the collapse of American sociopolitical and technological power abolishes the class distinctions, and thus makes possible a new start and innocence leading to the defeat of the new, anti-utopian would-be usurpers by the complementary forces of a new communal and personal order. These forces are aptly symbolized by the homunculus Bill—perhaps Dick's most endearing character—who is both person and symbiotic creature:

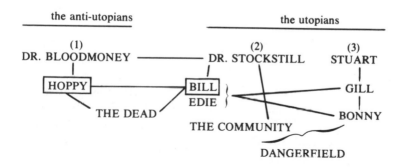

In this light, the ideological movement of the book is complete when Bonny, the all-embracing Earth Mother figure, has forsaken the old danger, Bloodmoney, and when her son Bill—coeval with the innocence and power of the new order (much as his feebler prototype, Mrs. Grayles in Walter M. Miller's *A Canticle for Leibowitz*)—has defeated the new danger, Hoppy. Fredric Jameson identified the new danger convincingly with a neo-pragmatic stance connected with modern electronics and the United States,[2] just as the old danger was the classical mad scientist of the Dr. Strangelove type connected with nuclear physics and Germany. Jameson's essay, as well as the analyses of *Martian Time-Slip* by Brian Aldiss (reprinted in this volume) and Carlo Pagetti (in *Science-Fiction Studies*, March 1975) make it possible to cut short here the discussion of narrative foci in these two master-pieces of Dick's. It only remains to notice that a Rousseauist utopianism cannot finally fuse personal happiness and harmonious community—at the utmost it can run them in tandem, or as the horizons of two successive generations and historical stages.

2. AM-WEB: POLITICS AND ONTOLOGY

The disintegration of the social and economic system had been slow, gradual, and profound. It went so deep that people lost faith in natural law itself. (*Solar Lottery*, 2)

There remains, in Dick's middle period, the important if ambiguous *The Three Stigmata of Palmer Eldritch*, the discussion of which will require shifting the emphasis to what are for Dick the horizons of human destiny. *Palmer Eldritch* is the first significant Dick novel to allot equal weight to politics and ontology as arbiters of its microcosm and its characters' destinies. I shall deal first with politics.

Up to the mid-60s Dick could be characterized as a writer of anti-utopian science fiction in the wake of Orwell's *1984* and of the menacing world-war and post-Bomb horizons in the pulp "new maps of hell" by Bradbury, Heinlein, Blish, and Pohl (to mention those who, together with van Vogtian plotting and Besterian ESPers, seem to have meant most to him). The horrors of Cold War politics, paranoiac militarism, mass hysteria organized by politicians, and encroaching government totalitarianism are broached in the stories of the mid-50s such as "Breakfast at Twilight," "War Veteran," or "Second Variety"; in one of the best, "Foster, You're Dead," the militarist craze for bomb-shelters is further seen as a tool for commercial twisting of the everyday life of little people. In Dick's early novels the dystopian framework is developed by adding to a look at the dominated humble people an equally inside look at the ruling circles—the telepaths and quizmasters in *Solar Lottery*, the secret police in *The Variable Man* and *The World Jones Made*, the mass-media persuaders in *The Man Who Japed*, the powerful bureaucrats in *Vulcan's Hammer*. Indeed, *Eye in the Sky* is the formalization of a literally "inside" look at four variants of dystopia, and carries the message that in the world of modern science we are all truly members of one another. Up to *Palmer Eldritch* then, the novels by Dick which are not primarily dystopian (*The Cosmic Puppets*, *Dr. Futurity*, *The Game-Players of Titan*) are best forgotten. Obversely, political dystopia has remained a kind of zero-level for Dick's writing right to the present day (e.g., in *Flow My Tears, the Policeman Said*), at times even explicitly connecting the early stories to the later second-line novels by taking over a story's theme or situation and developing it into the novel's mainstay (e.g., "The Defenders" and *The Penultimate Truth*, or "Shell Game" and *Clans of the Alphane Moon*).

The culmination and transmutation of political horizons occurs in Dick's "plateau tetralogy," from *The Man in the High Castle* to *Dr. Bloodmoney*. *High Castle*, with its superb feel of Nazi psychology and of life in a world of occupiers, occupied, and quislings overshadowed by it, is the high point of Dick's explicitly political anti-utopianism. Paradoxically if precariously balanced by ethical optimism, it is, because of that confident balance and richness, in some ways Dick's most lucid book. It is also the first culmination of the Germanic-paranoia-turning-fascist theme which has been haunting Dick as no other American science-fiction writer (with the possible exception of Vonnegut) since *The Variable Man* with its Security Commissioner Reinhart, and the seminal *Man Who Japed* with its German-American Big Brother in the person of Major Jules Streiter, founder of the Moral Reclamation movement. The naming of this shadowy King Anti-Utopus is an excellent example for Dick's ideological onomastics: it compounds allusions to the names and doctrines of Moral Rearmament's Buchman, Social Credit's Major Douglas, and the fanatic Nazi racist Jules Streicher. The liberalism of even the seemingly most hard-nosed dystopian science-fiction in the American 1940s–50s, with its illusions of Back to the Spirit of 1776, pales into insignificance beside Dick's pervasive, intimate, and astoundingly rich understanding of the affinities between German and American fascism, born of the same social classes of big speculators and small shopkeepers. This understanding is embodied in a number of characters who span the death-lust spectrum between political and psychological threat. Beginning with the wholly American Childan (who is, correspondingly, a racist out of insecurity rather than fanaticism, and is allowed a positive conversion) and the German assassin Joe masquerading as an American in *High Castle*, through Norbert Steiner and Otto Zitte as well as the vaguely Teutonic-American corrupt bigwigs Leo Bohlen and Arnie Kott in *Martian Time-Slip*, such a series culminates in Dr. Bruno Bluthgeld/Bloodmoney (descended from von Braun, Teller, et sim., both through newspapers and through Kubrick's mad German scientist Dr. Strangelove). It finally leads to a German takeover of the Western world by means of their industries and androids in *The Simulacra*, and of the whole planet through the UN in *The Unteleported Man*. In this last novel, the revelation that UN boss Horst Bertold (whose name and final revelatory plea are derived from Bertold

Brecht, the antifascist German whose name would be most familiar to the music and drama lover Dick) is a "good" German, on
the same side of the political fence as the hounded little man
Rachmael ben Applebaum, effects a reconciliation of powerful
German and powerless Jew.

These politico-national roles or clichés had started poles apart
in *High Castle*. But by the end of Dick's German-Nazi theme and
cycle the year was 1966, and the sensitive author quite rightly
recognized that the world, and in particular the United States,
had other fish to fry: the ubiquitous fascist menace was no longer
primarily German or anti-Jewish. Already in *Martian Time-Slip*,
the lone German killers Steiner and Zitte were small fry compared
to the Americans of Teutonic descent, Leo and Arnie. In *Dr.
Bloodmoney*, therefore, the Bluthgeld menace is supplanted by
the deformed American obstinately associated with the product
of Bluthgeld's fallout—the Ayn Rand follower and cripple
Hoppy, wired literally up to his teeth into the newest electronic
death-dealing gadgets. Clearly, Bluthgeld relates to Hoppy as the
German-associated World-War-II and Cold-War technology of
the 1940s and 50s to the Vietnam War technology of the 60s. It is
the same relation as the one between the Nazi-treated superman
Bulero and the reality manipulator Eldritch, and finally between
the Krupps and Heydrichs of *High Castle* and the military-
industrial complex of American capitalism: "it was Washington
that was dropping the bombs on (the American people), not the
Chinese or the Russians" (*Dr. B,* 5). The transformation or transubstantiation of classical European fascism into new American
power is also the theme of two significant stories Dick wrote in
the 60s, "If There Were No Benny Cemoli" (read—Benito Mussolini) and "Oh, to Be a Blobel!" (where an American tycoon
turns Alien while his humbler employee wife turns human). The
third significant story, "What the Dead Men Say"—which stands
halfway between *Palmer Eldritch* and *Ubik*—features half-life as
a nonsupernatural hoax by American economic and political to-
talitarians on the make.

By the *Martian Time-Slip* phase, Dick's little man is being
opposed not only to political and technological but also to
economic power in the person of the rival tycoons Leo (representing a classical big speculators' syndicate) and Arnie (whose capi-

tal comes from control of big trade-union funds), while on the horizon of both Terra and Mars there looms the big cooperative movement, whose capital comes from investments of members. In the corrupt microcosm of *Martian Time-Slip* these three variants of capitalism (classical *laissez faire*, bureaucratic, and demagogically managerial), together with the state capitalism of the superstate UN disposing of entire planets, constitute what is almost a brief survey of its possible forms. The slogan of the big cooperative-capitalist movement, which Manfred sees crowning his horrible vision of planetary future in decay, is AM-WEB, explained in Dick's frequent record-jacket German as "Alle Menschen werden Brüder"—"All men become brothers" (from Schiller through Beethoven's Ninth). But of course this explanation is half true and half disingenuous—the proper acronym for the slogan would, after all, be AMWB with no "E" and no hyphen. Thus, within Dick's normative Germano-American parallelism, AM–WEB is also, and even primarily, an emblem of the ironic reversal of pretended liberty, fraternity, and equality—it is the *American Web* of big business, corrupt labor aristocracy, and big state that turn the difficult everyday life of the little man into a future nightmare. As Mr. Aldiss remarks in this book, the whole of *Martian Time-Slip*—and beyond that, most of Dick—is a maledictory web. The economico-political spider spinning it is identified with a clarity scarcely known in American science fiction between Jack London's Oligarchy and Ursula LeGuin's Propertarians. The Rousseauist utopianism of *Dr. Bloodmoney* is an indication that the urge to escape this cursed web is so deep it would almost welcome an atomic holocaust as a chance to start anew: "We are, Adams realized, a cursed race. Genesis is right: there is a stigma on us, a mark" (*The Penultimate Truth*, 13).

The three stigmata of Palmer Eldritch, the interplanetary industrialist who peddles dope to enslave the masses, are three signs of demonic artificiality. The prosthetic eyes, hands, and teeth, allow him—in a variant of the Wolf in Little Red Riding Hood—to see (understand), grab (manipulate), and rend (ingest, consume) his victims better. Like the tycoon in "Oh, to Be a Blobel!" this eldritch palmer or uncanny pilgrim towards the goal of universal market domination is clearly a "mad capitalist" (to coin a term parallel to mad scientist), a miraculous organizer of production wasted through absence of rational distribution *(3SPE,*1) who turned Alien on a power trip. But his peculiar terrifying force is that he turns his doped manipulees not only into a captive market (see Dick's early story of that title) but also into partial, stigmatized replicas of himself by working through their ethical and existential weaknesses. The Palmer Eldritch type of supercorporative capitalism is in fact a new religion, stronger and more pervasive than the classical transcendental ones, because "GOD PROMISES ETERNAL LIFE. WE CAN DELIVER IT" *(3SPE,* 9). What it delivers, though, is not only a new thing under the Sun but also false, activating the bestial or alien inhumanity within man: "And—we have no mediating sacraments through which to protect ourselves . . . . It [the Eldritch Presence] is out in the open, ranging in every direction. It looks into our eyes; and it looks *out* of our eyes" *(3SPE,* 13). Dick moves here along jungle trails first blazed by William S. Burroughs: for both, the hallucinatory operators are real.

The narrative structure of *Palmer Eldritch* combines multifocality with a privileged protagonist-antagonist (Mayerson-Eldritch) axis and with the division into power levels:

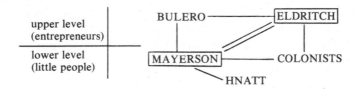

However, the erstwhile normal conflict between the upper and the lower social levels is here superseded by the appearance of a new-type antagonist, Eldritch, who snares not only the little people—Mayerson and other Mars colonists—but also the established power of Bulero, and indeed subverts the whole notion of monadic, individualistic characters of the nineteenth-century kind upon which Dick's, like most other, science-fiction had so far reposed. The appearance of Eldritch, signalized by his stigmata, *inside* the other characters shifts the conflict into their psyches—can they trust their reality perceptions? The political theme and horizon begin here to give way to the ontological.

While the ontological dilemmas have a clear genesis in the political ones, they shift the power relationships from human institutions to mysterious entities, never quite accounted for or understood in the narration. *Palmer Eldritch* is thus that first significant station in Dick's development where the ontological preoccupations begin to weigh as heavily as, or more heavily than, the political dystopianism.

Such preoccupations can, no doubt, be found in Dick's writing right from the beginning. "Foster, You're Dead," the story of a boy alienated by conformist social pressures, is already halfway between Pohl's satires (it was published by Frederick Pohl in *Star SF 3*) and the suffering alienated boy Manfred in *Martian Time-Slip* who erects an alternative reality as refuge, and can serve as a key to Dick's theme of mental alienation connected with reality changes. Parallel to that, "Adjustment Team" is a first tentative try at evolving Pohl's "The Tunnel Under the World" situation of total manipulation (also the kernel of *Palmer Eldritch*) toward metaphysics. The mysterious failure of memory, or missing interval of consciousness accompanied by headache, which is a sign of dissolving realities and is often found in combination with drug-taking, recurs from *The Man Who Japed* through *Martian Time-Slip* to *Palmer Eldritch*. Tagomi's great vision in *High Castle* and Manfred's AM-WEB vision in *Martian Time-Slip* can already be interpreted not only as trance-like insights but also as actual changes in collective reality. These are changes in being (ontological, as already in *Eye in the Sky*) rather than only in foreknowledge (gnoseological, as in *The World Jones Made*) or, even more simply, fraudulent-cum-psychotic ones (as in *Time Out of Joint*). Indeed, the storytelling microcosms, the depicted planetary realities of both *High Castle* and *Martian Time-Slip* are analogies for reality changes immanent in the author's here-and-now and already showing through it, like Eldritch's stigmata. *High Castle* is an alternative world explicating a California, USA, and globe fallen prey to fascism. *Martian Time-Slip* substitutes the more general physical category of entropy for its political particular case: Dick's Mars is a run-down future, "a sort of Humpty-Dumpty" where people and things have decayed "into rusty bits and useless debris" (*MTS*, 6), a space and time leading—in ironic repudiation of Bradbury's nostalgia for the petty-bourgeois past and Clarke's confidence in liberal scientism—to the dialectical interplay between Manfred's devolutionary vision of "gubble" (rubble, rubbish, crumble, gobble) invading everybody's reality and vitality and Jack's struggle against it. The totalitarian manipulation and the entropic human relations are to be found in *Palmer Eldritch* together with and flowing into a false, profit-making religion.

However, the shift from politics to ontology, which was only hinted at in *High Castle* and will culminate in *Ubik*, is in *Palmer Eldritch* not consistent. The referents of this lush novel are overdetermined: Eldritch, the allegorical representative of neocapitalism, is at the same time the bearer of an "evil, negative trinity of alienation, blurred reality and despair" (*3SPE*, 13) of demonic though unclear origin. An orthodox religious and an orthodox politico-economic reading of *Palmer Eldritch* can both be fully supported by the evidence of the novel; but neither of these complementary and yet in some ways basically contradictory readings can explain the full novel—which is to boot overburdened with quite unnecessary elements such as Mayerson's precog faculties, the garden-variety theological speculations, etc. Politics, physics, and metaphysics combine to create in *Palmer Eldritch* a fascinating and iridescent manifold, but their interference also, to my mind, makes for an insufficiently economical novel. It starts squarely within the political and physical field (clash of big drug corporations, temperature rise, colonization of Mars) and then drags across it the red herring of ontologico-religious speculations grafted upon van Vogtian plot gimmicks (here from Leigh Brackett's *The Big Jump*, 1955) which shelve rather than solve the thematic problems.

3. ALL WE MARSMEN: CHARACTEROLOGY AS MORALITY AND COGNITION

We do not have the ideal world, such as we would like, where morality is easy because cognition is easy. (*MHC*, 15)

In Dick's anthropology, the differentiation between upper and lower politico-economic power statuses is correlative to a system of correspondences between profession, as relating to a specific type of creativity, and ethical goodness or evil. This reposes on a more general view of human nature and species-specific human conduct, for which morality and cognition are closely allied, and which will be discussed in this section. Such an alliance breaks down in *Ubik;* this is to my mind the explanation of Dick's difficulties after 1966.

From Dick's earliest writings, aggressiveness is identified not only with militarism but also with commercialism (as in "Nanny"), and villainy with either totalitarian or capitalist rulers (as in "A Present for Pat," and in the stories of the 60s mentioned in Section 2). Opposed to the unscrupulous tycoons and other bigwigs (Verrick in *Solar Lottery,* the terrifying roster of Führer candidates in *High Castle,* Leo Bohlen and Arnie Kott in *Martian Time-Slip,* Leo Bulero and Palmer Eldritch in *Palmer Eldritch,* the Yancy Men in *The Penultimate Truth,* etc.) are the little people. The two ends of the politico-economic and power scale relate as "have-nots" to "titans" (*The Unteleported Man,* 14), but also as creators to destroyers. For, Dick's protagonists are as a rule some variant of immediate producer or direct creator. They are not industrial workers engaged in collective production—a class conspicuous by its absence here as in practically all modern science fiction. On the contrary, Dick's heroes are most often the new individual craftsmen, producers of art objects or repairmen of the most sophisticated (e.g., cybernetic) Second-Industrial-Revolution products. They are updated versions of the old-fashioned handyman (who is celebrated in the "Fixit-cart," nonstatistical, unquantifiable, "variable man" of the eponymous story) for a contemporary, or near-future, highly industrialized society; and their main trait is a direct and personalized relationship to creative productivity as opposed to standardized mass-production with its concomitant other-directedness, loss of self-reliance, and shoddy living (a key to this is to be found in the story "Pay for the Printer," a finger-exercise for *Dr. Bloodmoney*).

This characterology is not yet quite clear in the earlier novels, which deal more with the Ibsenian theme of social deceit versus individual struggle for truth than with the theme of destruction versus creation. Of *Solar Lottery's* two heroes one, Benteley, is a classical "cadre," a biochemist, and only the other, Cartwright, is "electronics repairman and human being with a conscience" (*SL*,2). Similarly, the hero of *Eye in the Sky* turns only at the end of the book from chief of missile lab to builder of phonographs, switching from Dick's chief dislike, militarism, to his chief love, music. But already in his early works there appears a populist or indeed New Left tendency to distrust rational intelligence, contaminated as it is by its association with "the cult of the Technocrat . . . run by and *for* those oriented around verbal knowledge" (*Vulcan's Hammer,* 14), and to oppose to it spontaneous action guided by intuition—a politics of the "do your own thing" type. Thus in *Time Out of Joint,* Ragle is a creative personality who dislikes the nine-to-five drudgery of the huge conformist organizations, regimented like armies (*TOJ,* 1), and who can "sense the pattern" of events through his artistic abilities (*TOJ,* 14). Though the traces of this dichotomy can be felt even in the *High Castle* heroes Tagomi and Frink—who are juxtaposed as mind and hand, intellectual visionary from the upper power level and intuitive creator from the powerless depths—it is fortunately absent from his most mature creations, the "plateau masterpieces" in which his ethico-professional pattern of characters emerges most clearly. In *Martian Time-Slip,* Steiner and Zitte are small speculators who exploit the work of others, just as the small shopkeeper Childan in *High Castle* exploited the creativity of the artificer Jew-Gentile pair, Frink and McCarthy; like him, Steiner and Zitte are unable to face reality and so resort to sexual fantasies alternating with suicidal/homicidal moods. At the other end of the power scale, Arnie Kott fuses the financial role of the big speculator, represented in pure form by Leo, with Zitte's role of sexual exploiter.

This quasi-robotic role of a sexually efficient but emotionally uncommitted *macho,* for Dick an ethical equivalent of economic exploitation, is to be found in his negative characters from the android of "Second Variety" to such "titans" as Verrick in *Solar Lottery* or Arnie Kott in *Martian Time-Slip* who use their female employees and mistresses as pawns in power maneuvers. Opposed to them are the sincere little people, here the repairman Jack Bohlen, who fight their way through the sexual as well as the economic jungle step by laborious step. In *Palmer Eldritch,* the character spread runs from the capitalist destroyer Eldritch to the suffering artist-creator Emily; and the central hero Mayerson's fall from grace begins by his leaving Emily for success's sake and is consummated when he refuses her creations for personal revenge, thus becoming an impediment to human creativity and falling into the clutches of Eldritch's false creations. Emily's husband Hnatt is midway between her and Mayerson: he is her co-worker, the vendor of her products, but his ambiguous position in the productive process finally brings about her creative regression in the novel's rather underdeveloped subplot of false creativity through forced intellectual evolution (this subplot is carried by Bulero, the old-fashioned tycoon). Similarly, in *The Penultimate Truth* the weak and less sympathetic characters are the wordsmiths who have forsaken personal creativity to be abused for the purposes of a regressive political apparatus (Lindblom). This novel divides into two plots, the ruling-class and the subterranean one. The first centers, alas, around a van Vogtian immortal and the intrigue from *The House That Stood Still* (1950), marring one of Dick's potentially most interesting books. For the hero of the other plot, Nick, is the democratically elected president of an oppressed community, whose creativity is manifested by political persistence in securing the rights of an endangered member. Thus Dick's concept of creativity, though it centers on artists, encompasses both erotic and political creative ethics.

Beside the professional roles, Dick has three basic female roles, also clearly present in *Palmer Eldritch* as Roni, Emily, and Anne around Mayerson. The first role is that of castrating bitch, a female *macho,* striving to rise in the corporative power-world (also Kathy in *Now Wait for Last Year,* Pris in *We Can Build You,* etc.); the second that of weak but stabilizing influence (also Silvia in *Martian Time-Slip,* etc.); and the third, crowning one that of a strong but warm sustaining force. Although Dick's female characters seem less fully developed than his male ones, such an Earth Mother becomes the final embodiment of ethical and political rightness in his most hopeful novels (Juliana in *High Castle,* Bonny in *Dr. Bloodmoney*); conversely, the Bitch is developed with increasing fascination in his third phase.

As suggested above, the totally unethical and therefore inhuman person is often an android, what Dick, with a stress on its counterfeiting and artificial aspect, calls a *simulacrum* (see his very instructive Vancouver speech in *SF Commentary,* no. 31). Already in his first novel, this is associated with modern science being manipulated by power-mad people, who are themselves the truly reified inhumans and therefore in a way more unauthentic than their simulacra. An interesting central anthropological tenet is adumbrated here, halfway between Rousseau and Marx, according to which there is an *authentic core* identical with humanity in Homo sapiens, from which men and women have to be alienated by civilizational pressures in order to behave in an unauthentic, dehumanized way, so that there is always an inner resistance to such pressures in anybody who simply follows his or her human(e) instinct of treating people as ends, not means. That is why Dick's heroes rely on instinct and persistence (several of them, such as Jack in *Martian Time-Slip* or Nick in *The Penultimate Truth* are characterized as permanently "going to keep trying"). That is why social class is both a functionally decisive and yet not an exclusive criterion for determining the humanity of the characters: the more powerful one is, the more dehumanized one becomes, and Dick's only real heroes tend to be the creative little people, with the addition of an occasional visionary; yet even the literally dehumanized alien such as Eldritch has inextinguishable remnants of humanity within him which qualify him for suffering, and thus for the reader's partial, dialectical sympathy for his (now alienated) human potentialities. That is why, finally, there emerges the strange and charmingly grotesque Dickian world of semianimated cybernetic constructs, which makes stretches of even his weaker novels enjoyable light reading: e.g., the fly-size shrilling commercial and the hypnotic surrogate-"papoola" of *The Simulacra,* the Lazy Brown Dog reject carts in *Now Wait for Last Year,* the stupid elevators and grumpy cybernetic taxis such as Max the auto-auto in *The Game-Players of Titan,* etc. Together with a few interesting aliens, the all-too-human inhumans culminate in the menace of *Palmer Eldritch* and in Dick's richest spectrum of creatures in *Dr. Bloodmoney,* which runs from the stigmatic psi-powers of Bluthgeld and cyborg booster-devices of Hoppy to the zany and appealing new life-cycle of homeostatic traps and evolved animals. At the center of *Dr. Bloodmoney* is the homunculus Bill, who is in touch with humans, animals, and even the dead, and unites the kinaesthetic and verbal powers in the universe of that novel.

I have left *Ubik* for the end of this discussion both because it seems to me Dick's last major work to date and because in it the analogies between morality and cognition suffer a sea-change. The Dickian narrative model, as discussed here, is in *Ubik* extremely simplified and then recomplicated by being twisted into a new shape. The character types remain the same and thus link the new model with Dick's earlier work: the bitch Pat, the redeemer Ella, the bewildered old-fashioned tycoon Runciter, the shadowy illusion creator Jory, losing in precision but gaining in domination in comparison to Eldritch, and, most important, the buffeted but persistent *schlemiel* Joe Chip. But the shift from social to ontological horizons around the axis connecting the two main narrative foci of Runciter and Chip results in a world without stable centers or peripheries, where the main problem is to find out who is inside and who outside the unstable circles of narrative consciousness, liable to an infinite receding series of contaminations from other—often only guessed at—such centers. The characterological equivalent of this uncertainty is the half-life, a loss of sovereignty over one's microcosm. After the explosion on the Moon, is Chip, or Runciter, or neither, or both in that state? The most all-embracing explanation would be that both are in the moratorium with different degrees of control, and acted on by the rival forces of destruction and redemption of Jory and Ella. However, no explanation will explain this novel, about which I have to differ fundamentally with what seem to me the one-sided praises of Stanislaw Lem and Peter Fitting.[3] No doubt, as they convincingly point out, *Ubik* is a heroic effort with great strengths, particularly in portraying the experiences of running down, decay, and senility, the invasion of entropy into life and consciousness, amid which the little man yet carries on: *impavidum ferient ruinae*. This experience of manipulated worlds, so characteristic of all our lives, is expressed by a verbal richness manifest, first, in a whole fascinating cluster of neologisms connected with the half-life, and second, in the delicious satire centered on the thing Ubik—the principle of food, health, and preservation of existence, of anti-entropic energy—which is promoted in kitschy ad terms parodying the unholy capitalist alliance of science, commercialism, and religious blasphemy. Dick's basic concern with death and rebirth, or to put it briefly with *transubstantiation,* has here surfaced perhaps more clearly than anywhere else in his opus. Yet it seems to me that—regardless of how far one would be prepared to follow Dick's rather unclear religious speculations—there is a serious loss of narrative control in *Ubik.* The "psi-powers" signifier has here become not only unnecessary but positively stultifying—e.g., has anybody in the book ever got back on the original time-track after Pat's first try-out?; did Pat engineer also her own death? etc. Further questions arise later: why isn't Pat wired out of the common circuit in the moratorium?; why isn't Jory?; etc. There is a clumsy try at subsidiary narrative foci with Vogelsang and Tippy (Chapters 1 and 5); Jory "eats" Wendy just when Pat was supposed to have done it; etc. The net result seems to me one of great strengths balanced by equally great weaknesses in a narrative irresponsibility reminiscent of the rabbits-from-the-hat carelessness associated with rankest van Vogt if not "Doc" Smith: the false infinities of explaining one improbability by a succession of ever greater ones.

The deconstruction of bourgeois rationality for which Peter Fitting argues seems thus not to result in a new form but in a nihilistic collapse into the oldest mystifying forms of science-fiction melodrama, refurbished, and therefore rendered more virulent, by some genuinely interesting new experiences. This is, of course, not without correlation to Dick's ideologies after the mid-60s, his drug-taking experiences, and his (often very ingenious) God-constructions; and one must assume that this was validated by the feeblest and least useful aspects of the late-60s counterculture, by the mentality despising reason, logic, and order of any kind—old or new. Thus the heroic effort of *Ubik* seems to me, in spite of its many incidental felicities, to be the *Palmer Eldritch* experience writ large: in some ways among the most fascinating science-fiction books of its time, it is finally, I fear, a heroic failure. In art, at least (and I would maintain in society, too), there is no freedom without order, no liberation without controlled focussing. A morality cut off from cognition becomes arbitrary; as Dick's own words in the epigraph to this section imply, it becomes in fact impossible.

My argument may perhaps gain some additional strength if it is
accepted that Dick's writing around and after *Ubik* has not been
on the order of his first-rate novels. From *Now Wait for Last Year*
on, it has withdrawn from the earlier richness into an only frag-
mentary use of his already established model, it has centered on
one protagonist and his increasingly private and psychoanalytic
problems, or, as the other side of the same coin, on a Jungian
collective unconscious. In *We Can Build You,* for example, the
erstwhile characteristic Dickian theme of the simulacrum Lincoln
is left to fizzle out in favor of the Jungian theme of Pris—though
the conjuring up of the past probity from the heroic age of the
United States bourgeoisie against its present corruption cries out
for more detailed treatment. While the touch of the master shows
in incidental elements of these late novels (e.g., the comics society of *The Zap Gun,* or the imitations of Chaplin's *Great Dictator*
in *Now Wait for Last Year*) there are also outright failures, such
as *Do Androids Dream of Electric Sheep?,* with its underlying
confusion between androids as wronged lower class and as inhuman menace. Indeed, Dick's last novel, *Flow My Tears, the
Policeman Said,* raises to my mind seriously the question of
whether he is going to continue writing science fiction or change
to "realistic" prose, for its properly science-fictional elements
(future Civil War, the reality-changing drug, the "sixes") are
quite perfunctory in comparison to its realistic police-state situations.

4. THE TIME IS OUT OF JOINT: INSTEAD OF A CONCLUSION

"Oh no," Betty disagreed, "no science in it. Science fiction deals with
future, in particular future where science had advanced over now.
Book fits neither premise."
  "But," Paul said, "it deals with alternate present. Many well-
known science fiction novels of that sort." (*MHC,* 7)

A number of very tempting subjects have to be left undiscussed
here: the uses and transubstantiations of stimuli from movies and
music (especially vocal music concerned with transcending the
empirical world—e.g., in Bach, Wagner, or Verdi); the uses of
literature—from Shakespeare, Aesop, and Ibsen through

Hemingway, Wells, Orwell, and the comics to the science fiction of the 40s and 50s; the strange coexistence of dazzling verbal invention with sloppiness and crudities; etc. Also, no conclusion · will be attempted here. That would be rather an impertinence in the case of a writer hopefully only in the middle of his life's path, who has grown and changed several times so startlingly, outstripping consistently most of his critics (so that he will, hopefully, also prove my gloomy opinions about his latest phase wrong).

For a conclusion, the reader is referred to the special issue on Philip K. Dick of *Science-Fiction Studies* 5 (March 1975), and to a rereading of Dick. But instead of it, I would like to indicate that in his very imperfections Dick seems typical. All his near-futures and alternate presents are parabolic mirrors for our time, which he has always deeply felt to be "out of joint." His political acumen was a good dozen years in advance of his fellow Americans, not so much because he mentions Richard Nixon both as President and as FBI Chief in his earliest works, when Nixon was still Vice President, as because, for example, in his first novel, *Solar Lottery*, he asks: "But what are you supposed to do in a society that's corrupt? Are you supposed to obey corrupt laws? Is it a crime to break a rotten law . . . ?" (*SL*, 14). His ontologico-religious speculations, while to my mind less felicitous, have the merit of taking to some logical science-fictional limits the preoccupations a great number of people have tried to express in more timid ways. It is when Dick's view is trained both on Society and Reality in their impact upon human relationships, with the ontology still clearly grounded in the sociology, that I believe Dick's major works, from *The Man in the High Castle* to *Dr. Bloodmoney*, have been written. His concerns with alienation and reification, with one-dimensional humans, parallel in science-fiction terms the concerns of a whole generation, expressed in writings such as those of Marcuse or Laing. His concerns with a social organization based on direct human relations parallel the movements for a radical democracy from the Berkeley Free Speech movement (the scene of his most fully utopian work, *Dr. Bloodmoney*) to the abortive youth–New Left movement of the late 60s. His deep intuitive feeling for decline and entropy raises the usual Spenglerian theatrics of space-opera science fiction to the "Humpty-Dumpty" landscapes of *Martian Time-Slip, The Three Stigmata of Palmer Eldritch,* and *Ubik.* He always speaks directly out of and to the American experience of his generation, most so when he uses the parabolic mirror of Germans and Nazis. He has the strengths and limitations of his existential horizons, which are identical to that of his favorite hero—the artificer, including the verbal craftsman. His books are artifacts, refuges from and visions of reality—as are Abendsen's book *The Grasshopper Lies Heavy* (in *High Castle*) and Lederman's *Pilgrim Without Progress* (in *Palmer Eldritch*). In fact, only a fiction writer could have embarked on the Pirandelloesque ontology of *Ubik,* whose characters search not only for their Author but also for their world. Explicating the message in terms of the form, half a dozen works by Dick, at least, are science-fiction classics. That is equivalent to saying that they are significant humanistic literature.

5. Dick's Maledictory Web*

BRIAN W. ALDISS

The trail levelled out and became wider. And all was in shadow; cold and damp hung over everything, as if they were treading within a great tomb. The vegetation that grew thin and noxious along the surface of rocks had a dead quality to it, as if something had poisoned it in its act of growing. Ahead lay a dead bird on the path, a rotten corpse that might have been there for weeks; he could not tell.

(Martian Time-Slip, 15)

ARNIE KOTT is on his way back into a schizoid variant of the recent past. Philip K. Dick is in the middle of one of his most magical novels, *Martian Time-Slip.*

The setting is Mars, which is now partly colonized. Colonists live along the water system, where conditions of near-fertility exist.

This web of civilization is stretched thin over utter desolation. There is no guaranteeing that it can be maintained. Its stability is threatened by the Great Powers back on Earth. For years they have neglected Mars, concentrating dollars and man-hours on

*This chapter appeared, in slightly different form, as the "Introduction" to the British edition of *Martian Time-Slip* (London: New English Library, 1976). "Introduction" copyright © 1976 by Brian W. Aldiss. It also subsequently appeared in *This World and Nearer Ones: Essays Exploring the Familiar* (London: Weidenfeld & Nicholson, 1979).

further exploration elsewhere in the system; now they may interfere actively with the balance of the colony.

Behind this web exists another, even more tenuous: the web of human relationships. Men and women, children, old men, Bleekmen—the autochthonous but nonindigenous natives of Mars—all depend, however reluctantly, on one another. When poor Norbert Steiner commits suicide, the effects of the event are felt by everyone.

Behind these two webs lies a third, revealed only indirectly. This is the web connecting all the good and bad things in the universe. The despised Bleekmen, who tremble on the edge of greater knowledge than humanity, are acutely aware of this web and occasionally succeed in twitching a strand here and there, to their advantage; but they are as much in its toils as anybody else.

These three webs integrate at various coordinate points, the most remarkable point being AM-WEB, a complex structure which the UN may build some time in the future in the FDR Mountains. The structure is visible to Steiner's autistic but precognitive son, Manfred, who sees it in an advanced stage of decay.

Its function in the novel is to provide a symbol for the aspirations and failures of mankind. The structure will be a considerable achievement when completed; which is not to say that it is not ultimately doomed; and part of that doom may be decreed by the miserable political and financial maneuvers which form one of the secondary themes of this intricately designed novel.

Martian Time-Slip comes from the middle of one of Dick's most creative periods. *The Man in the High Castle* was published in 1962. In 1963 came *The Game-Players of Titan* and then, in 1964, *The Simulacra, The Penultimate Truth, Clans of the Alphane Moon*, and *Martian Time-Slip*. Although Dick is a prolific author, with some thirty novels appearing in fifteen years, his production rate is modest when compared with many other writers in the prodigal field of science fiction.

One of the attractions of Dick's novels is that they all have points at which they interrelate, although Dick never reintroduces characters from previous books. The relationship is more subtle—more weblike—than that. There is a web in *Clans of the*

Alphane Moon, made by "the world-spider as it spins its web of destruction for all life" *(CAM*, 6). The way in which Mars in *Martian Time-Slip* is divided up between various nationalities is reminiscent of the division of Earth into great estates in *The Penultimate Truth* and *The Game-Players of Titan*. The horrifying corrupt world of "gubble," reminds us of the tomb world into which John Isidore falls in *Do Androids Dream of Electric Sheep?* or of one of the ghastly fake universes of Palmer Eldritch in *The Three Stigmata of Palmer Eldritch*. When Jack Bohlen, in the first few pages of the novel, awaits the arrival of his father from Earth, change is about to creep in; and change is often paradoxically embodied in someone or something old, like Edwin N. Stanton lying wrapped up in newspaper in the back of Maury Rock's Jaguar, in the opening pages of *We Can Build You*. And so on.

Such building blocks are by no means neatly interchangeable from book to book; Dick's fictional kaleidoscope is always being shaken; new sinister colors and patterns are continually emerging. The power in the Dickian universe resides in these overlapping blocks, rather than in his characters; even when one of the characters has a special power (like Jones's ability to foresee the future in *The World Jones Made*), it rarely does him any personal good.

If we look at two of the most important of these building blocks and observe how they depend on each other for greatest effect, we can come close to understanding one aspect of Dickian thought. These blocks are the concern-with-reality and the involvement-with-the-past.

Most of the characteristic themes of science fiction are materialist ones; only the concern-with-reality theme involves a quasi-metaphysical speculation, and Dick has made this theme peculiarly his own. Among his earliest published stories is "Imposter" (1953), in which a robot, who is actually an agent of an alien invasion force, believes himself to be a man; the deception is so nearly perfect that even he cannot detect the truth until the bomb within him is triggered by a phrase which he himself speaks. Later, Dickian characters frequently find themselves trapped in hallucinations or fake worlds of various kinds, often without knowing it or, if knowing it, without being able to do anything about it. In *The Man in the High Castle,* the world we know—in which the Allies won World War II and the Axis Powers lost—is itself reduced to a hypothetical world existing only in a novel called *The Grasshopper Lies Heavy,* which the victorious Japanese and Germans have banned. (It should be noted that this hypothetical world is only partially congruent with the world as we know it.)

And it is not only worlds that are fake. Objects, animals, people may also be unreal in various ways. Dick's novels are littered with fakes, from the reproductions of guns buried in rock in *The Penultimate Truth* which later are used and so become genuine fakes, to the electric toad which can hardly be told from a real one in *Do Androids Dream of Electric Sheep?,* to the androids masquerading as humans in the same novel. Things are always talking back to humans. Doors argue, medicine bags patronize, the cab at the end of *Now Wait for Last Year* advises Dr. Eric Sweetscent to stay with his ailing wife. All sorts of drugs are available which lead to entirely imaginary universes, drugs such as the evil Can-D and Chew-Z used by the colonists on Mars in *Palmer Eldritch,* or the JJ-180 which is banned on Earth in *Now Wait for Last Year.*

The colonists on the Mars of *Martian Time-Slip* use only the drugs available to us, though those are generally at hand. In the very opening scene, we come across Silvia Bohlen doped up on phenobarbital. Here the concern-with-reality theme is worked out through the time-slip of the title, and through the autistic boy, Manfred Steiner.

Manfred falls into the power of Arnie Kott, boss of the plumbing union which, because water is so scarce, has something of a stranglehold on Mars (a typical piece of wild Dickian ingenuity). Arnie worries a lot. He asks his Bleekman servant, Heliogabalus, if he has ever been psychoanalyzed.

"No. Mister. Entire psychoanalysis is a vainglorious foolishness."
"How zat, Helio?"
"Question they never deal with is, what to remold sick person like. There is no what, Mister."
"I don't get you, Helio."
"Purpose of life is unknown, and hence way to be is hidden from the eyes of living critters. Who can say if perhaps the schizophrenics are

not correct? Mister, they take a brave journey. They turn away from mere things, which one may handle and turn to practical use; they turn inward to meaning. There, the black night-without-bottom lies, the pit . . ." (*MTS*, 6)

Of course, there are many ways of falling into the pit, one of which is to have too much involvement-with-the-past. Dick admits a fascination with the past, quoting lines of Henry Vaughan:

Some men a forward motion love
But I by backward steps would move . . .

While admitting how much he enjoys the junk of the past, Dick adds, "But I'm equally aware of the ominous possibilities. Ray Bradbury goes for the Thirties, too, and I think he falsifies and glamorizes them . . ." (*Daily Telegraph Magazine*, 19 July 1974). This casual remark reveals much; Dick perceives fiction as a quest, not a refuge.

Arnie Kott has an innocent fascination with objects of the past—he possesses the only harpsichord on Mars. In the same way, Robert Childan's trading Mickey Mouse watches and scarce copies of *Tip Top Comics* to the victorious Japanese (in *The Man in the High Castle*) is represented as entirely innocuous. Trouble comes when the interest with the past and all its artifacts builds into an obsession, like Virgil Ackerman's Wash-55 a vast regressive babyland which is featured in *Now Wait for Last Year*.

And this is indeed where Dick parts company with Ray Bradbury, and with many another writer, in or out of the science-fiction field. If he sees little safety in the future, the past is even more insidiously corrupting. So dreadful is Manfred's past that you can die in it. The past is seen as regressive; one of the most striking Dickian concepts is the "regression of forms" which takes place in *Ubik*, that magnificent but flawed novel in which the characters try to make headway through a world that is becoming ever more primitive, a world in which the airliner devolves into a Ford trimotor into a Curtis biplane, while Joe's multiplex FM tuner regresses into a cylinder phonograph playing a shouted recitation of the Lord's Prayer.

In *Martian Time-Slip*, the involvement-with-the-past is general, as well as being particularized in Manfred's illness. Mars itself is regarded by Earth as a has-been, and is patterned after has-been communities based on earlier versions of terrestrial history. Here it is especially difficult to escape damnation.

With the past so corrupting, the present so uncertain, and the future so threatening, we might wonder if there can be any escape. The secret of survival in Dick's universe is not to attempt escape into any alternate version of reality but to see things through as best you can; in that way, you may succeed if not actually triumph. The favored character in *Martian Time-Slip* is Jack Bohlen, whom we last see reunited with his wife, out in the dark garden, flashing a torch and looking for someone. His voice is businesslike, competent, and patient; these are high-ranking virtues in the hierarchy of Dickian theology. It is significant that Bohlen is a repairman ("an idiot who can fix things," says Kott)—a survival job, since it helps maintain the status quo. Similar survivors in other novels are pot-healers, traders, doctors, musical instrument makers, and android-shooters (since androids threaten the status quo).

The characters who survive are generally aided by some system of knowledge based on faith. The system is rarely a scientific one; it is more likely to be ancient. In *Martian Time-Slip*, it is the never-formulated paranormal understanding of the Bleekmen; Bohlen respects this vague eschatological faith without comprehending it, just as Kott despises it. The *I Ching*, or *Book of Changes*, the four-thousand-year-old Chinese work of divination, performs a similar function in the *The Man in the High Castle*, whereas in *Counter-Clock World* Lotta Hermes randomly consults the Bible, which predicts the future with an alarming accuracy. In both of Dick's two middle-period masterpieces, *Martian Time-Slip* and *High Castle*, this religious element—presented as something crumbling, unreliable, only to be figured out with pain—is well integrated into the texture of the novel.

Dick's next great book, *The Three Stigmata of Palmer Eldritch*, was written very soon after *Martian Time-Slip*; and the two are closely related, not only because Mars is in both cases used as a setting. To my view, *Eldritch* is a flawed work, overly complicated, and finally disappearing in a cloud of quasi-theology, whereas *Martian Time-Slip* has a calm and lucidity about it. But in *Eldritch* we also find an ancient and unreliable metastructure of faith, in this case embodied in the ferocious alien entry which fuses with Eldritch's being:

> Our opponent, something admittedly ugly and foreign that entered one of our race like an ailment—during the long voyage between Terra and Prox . . . and yet it knew much more than I did about the meaning of our finite lives, here; it saw in perspective. From its centuries of vacant drifting as it waited for some kind of life form to pass by which it could grab and become . . . maybe that's the source of the knowledge: not experience but unending solitary brooding. (*3SPE*, 12)

So muses Barney Mayerson. Jack Bohlen in *Martian Time-Slip* desperately needs a transcendental act of fusion; he is estranged from his wife, sold by his first employer, threatened by his second, and invaded by the schizophrenia of Manfred Steiner, the boy he befriends. Bohlen sees in this mental illness, so frighteningly depicted in the book, the ultimate enemy. From this ultimate enemy comes the "time-slip" of the title and that startling paragraph which seems to condense much of the feeling of the book—and, indeed, of Dick's work in general, when Bohlen works out what Manfred's mental illness means: "It is the stopping of time. The end of experience, of anything new. Once the person becomes psychotic, nothing ever happens to him again" (*MTS*, 11).

This is the maledictory circle within which Dick's characters move and from which they have to escape; although almost any change is for the worse, stasis means death—spiritual if not actual.

Any discussion of Dick's work makes it sound to be grim and appalling. So, on the surface, it may be; yet it must also be said that Dick is often amazingly funny. The terror and the humor are fused. It is this rare quality which marks Dick out. This is why critics, in seeking to convey his essential flavor, bring forth the names of Dickens and Kafka, earlier masters of Ghastly Comedy.

Martian Time-Slip is full of delightful comic effects, not the least of which is the way in which Norbert Steiner and the lecherous Otto Zippe ship illegal gourmet foods from Earth in unmanned Swiss rockets. Dick's fondness for oddball entities and titles is much in evidence, notably in the surreal public school, where homeostatic robot teachers named for the Emperor Tiberius, Sir Francis Drake, Mark Twain, and various other dignitaries talk to the boys. Below this easy-going humor lies a darker stream of wit. Arnie Kott's terrible and fatal mistake of believing that reality is merely another version of the schizoid past is also part of the comedy of mistakes to which Dick's characters always dance.

There is also a deeper resemblance to the work of Dickens and Kafka. Dick, like Dickens, enjoys a multiplotted novel. As the legal metaphor is to *Bleak House*, the world-as-prison to *Little Dorrit,* the dust-heap in *Our Mutual Friend,* the tainted wealth to *Great Expectations,* so is Mars to *Martian Time-Slip.* It is exactly and vividly drawn; it is neither the Mars as adventure-playground of Edgar Rice Burroughs nor the Mars as parallel of Pristine America of Ray Bradbury; rather it is Mars used in elegant and expert fashion as a metaphor of spiritual poverty. In functioning as a dreamscape, it has much in common with the semiallegorical, semisurrealist locations used by Kafka to heighten his Ghastly Comedy of bafflement. (Staring at his house standing in the meager Martian desert, Bohlen smiles and says, "This is the dream of a million years, to stand here and see this.")

Dick's alliance, if one may call it that, with writers such as Dickens and Kafka makes him immediately congenial to English and European readers. It may be this quality which has brought him reputation and respect on this side of the Atlantic before his virtues are fully recognized in his own country.

6. Philip K. Dick's Political Dreams

HAZEL PIERCE

She wanders in Eternal fear of falling into the indefinite,
For her bright eyes behold the Abyss. Sometimes a little sleep
Weighs down her eyelids; then she falls; then starting, wakes in fears
Sleepless to wander round, repell'd on the margin of Non Entity.
            —William Blake, *Vala* (III, 208-11)

THE NOVELS OF Philip K. Dick elicit ambivalent responses from readers, responses such as: "I don't like this novel, *but* . . ." Behind that last word lurks the intuitive realization that Philip K. Dick demands more of a reader than such a superficial affective response would indicate. True, one may be annoyed by a weak plot line, by scientific inconsistencies, or by the cavalier way in which Dick introduces, then summarily dismisses, some of his characters. Any reader with a strong urge to impose a firm and logical sequential structure on the events in Dick's novels will fight a losing battle. *But*—that word again—in the midst of the many shifts in reality, Dick does awaken our fears, shaking our complacent acceptance of the commonplace world as we think we know it. We sense an urgency in his appeal to our powers of imagination.

Critical commentary on Philip K. Dick also reflects this ambivalence to some degree. George Turner speaks of his own superficial enjoyment of Dick's work but of his dissatisfaction with it on deeper levels.[1] In a review of *Flow My Tears, the Policeman Said,* Turner further claims that Dick "achieves his own brand of forgettability," compounded from carelessness, hastiness, and obvious logical holes.[2] Robert H. Canary remarks on the "stigmata" in all of Dick's novels, those marks revealing "his long apprenticeship in Ace Double Novels."[3] Gérard Klein, on the other hand, lauds Dick's work as the "most important work in American SF at least until the end of the 60s,"[4] reflecting the esteem with which Dick's work is regarded in France. The ultimate accolade comes from Stanislaw Lem, when he labels Dick as a "visionary among charlatans" in an essay by that title.[5]

It appears self-evident that superficially Philip K. Dick satisfies something in all people, whether it is the need for a target to demolish or for a flag to raise. Perhaps the lack of unanimity is attributable to the absence of any single, generally accepted theory of science fiction by which to judge accomplishment or failure, as has been suggested by Lem in his critical salvos at the field in general. Despite the absence of such a theory, a serious reader must still face the nagging insistence of that small word, *but.* Philip Dick's work is all of these things which readers and critics say it is. However, he does demand more of us than flip dismissal, empty praise, or abstract labels. But just what *does* he want of us? And what has motivated him to assume the right to demand more of us?

Dick has sprinkled clues to possible answers to the above questions in several articles. In "Who Is an SF Writer?" Dick describes an individual who is in part a scientist, in part a believer in the magic of the written word, and in part a political dreamer. He considers the term *scientist* to refer to more than the possessor of a body of systematized knowledge derived from empirical investigation; instead, he focuses on the etymological basis of the word—*scientia*, having knowledge. The writer of science fiction possesses some knowledge which he must impart to his readers; he has that "grand drive of the true research scientist, to acquaint people with something heretofore overlooked."[6] To do this, he must struggle with what William Blake called "the stubborn structure of the language" while believing in its ability ultimately to achieve some change or to effect some awakening in that mind lulled to sleep by custom.

Motivating Dick's drive to acquaint us with something heretofore overlooked is a modern variation of an age-old philosophical concern: what does it mean to be a human being? Humanists of every age have discussed this question within the context of their own culture and society. Pre-Newtonian thinkers saw an orderly universe with a special place for man—a place of equal value with others in the eyes of God, but a place which warranted the special gift of reason. Shakespeare's Hamlet closely reflects the view of his age:

> What is a man
> If his chief good and market of his time
> Be but to sleep and feed? A beast, no more,
> Sure, He that made us with such large discourse,
> Looking before and after, gave us not
> That capability and godlike reason
> To fust in us unused.

Post-Newtonian man, escaping his prescribed place in a hierarchical universe, could assume a central place in the universe and find comfort in a belief in his own perfectibility.

But what of twentieth-century man? Technological man? Man living in a world of economic, political, and social complexity? That this is Philip K. Dick's very real concern is inescapable, for all of his writings—novels, short stories, essays, responses to reviews of his books, published letters—reflect it in one way or another. Perhaps the most open and detailed discussion of this concern appears in a speech, "The Android and the Human," which Dick gave in Vancouver, B. C., in March of 1972.[7] Whether on purpose or inadvertently, the mere arrangement of the two key words in the title betrays the focal problem for contemporary society. Amidst the twentieth-century reality of the increasing use of ever more complex mechanical and electronic constructs, is an "android" response to life taking precedence over the human one? Will the values associated with technological "behavior" encroach on humanistic values to the point of reducing people to the level of being mere extensions of their constructs? Dick would consider these questions to be phrased in the wrong tense. One should rather ask: *has* the android mentality *already* replaced authentic human behavior?

These two additional words—*authentic* and *human*—appear over and over in the Vancouver speech until they work on our conscious mind much as does water dripping on a stone, though more quickly. Slowly they wear into even the closed mind. Dick speaks of "unauthentic human activity" encouraged by present-day organization which relieves individuals of the responsibility for personal decisions. He finds hope for the "dying bird of authentic humanness" in those young persons who feel and express a "new and inner—and genuinely authentic—human desire." At last he lays out for us those telltale signs that might alert us to the encroachment of androidism. Comparing this state of mind with the more commonly understood schizoid personality, Dick warns us of the danger in the submersion of that which is authentic. When thought reduces feeling, when people are deprived of the opportunity for "making exceptions" or exerting choice, and when they fail to grow as a result of "agonizing situations," then there is a failure of sensitivity and the open avenue to androidism.

If the majority of people fail to notice these signs, the person with the spirit of the true research scientist and a firm belief in the word must act to alert them. Often this special knowledge will involve direct, stern criticism of situations generally labeled "good" or accepted as the status quo. Then the writer stands a fair chance of suffering considerable resistance, even of being labeled as a political activist. All too often the images evoked by this label tend to obscure and erode the validity of any message which the event may carry. The science-fiction writer, however, works as an "introverted activist." His protest, according to Dick, is a protest against "concrete reality," a protest that suggests neither a cause nor cure but rather alternate possibilities to that reality. Like William Blake's Los, the Poetic Imagination, "striving with Systems to deliver Individuals from those Systems," the science-fiction writer strives with his own special systems—the other realities which might exist, given the chance. With these alternatives, he can alert us to the "Systems" in our own experiential reality which threaten our humanity. In so doing he achieves his special deliverance. Perhaps this is the most solemn task of the science-fiction writer—that of *political dreamer*, or to apply Stanislaw Lem's term, of *visionary*.

Even though written in the decade before the Vancouver speech, those novels of Philip K. Dick published between 1962 and 1965 provide us with evidence of his intense concern with the political relationships that threaten authentic humanity. Obviously this concern operates first through the plot. Characters react to a sequence of events in such a way as to define their values; they fail or succeed insofar as those values harmonize with the surrounding social, political, or physical reality, whichever is most dominant. Tacitly invited to step into this fictional framework, a reader can test himself against the conflicts or challenges of this futuristic—usually near-future—society. Up to this point, Dick does little or nothing different from many science fiction writers—indeed, from any writer of fiction. But Philip K. Dick, as an "introverted activist," does more. He prods our complacency, fills us with a vague sense of uneasiness, and finally forces us to hold up the mirrors of his worlds and recognize the distorted reflections of our own world in them.

How does he accomplish this? Certainly not through the plot, for he demolishes time and sequence almost to the point of our total confusion at times. Nor through the diverse characters who flood his pages in profusion. Instead, Dick activates our minds by those often small but telling images which remind us of something familiar but which are slightly out of focus for us. As we strive to bring these images into focus, they penetrate our consciousness and remain to change our outlook from that point on. This technique works much as do those rapid, montagelike films which purport to show all of American History or the sweep of the world's art in sixty seconds. We sense the continuity but cannot absorb the totality of each frame. What *does* stay with us is some eye-catching detail like the pose of a head signalling authority, or a drop of blood encompassing all of the pain of war, or the glowing eye of a newborn baby suggesting hope and life. Imagine such an imaginary film running from *The Man in the High Castle* (1962) to *Dr. Bloodmoney* (1965). Certain images and phrases impinge upon our awareness as they are whisked rapidly by: an end of the idea of place; the "web of the world-spider" suggesting the interconnectedness of all life counterbalanced by AM-WEB with its harsh reality; the many simulacra built to order; adults escaping from their untenable existence by playing with dollhouses. . . The images go on and on, living a potent existence completely apart from the fictional plot. When they do not go away, they remain to urge the reader to ask: What does it mean to be a person in twentieth-century America? What is the contemporary idea of place? Are we adults playing with "toys" or with our special artifacts of material existence? How tenuous is the peace of the human relations we so take for granted? If we are pushed to answer these and the many other disquieting questions which Philip K. Dick arouses in us, he has succeeded in his introverted way in activating a sense of awareness in us.

At first glance, *The Man in the High Castle* seems little more than another treatment of a science-fiction cliché. It asks a standard question: what if the losers of a past war in our history had been the winners? In *High Castle* the war is World War II. After their victory the Axis powers, Germany and Japan, have partitioned a conquered United States into three parts, two spheres of influence separated by the Rocky Mountain States (RMS) as a buffer zone. The Pacific States of America (PSA), now Japanese-occupied, has not advanced as far technologically as has the German-dominated United States of America (USA) on the East Coast. (The Italians have declined in political power and do not figure in the narrative.) Japanese customs and cultural attitudes permeate the social structure of the PSA. For instance, pedecabs transport people in the city; ritualized public manners (bowing) smooth over the roughness of human contact. The most pervasive attitude is one of deep interest in and reverence for the past, as evidenced in the acquisition of "native" artifacts from prewar America and the dependence on the *I Ching*—an ancient sacred text which provides a system for divination based on the possible configurations of yarrow stalks—for guidance in vital personal and social decisions. This cultural mind-set, obviously rigid in its social demands, discourages any resurgence of prewar initiative or creativity on the part of the conquered peoples. It does, on the other hand, result in a fairly stable, comfortable social and political atmosphere.

There are no scenes described in the novel which occur in the

USA, the German-occupied territory. Nevertheless Dick repeatedly hints that the atmosphere in the USA is the antithesis of that found in the PSA. The engineering genius of the German elite creates—indeed, suffers—an obsessive need to build, to tear down, and to rebuild. They spread this zeal into all areas. In a prodigious effort of engineering skill they drain the entire Mediterranean Sea for agricultural purposes. Even outer space is not off limits as German energy sends rockets to the Moon and then Mars. Meanwhile, the darker side of their Teutonic nature continues its drive to eliminate the "lesser" peoples of the world, especially the Jews, and the African peoples are almost entirely decimated in a wild attempt to clear a continent for remaking. Only the Japanese-dominated area and the buffer of the RMS seem safe temporarily from this mechanical push to remold Earth.

At this point, we may wonder if the novel is promising to be the usual set piece of two great powers, toe-to-toe, ready to start pushing one another into their respective oceans. Dick, however, does not handle his material as a textbook exercise in the writing of science fiction. The simple device of partition affords him three separate and distinct realities or environments. Each area supports a social structure with a value system highly divergent from the other two. The clash of these three value systems affords Dick the occasion for both dramatic action and ideological discussion.

He is able to sidestep the dilemma of choosing between three alternatives by adding further alternatives. When Hawthorne Abendsen, a novelist living in the relatively free RMS zone, publishes a novel entitled *The Grasshopper Lies Heavy,* a fourth "reality" is created. The novel presents a world in which the Allied forces have won World War II. The Russia of this novel-within-a-novel is a second-rate power, unable to sustain political equivalency with the other victors. A possible fifth reality fleetingly offers itself for our consideration when Mr. Tagomi, a high-ranking Japanese trade official in the PSA, experiences a nightmarish vision of an alternate-world San Francisco. Gone are the pedecabs so familiar to Mr. Tagomi. This visionary San Francisco is smothered in a cacophony of running motors, strangled in a net of "freeways" (a term unfamiliar to Tagomi), and beset by churlish human behavior that is quite the opposite of the mannered, ritualistic politeness to which he, as a citizen of the PSA, has been accustomed. The alternate San Francisco which Tagomi fleetingly sees may or may not be congruent with the world that we know. Likewise the world of Abendsen's novel is only partially congruent with the world of today. But both of these alternate realities at least hint at the reality we know.

Moving through this montage of world models, the characters form intricate relationship patterns, some of which verge on literary clichés. If we were to convert the east–west movement of Frank Frink into a south–north movement, we would have a stereotypical situation so common to stories about escaped slaves, stories which have been popular since the time of *Uncle Tom's Cabin* (1852). The wicked owners (the German conquerors in the USA) send their fierce dogs (the quasi-stormtroopers) to recapture the escaped slave (Frank Fink, alias Frink, a Jew from the USA who has slipped into the PSA via the RMS). Juxtaposed with that pattern is the cliché of the lonely artist (Frink and his partner, Ed McCarthy) struggling in a garret (a small shop unconnected to the mainstream of commerce) to produce the perfect object of art against the tide of current taste (handcrafted, artfully asymmetric jewelry for a market absorbed with antiques and artifacts of a bygone era).

Then there are the patterns of conformity in which many of the individuals in the novel are trapped. Robert Childan, purveyor of the above artifacts, wistfully muses on the "end of place" as he enjoys a moment of shared human warmth and artistic appreciation with a customer. Wistful contemplation is the limit of his nonconformity as he weakly slips back into the rut of expected behavior. He apes the language pattern of the Japanese conquerors, imitates their body gestures, and obeys the code of "place." By so doing he abrogates his right to be a complete human being; instead, he becomes a mere functionary—a lackey, shopkeeper, or puppet. This particular pattern appears repeatedly: the *pinoc* (or white authorities) in the PSA; the factory owner Wyndham-Matson; the Waffen SS men; Consul Reiss, the well-oiled model of the perfect diplomat; Joe Cinnadella, the undercover would-be assassin of Abendsen.

Only when these functionaries awaken to their dependence on social programming do they stir themselves to a degree of independent action; they sometimes do act humanly, though feebly so. Joe Cinnadella, his program brought to a jarring halt by his own imminent death at the hands of Juliana Frink, becomes human as he cries out in vain for aid. Robert Childan, risking business disaster, feels the faint stirring of national pride in Frink's native creativity when he agrees to try to sell the Edfrank jewelry, though the terms of his agreement are largely unfavorable to Frink. This group of newly awakened but still weak reformers of self is perhaps best represented by Mr. Tagomi. Even though he should feel secure in his position as a trade official, Tagomi very humbly recognizes the chinks in his social and political armor. He continually worries about doing the right thing at the right time in the prescribed way. After his vision of an alternate world made harsh by technological progress, Tagomi faces up to the choices he must inevitably make. He chooses a personal, humane approach rather than the safer, prescribed path of his cultural tradition.

The plot incidents and character movements previously discussed engage the reader on the first level of the story. Dick, however, also provides us with another level; almost subliminal in its effect, this second level activates our latent consciousness of certain portents in our own social and political milieu. Are we actively aware of those imposed expectations which may sometimes support but more often cripple or completely erase our sense of entity? With insistent but purposeful repetitiveness, Dick insinuates certain words into our consciousness: *forgery, ersatz, bluff, mask.* These words attach themselves to images which catch at the mind. In the diplomatic arena the Japanese officials mask messages by use of a metaphor-based cipher, to prevent their more literal-minded former allies, the Germans, from understanding their true intentions. Metaphor, formerly the language of poetry, becomes ersatz language, bled of its beauty and richness for insidious purposes. Also pervasive in PSA society are the actual forgeries: the flood of fake Colt .44 revolvers of the American frontier days, the counterfeit Mickey Mouse watches, and the valuable *"framed signed picture of Jean Harlow" (MHC, 1).* It does not matter whether physically forged material objects or psychologically forged values are involved; the effect is the same in either case—falsity, a willful divergence from what is real. The emphasis is not on the still vital values of history but on the mere *historicity* of an object, regardless of its original value.

Fake objects are a burden that can be endured without too much difficulty, subject to the whims of their owners; but what of the human "forgeries" or those people who willfully and even knowingly surround themselves with false values? Joe Cinnadella, a Swiss-born former German soldier posing as an Italian truck driver, a once-proud fighter now underground assassin, becomes his own forged or ersatz identity until faced with that final and exquisitely natural experience, death. Mr. Baynes and General Tedeki represent well-known examples of human deception—agents traveling incognito to assure their safety while on a mission. Although they are at least in part political dissidents rebelling against the totalitarian grip, they temporarily mask their true identities in order to preserve themselves from extinction. Frank Frink, partly by choice and partly by chance, rejects his social role as an ersatz person by repudiating his previous occupation as a forger of false antiques. Once he has made this crucial move, he can now give free rein to his creative, imaginative spirit.

The most affecting image of all is that which flicks at us in a brief scene when Juliana Frink picks up an issue of *Life* magazine containing an article, "Television in Europe: Glimpse of Tomorrow." Idly looking at the illustrations to the article, she notes one of German electronic engineers. They are in New York supervising the construction of what, with the aid of local personnel, is to be the first television station in America. Juliana regards the Germans as having "that healthy, clean, energetic, assured look." The Americans, she observes, "just looked like people"(*MHC*, 6). Which type will gain the advantage in the world of tomorrow—the human forgeries who are nothing more than mechanical, structured embodiments of stereotypic perfection, or those who "just look like people" with all of their complex humanity and worth? The answer, which Dick does not give us, can only come from each politically and socially aware individual who recognizes the masks or forgeries that replace the genuine.

In 1963, following *High Castle*, Dick published *The Game-Players of Titan* and *Martian Time-Slip*, the titles of which suggest a shift to conventional space opera. In these novels he does utilize several conventions of this older strain of science fiction—space travel, alien life forms, robots (or "simulacra," to use his term), and a highly advanced technology in which machines function almost at human levels, sometimes more efficiently. In both novels the humans have met with aliens a considerable time before the action begins and have at least come to terms with them, unstable though those terms may be. Dick does not revel in the mere delight of building a futuristic world. His conapts, auto-autos, vidphones, homeostatic maintenance machinery, teaching simulacra, and so on serve as props for the initial reality he invites us to enter. The space travel itself holds no comparison to that found in early space opera; there are no star drives, no time travel, no far-flung fields of stars to wax about poetically. In *Martian Time-Slip* the trip is a "milk-run" to bring in supplies from a mother planet (Earth) to her less affluent child (Mars)—or for doing a bit of lucrative smuggling. In *Game Players* the characters travel through space by mental projection, being flung through hyperspace by mental and psychic forces that are never precisely described.

Similarly, Dick does not strive too hard to make his worlds scientifically accurate or to explain the details of how his machines operate. In *Martian Time-Slip* Mars offers the first serious obstacle for the person who expects an author to take the traditional tenets of genre science fiction seriously. While Dick's Mars has canals, a lingering legacy of the timeworn mistranslation of Schiaparelli's *canali* (channels), water runs through them to serve the homes and growing areas. Oxygen seems to be no problem. Rockets come and go from Earth to Mars with the conventional ease of our transcontinental jet flights, as witness the comfort of the elderly Bohlen in *Martian Time-Slip*, who takes off from Earth for a short visit with his son and family as well as for a small interworld business transaction. In *Game-Players* the aliens do not suffer at all in the oxygen-rich atmosphere of Earth, in large part due to their shape-changing ability. They function in an awkward way, a fact that we do not recognize until we are given a brief vision of their natural existence as "glowing weightless presences" (*GPT*, 16). The machinery of these futuristic worlds exists mainly to relieve the characters of a tedious preoccupation with everyday existence. An "auto-auto" (robot auto) talks back saucily to its owner and a medicine cabinet offers parental advice on drug consumption; clearly we cannot regard such machines as serious technological extrapolations, but rather as whimsical caricatures of trends in present-day society.

What one *does* take seriously is Dick's concern with the nature of political power and with structures of government. Dick again presents us with a vision of power relationships and struggles, with political events occurring not only on a national level but on a personal and cosmic level as well. Again we are presented with questions which we must answer for ourselves: What is the most equitable balance between an individual and these social mechanisms he employs? At what point do these mechanisms cease to function as liberating disciplines and become onerous constrictions?

In *The Game-Players of Titan,* the human race is shrinking in numbers. Some years before the novel opens, there was a war with Titan, during which the Red Chinese released a bomb which had the unhappy effect of sterilizing most of the human population. To some extent doctors have been able to relieve the problem with a glandular operation which has extended human life expectancy into a second century. The real hope for continuance of the race lies in the few remaining fertile persons. Surprisingly enough, even though medical scientists have produced a test for pregnancy in rabbits that is effective within a day or two after a successful mating, it has not been able to test the human population for fertility. In the effort to find the perfect matches for *luck* (a euphemism for pregnancy), couples constantly shift alliances. This constant concern with the survival of the species leaves people with little desire to maintain any loving relationships.

The key political institution in this future society is the Game, a futuristic version of Monopoly. Played in small, tightly organized groups representing specific regions, the Game ostensibly serves a great purpose. It confers prestige to its participants. It is a mechanism for redistributing property ownership for the economic benefit of the group. It allows a socially acceptable mechanism for exploiting the mathematical possibilities of matching compatible, fertile people. Rigid rules of conduct govern the Game. Only bindmen (property owners similar to medieval lords of the manor) and their wives are allowed to play. The stakes are actual properties: San Francisco, all of Marin County, a group of adjacent counties in Kansas, or comparable blocks of land. When a player loses, the loss includes not only his properties but also the player's wife, thus allowing for economic and genetic distribution simultaneously.

The ultimate power behind the Game lies not with the human players but with their Titanian conquerors, whose Terran appearance is that of a jellylike form with telepathic abilities. Termed "vugs" by the defeated Terrans, they receive unexpected treatment from the humans. Ordinarily one would not expect a defeated people to keep weapons ("vugsticks") in their homes for use in prodding unwelcome representatives of the victorious group out of their homes, but this is what in fact occurs.

Such treatment occurs because the opacity of the earthbound, provincial human mind precludes it from grasping the truth. Gradually the most sensitive of the Terran Game-players, Peter Garden, rids himself of that opacity. He begins to see his associates as multidimensional beings, sharing qualities both of human and vug. His insight serves him well when the Titanians challenge the Terrans to play the Game on an extraterrestrial level. The vugs first enter as simulacra of their human opponents but finally assume their own special Earth-forms, only to merge gradually into one form, "ancient and slow in its actions, but infinitely determined. And wise" (*GPT*, 16). Later, in a highly dramatic expansion of their awareness to an almost cosmic perspective, Garden and his friend Schilling experience the Titanians in their natural environment, one in which the humans can exist only as disembodied, sensitive awareness; in this environment, the humans encounter the shape-changing vugs in their true form—as disembodied, radiant essences.

This protean capability (whether attributable to the Titanians or to the power of the human mind) results in numerous shifts of perspective. The vugs are the old enemy, the present victor, but the everyday inferior. The vugs are old and wise in the Game but simultaneously amoral and unrestricted by the very ethical rules they have established. The metamorphosis of human into vug carries the judgment of untrustworthy; the metamorphosis of vugs into their ancient form elicits awe. After these several transmutations, the more sensitive of the humans—Garden, Schilling, and Mary Anne—begin, like Saint Paul, to see "through a glass darkly." Gradually they sense the presence of an outside agency greater than they, one that is somehow artfully rearranging their individual identities into a collective entity. A Master Game-player operates the Game according to rules they do not come close to understanding. But who is this Master? A Titanian? An evil spirit, the Other, loose in the universe? The First Cause with its infinite determination? The Absolute of all-enveloping truth? Or is this alien psyche the infinite and eternal consciousness of which all of us are only finite bits and pieces in "frightened, hating isolation" (*GPT*, 17)?

Again, as in *High Castle,* Dick offers an almost nightmarish vision of human existence. It comes as if in answer to Robert Burns's wry request: "O wad some Power the giftie gie us/ To see oursels as ithers see us!" Whether Dick's "giftie" will free us from "mony a blunder" or not is debatable, but he does thrust us momentarily into a revealing awareness of how some higher forms of life may see us. At one point during the cosmic Game, the vugs have disoriented and separated the human players, shifting them out of earthly reality into psychic isolation. It is the ancient military technique of divide and conquer. Somehow Pete, Joe, and Mary Anne manage to keep in touch with each other mentally. It is Mary Anne, who has special psychic powers, who is given the glimpse of human degradation.

For this glimpse Dick uses a standard literary convention of vision-literature—aesthetic distance provided by height, physical removal, or translation into a dream. In a classical example, *Scipio's Dream,* Africanus shows Scipio an orderly cosmos with the planets circling in their prescribed paths, the stars in their ceaseless courses, all enveloped by the embrace of a spiritual force and soothed by the music of the spheres. In the medieval poem *The Vision of William Concerning Piers Plowman,* the dreamer takes comfort in the "field of folk" living out their homely lives for the glory of God and mankind, while learning at the same time of the threats to that comfort in the presence of sin and evil. According to the Bible and Milton, on a lofty mountaintop Satan invites Christ to consider the panorama of the world over which He can yield power if only He will yield to satanic power. Today satellite pictures provoke a far different vision, one aptly summed up in R. Buckminster Fuller's phrase, "our little Spaceship Earth."

Dick achieves aesthetic distance and dramatic impact by exploiting the paradox implicit whenever one equates appearance with reality. Seeming to look down from a great distance, the disembodied consciousness of Mary Anne gazes at "stunted, alien creatures, warped by enormous forces" (GPT, 17). The human race is a waning one made up of blind, malformed organisms going about their pointless activities in the light of a dying sun. All of this is presented from the perspective of an alien consciousness composed of unrestricted and pure essence. But Mary Anne also must look within. Is the human race truly stunted, limited, and hopeless in the grip of universal forces beyond its control? Mary Anne—and with her any thinking person—grasps for the only explanation available to our limited comprehension: one reality is as valid as another. Perhaps we are stunted and warped; on the other hand, within that malformed organism there exists a will to reinforce a precious individuality against all odds.

Precious individuality is a commodity of little value in Martian Time-Slip, published the same year as Game-Players. The colony on Mars depresses us with an uncanny accumulation of all the false patterns of human relationships which we would like to sweep under the rug of memory. The Bleekmen, generally regarded as remnants of the native Martian race, so evocative of the American Indian or Australian aborigine, wend their weary ways over the harsh Martian terrain. Only a few of them, such as Heliogabalus, have achieved a degree of assimilation into human culture. Their poetic greetings such as "rains are falling from me on your valuable person" (MTS, 6), sharply outline the cruel disregard which Terrans in general direct toward the Bleekmen. One of these "valuable persons" could be the union leader Arnie Kott, a spiritual descendant of all the sharp entrepreneurs in Western business circles, who finds Mars the perfect base for his operation. He regards the Bleekmen as less than human and refuses to accept the anthropologists' theory that Bleekmen and humans alike had common ancestors out among the stars. The legal authority on Terra also finds Mars a perfect arena for one of its less admirable operations—the tucking away out of sight and the ultimate disposal of human beings who deviate from accepted physical or mental norms. Manifest destiny, "good" business, and a futuristic brand of Aryanism, all combine to negate the value of the precious humanity that is supposedly a part of all of us.

Or so it would seem—until Dick lifts the curtain on the stage and proceeds to dissect the irrationality of these misconceived realities. One by one he demolishes our sacred cows: education, business, the myth of progress, the sanctity of the individual—all those institutions and ideas which support our political dream. In the wake of the demolition, Dick leaves us with a string of nagging questions.

The school on Mars appears to provide an ideal answer to the educationist's dilemma: How can we educate our children for the future, retain what is valuable from the past, but still serve the status quo of the present? To accomplish this, the Martian colony uses teaching machines. These are not the simple devices of the twentieth-century school, but a total teaching environment, unfortunately programmed to fit a reality more serviceable to Earth than to Mars. It is a false reality in several ways. Literally half of this environment is ersatz, being "peopled" by simulacra who do the actual instruction and serve in various administrative capacities. Even the simulacra are false, being imitative of stereotypes which rarely existed outside romantic myth: the Angry Janitor; the female Authority Figure; the kindly, homespun philosopher with a rural midwestern dialect; and the ideal "Abraham Lincoln." They represent a pseudoculture transplanted into the memory banks of mechanical men who in turn attempt to mold the behavior of human children. Fortunately the strength of the young mind, its resistance to social indoctrination and informational force-feeding, runs high and tough, as any teacher in a contemporary public school may well testify. For Jack Bohlen, the adult technician who is summoned to the Martian Public School to fix a recalcitrant simulacrum, the experience only serves to weary him and to provide him with dark insight into the deadening effects of these human facades.

Martian Time-Slip, through the character of Arnie Kott, poses questions pertaining to morality and business. If a human being has values, does that impose codes of conduct on both parties, or is the only code that of practicality in the manner of Machiavelli's advice to his prince? Does anything go as long as it results in the achievement of the primary responsibility, to take care of one's own? One must be practical, thinks Arnie Kott, Supreme Good-member of the Water Workers' Local, Fourth Planet Branch. What is good for Arnie Kott is good for the Colony. And what is good for Arnie Kott is success. Success may mean smuggled gourmet foods for Arnie's comfort; his conspicuous consumption of that most precious Martian commodity, water; or the tempo-rary exploitation of one of the defective children housed in the large, restricted conclaves.

True to his basic political orientation, Arnie Kott plays both the lion and the fox. He acts as the lion to terrify those persons who might possibly challenge his place in the Martian business hierar-chy, regardless of how small a threat they represent. Witness the peremptory way in which he disposes of the small-time smuggler Otto Zitte. All Otto asks is to "live the American way of life, instead of just talking about it" (*MTS*, 6). This, translated, means simply being a successful small businessman, having a one-man operation that allows him the satisfaction of self-reliance. But Otto does not even have a chance to show Kott that he might keep the faith with him; the fox in Arnie Kott sees Otto as a snare and a threat to his own on-the-side personal smuggling.

But Arnie Kott is not capable of broadening his political under-standing of the way in which a merchant prince, let alone a prince of the blood, should work. He has not studied Machiavelli and so is betrayed by his own greed. He neglects to find out that Machiavelli advised a prince always to *appear* to keep faith with others. With Bohlen, Doreen, Dr. Glaub, and most especially with Manfred, the autistic child he tries to use, he fails to be "altogether merciful, faithful, humane, upright and religious."[8] He might have survived the deceptions he perpetrated upon the first three persons, but his relationship with Manfred proves to be his undoing.

Manfred Steiner differs greatly even from those other disabled persons with whom he lives. What does it mean to be different in a society whose standards of acceptable individuality may prove to be counterfeit and hollow? For one thing labeling occurs: It is easier to categorize individuals than to regard them as unique. Labels, being abstract entities, are easier to destroy than people. What does it matter if in eradicating a label one does away with the container on which it has been erroneously pasted? An empty bottle might appear to be useless; it is often easier to throw an empty bottle out than to attempt to fill or recycle it. Manfred, along with the other "abnormal" children in Camp Ben-Gurion, is an empty container as far as the bulk of the human—Terran as well as Martian—population is concerned. A concerned parent like Norbert Steiner may visit periodically, but mere concern is not enough.

Even someone who is motivated by an enlightened concern may find the bottle not empty, but filled with a reality which most of us do not have the capacity to enter. "Five windows light the cavern'd Man," sings the Fairy in William Blake's *Europe*; the five windows are the five bodily senses through which the rational man may experience only "small portions of the eternal world that ever groweth." Is it possible that those we reject as empty have other senses through which they can experience the eternal world? Manfred Steiner possesses just such a sense, a special sense of time. His "inner clock" is so adjusted that he perceives normal movement as jerky and frenetic, normal speech as dissonant and meaningless. Instead, he possesses the ability of precognition and seems even to possess the ability to travel into the recent past and set alternate realities into motion. But he is unable to subject these abilities to conscious or rational control.

Ever alert to the opportunity to use a situation to his special advantage, Arnie Kott jumps at the chance to use Manfred. Hearing rumors of a government plan to buy up seemingly useless land for the construction of a large new population center, Arnie tries to use Manfred to manipulate the past in his favor so that he may pre(post)-file claims on the land. In his eagerness to push his claims, Kott discounts Manfred's vision of the future of those huge living complexes, the AM-WEB, as decaying "storage cells" for the very old and rejected members of society. Instead, the vision provokes quite a different chain of events. Arnie Kott's tunnel vision with regard to business, his total lack of concern for Manfred's humanity, and his failure to recognize Manfred's irreducible uniqueness betray him into a critically disturbed flow of time and into a reality that holds his own death.

The deep-lying concern for human individuality and human dignity when faced with a threatening source of power continued to engage Dick throughout 1964, a prolific publishing year for

him.[9] While the fertility of his imagination allows him to continually reexamine the old theme of appearance and reality in the
guise of new plot lines, he reuses many of the techniques and
devices found in his earlier works. Again we find provision for
aesthetic distancing by extending Terran society either into outer
space or into a time not too far distant from our own. The locales
may seem different, but they serve the same purpose: Fomalhaut
in *The Unteleported Man* and the Alphane moon of *Clans of the
Alphane Moon* give us off-earth versions of (respectively) the all-
too-well-known concentration camp and insane asylum. The 2014
date of *The Unteleported Man* is too close in time for comfort. It
is only too easy to extrapolate the contemporary power struggles
between Big Business and Big Government to that date. We are
being faced again with the uncomfortable possibility that the
proverbial "history repeats itself" may be true.

Are we so chained to the circle as a dominating symbol that we
must accept a cyclical view of human history? What if we substitute the metaphor of a tree for the circle? On this tree can grow
innumerable branches or possibilities; perhaps even an entirely
new branch, a new combination of events and beings, will evolve
to tender a more viable arrangement for political harmony. In
Clans of the Alphane Moon, Dick offers one such possibility. In
this slight novel, not often given critical attention, Dick submits a
unique alternative to his more obvious political structures dependent on the tension between two power centers. True, there
may be burgeoning power centers, but they usually suffer impo-
tence because of their smallness or their idealistic base. Whether
the tension is between business and government or between two
strong military and racial political powers, the genesis of that
tension stems from an either/or philosophy. In *Clans* Dick
explodes the Aristotelian stand-off into seven, and eventually
eight, possible foci.

Imagine, if you will, a world in space, populated with those
human beings whose mental states the "normal" world in its
infinite wisdom has labeled *aberrant*. On the Alphane moon live
seven groups of people, each group in a separate conclave or city.
The names of the cities suggest not too subtly the fondness of
contemporary developers for indulging in semantic floweriness
when naming their latest developments. On the Alphane moon

there are a DaVinci Heights, a Cotton Mather Estates, and an Adolfville, for example. A unique mental bent marks each population—schizophrenia, hebephrenia, depression, manic depression, paranoia, polymorphous schizophrenia, or compulsive obsession. The clans are likewise named after the mental state they represent: the Heebs, Pares, Manses, etc. Although physically and mentally separated the clans do enjoy a loose confederation in the form of a council of seven members on which each group has one representative. Under ordinary circumstances this confederation does not really accomplish much, since the member groups organize reality within seven incompatible frameworks. However, when their moon faces a threatened invasion by "normal" people—scientists sent from Terra to study them as a preface to the imposition of treatment—the groups unite in strength to resist. Each group contributes the insights gained from its specialized reaction to the world to benefit the confederation as a whole. In the end a new city is founded and accepted into the confederation: Thomas Jeffersonburg, for those labeled *normal*.

The labels absorb the characters in *Clans* to such an extent that we lose interest in them as surrogate human beings. However, what Dick succeeds in presenting here is a science-fictional version of the old morality play of *Everyman*. In *Everyman* the characters representing the various moral components of a man's existence fail to sustain him on his journey to death because he has neglected them during life. Instead of the attributes of Beauty, Fellowship, or Worldly Goods that were found in *Everyman*, Dick offers groups of humans who function as symbols for a variety of mental states. These can help Mr. Normality on his journey through life if only he will recognize and utilize their special knowledge of the human condition, instead of trying to eradicate them in favor of an equally unbalanced state, that of complete, unbending logicality and rationality. Just as an unused hand or heart will atrophy leaving an impaired physical body, just as heedlessly used good works or worldly goods make for an imperfect moral being, so does an inflexibly hierarchic mode of thinking produce an incomplete political being. Translated into practical terms, Dick's political alternative in *Clans* challenges the long-established and firmly entrenched primacy of reason.

In *The Simulacra* Dick returns to a variation on the world presented in *High Castle,* a world split between and dominated by two contrasting social orders. Though a Communist power has replaced the Japanese of *High Castle,* the USEA of *The Simulacra* bears a great resemblance to the German-dominated zone in *High Castle.* Those earlier clean-cut, energetic German engineers have their counterparts in the German business community of *The Simulacra.* Raised to an almost mystical level by their poetical name *Geheimnisträger* or "bearers of the secret," the Ges constitute the upper level of society. The secret which they bear is power and the tools with which to sustain that power. But power is not enough unless one is willing to bear the brunt of its effects. Consequently, Dick presents us with analogues to those characters in *High Castle* who "just looked like men." These are the Bes, the *Befehlträger* or "carriers out of orders"—those who follow directions without question and carry out the plans of the power elite.

From the beginning the novel invites the reader to focus upon political matters by its not-too-subtle evocation of the Hitlerian era. The USEA, ostensibly a continuation of the conventional American democratic structure, has an elected president, *der Alte* ("the old man"). Despite his elective status, *der Alte* ranks second in popularity behind his wife, Nicole Thibodeaux. A charismatic woman, Nicole has captured the imagination and affection of the nation. Helped by the sympathetic eye of the television camera, she functions variously as a mother image, a love object, the repository of the nation's ideals, and the protector and mentor of its cultural life. The actual power of the land, however, lies with the large German business combines—that is, until Big Government decides to challenge Big Business when a new *der Alte* is up for reelection. A cabal of high officials decides to bring back Hermann Goering from 1944 by use of the von Lessinger equipment, involving a sophisticated process in the lineage of H.G. Wells's time machine. Putting his experience with assassination to good stead, the modern group rids itself of powerful opponents, especially the cartel officers of the company which constructs *der Alte.* This is the more concrete "secret" born by the Ges: *Der Alte* is an android, or simulacrum, the mechanical mouthpiece for Ges policy which has been in existence in various forms for fifty years.

Appearance versus reality—the appearance of great benefits

masks the underlying reality of exploitation. The Ges have thrust an ersatz reality upon the Bes. *The Simulacra,* true to the plural of its title, presents us with a simulacrum of an entire society, replete with multiple simulacra wherever one turns. This is a society in which the authenticity of human life is barely discernible. A large segment of the population lives in communal apartments where rules rigidly control the social and personal lives of the inhabitants. Each occupant must pass a "relpol" test in order to remain there. Security committees work each complex in a constant search to rout out misfits, such as those who refuse to attend the required cultural evenings or who keep pets that make noise, even the natural peeps, woofs, and meows of our conventional pets. Ironically the name of one of these complexes is the Abraham Lincoln, the traditional symbol of human freedom. An alternative to this regimented living lies in an unauthorized escape via "Looney Luke" jalopies to Mars. Even in this alternative lie the seeds of conformity and false fronts, for there is a lively traffic in *famnexdos,* a family-next-door set of simulacra to give the illusion of human society in a socially sterile and alien world. Unfortunately these "neighbors" reflect only the thoughts and fantasies of their human owners, thus encouraging an ingrown point of view very similar to that imposed by the communal living on Terra.

In *The Simulacra* the author pushes rather than leads the reader, shouts rather than hints at the overt manipulation of our minds and our behavior by the advertising industry with its hard-and soft-sell techniques. The "Nitz commercial," a synthetic but organic life form programmed to deliver a message, forces its way into vehicles and homes; it can attach itself to a hapless person and screech out its message over and over. The message sells fear of personal rejection so persuasively that it sometimes induces phobic reactions in especially ill-balanced minds. In the hands of a clever salesman, the papoola—a simulacrum of an outwardly benign and lovable Martian creature—becomes a tool for mind-bending. While depriving the listener of the opportunity for free choice, it infuses him with feelings of warmth and love. The effectiveness of these two devices alone bids fair to put Vance Packard's "hidden persuaders" into a museum. The only saving grace is the fact that wary persons recognize both the Nitz commercial and the papoola for what they are and do. There is a margin of safety from them, for once identified they can be destroyed or rejected.

While the communal living encourages the stagnation of human free will and the advertising gimmicks negate it completely unless one is on guard against them, the most insidious force is the vaunted Ges combine of business coupled with government. It takes a special brand of person to operate successfully at these rarefied levels, the kind of person that Dick presents dramatically in a brief encounter between the head of the powerful Karp cartel and one of the strong men of the government. McRae accuses Karp of not being "authentically a political person" because he has the idea that truth is still a valid commodity. McRae can see that Karp is a coward when he fails to ask about plans concerning the next presidential simulacrum. Karp has been morally emasculated in accordance with present-day requirements for membership at the power center of the German business community. Ironically, in a later interview with Nicole, this same McRae justifies his own part in the use of the simulacrum by soothing himself with the statement that the fraud is legal and is in the best interests of the people, thereby revealing his own spiritual and moral emasculation.

In its total commitment to maintaining false fronts, the power elite accepts its right to perpetuate any fraud in the name of legality. The chief executive is a dummy, a mechanical construct which issues orders emanating from spiritually and morally depraved people. Only Nicole recognizes the truth that the legal front is a face-saving device. Even so, she participates in the fraud in a multitude of ways. A young and beautiful woman, she plays her part as tastemaker by feeding the public, in some cases force-feeding, the current line regarding cultural excellence. Above all, she is a person of considerable political acumen, recognizing the harsh political realities of a power center divided within itself and threatened by an insurgent group driven by much native vitality. Even in the person of Nicole, Dick does not allow us to find a saving crust of normality to nourish us. In the end comes the revelation that even Nicole is ersatz, the original Nicole being almost a century dead and the contemporary one another in a series of clever actresses assuming the role and completely without real power. Like *der Alte* and the members of Ges, she too is unreal.

How can one escape this mad, absurdist world? It might be possible to migrate to a virgin environment and attempt to reconstruct from the bottom up the very same society you escaped, improving it through the hindsight of prior experience. Or one might retreat into social invisibility, living a life of psychological isolation and tainted freedom in the midst of the crowd. A third alternative is the complete destruction of civilization so that a more primitive social group may have the chance to set the stage with new hopes and new directions. To his various characters in *The Simulacra*, Dick has offered each alternative, together with its accompanying pain. With the final clash resulting in all-out conflict he introduces us to the "chuppers," beings vaguely reminiscent of Stone-Age man. Is his answer to the political problem the dismal one that *Homo sapiens* has had his time at bat, so it is now time for another team to take over?

The novels of 1965 resume Dick's disintegrative view of human history. Both *The Three Stigmata of Palmer Eldritch* and *Dr. Bloodmoney*, subtitled *How We Got Along After the Bomb*, indict subtly by again presenting alternatives that are so close to our everyday reality that we easily fit them to our needs and perspective. Some events in the plots conjure up our not-so-distant past, while even those in an apparent future carry an air of familiarity. With this novel Dick reminds us forcibly of a conclusion of Saint Augustine, that wise man of the Christian visionary tradition:

> If future and past times exist, I wish to know where they are. But if I am not yet able to do this, I still know wherever they are, they are neither as future nor as past, but as present.[10]

We can interpret *Dr. Bloodmoney* and *Palmer Eldritch* as referring to the present, for both works cause us to scrutinize our given conventions and traditions and to look more carefully at the next step our society seems to take.

In *Dr. Bloodmoney,* first published in 1965, the dates upon which Dick hinges his events demand initial attention. One might expect to find the references to events said to have occurred in 1972 a disconcerting annoyance for a post-1972 reader, especially in a novel which does not purport to be realistic; but that date, with its subsequent description of incidents foreign to our known flow of history in no way negates the impact of the story. In the first two chapters, various epithets for that date command attention: "the first great accident" of 1972; the "tragic error" of 1972; Bluthgeld's "miscalculation back in 1972"; the time of the "high-altitude blast which wasn't supposed to hurt anyone"; the "fiasco"; and finally, the "faulty calculation" which was "faulty in relationship to the reality situation." Similar, though less frequent references to 1972 occur in subsequent chapters. These phrases hurt as we read them in the context of the news stories of our world of 1977, stories of radiation clouds drifting at high levels over the Great Lakes or of the strontium level in the milk of cows in certain parts of the United States. Even now, we are told these are not great enough quantities to hurt anyone. *Dr. Bloodmoney* does not suffer from its initial date; it may go so far as to transform a political dream into a recurrent nightmare.

The main action of the novel, however, starts at a second date, 1981. The United States of 1981 is recognizable. The stores in the San Francisco area open for business as usual on this beautiful, sunny morning. Although a few unsettled people are keeping appointments with their psychiatrists, the many others look forward to a fine week of buying and selling, working and playing, getting along or advancing in the world. And then it happens. A bomb attack demolishes the expected forward progression of the nation and its economy with everything "booming from the start, where America got bigger and stronger and everybody took more home" (*Dr. B.*, 1). That world gives way abruptly to the world of 1988, seven years after the second great miscalculation. The society of *Dr. Bloodmoney* has for the most part reverted to a state of preelectrical technology, the days of the small artisan and farmer. A notable exception to this is the handyman of each small community, that rare person who is able to repair the few machines that still operate. A 1988 version of cottage labor exists in places such as Andrew Gill's tobacco factory in Petaluma where eight employees roll cigarettes by hand. There is even evidence of the resurgence of labor exploitation, for Andrew Gill "paid his employees almost nothing; they were glad to have jobs at any salary" (*Dr. B.*, 11). Despite the drawbacks to comfortable living the small communities have managed to establish a "fragile structure of maladaptation'' (*Dr. B,* 12), to borrow a Dickian phrase applied to Bruno Bluthgeld. *Dr. Bloodmoney* treats us to the politics of survival in a world where just enough reminders of the good old days are left to taunt the survivors.

Daily the survivors are faced with the irreversible effects of the Emergency. Radiation freaks, funny people, and sports—all kinds of mutations, both man and animal—are integral parts of this world and must be dealt with equitably. These people and animals possess powers which compensate for the abnormalities they carry. Hoppy Harrington, the handyman without arms or legs, possesses the power to move objects and to heal breaks in metal with his mind. Mr. Tree's dog Tom has mastered a rough command of the English language. Rats in the cities have sharpened intelligences and even artistic propensities, as evidenced by one who plays a nose flute! Overhead floats a major reminder of the Emergency: the perpetually orbiting spaceship of Walt Dangerfield. Dangerfield and his wife, Lydia, are the first couple chosen to migrate to Mars, an undertaking which fires the imagination of the populace. After a successful lift-off but eight minutes before the firing of the fourth-stage rocket which would free them of Earth's gravitational pull, the bombs drop, destroying forever the mechanism which could release them from Earth orbit or return them to the ground. All Dangerfield can do is to watch his old world fall apart because those at the center of power are no longer able to hold it together.

Ironically, in this post-Emergency world Walt Dangerfield comes to assume a central significance. To preserve his sanity, particularly after the death of Lydia, Walt continues to transmit messages regularly to the few radios still in operation on Earth. For the earthbound listeners, this event comes to have not a cultural but a communal significance. They gather together to listen to his scraps of folk wisdom which are actually more applicable to a pre-Emergency society than now, or for the playing of popular pre-Emergency songs from his store of old recordings. A favorite program is his reading of Somerset Maugham's *Of Human Bondage,* the irony of the title remaining unappreciated by any of his listeners. As the years pass, the transmissions become more devoted to mention of Dangerfield's deteriorating health and his fear of impending death.

Dangerfield, the central figure upon whom they so depend for communal meaning and order in their lives is only too human. Again, the center of power and meaning cannot hold forever. Blinded by their own fears, they are ripe for being duped by those who fancy themselves as candidates to usurp Dangerfield's power. The two candidates, both motivated by twisted ideals, well fit Yeats's image of that "rough beast, its hour come round at last," and they slouch into the power vacuum left by Danger-field's deteriorating condition. Bruno Bluthgeld, the Dr. Blood-money of the novel's title, epitomizes the mad scientist. A focal point for the world's hatred after the "miscalculation" of 1972, Bluthgeld accepts the 1981 attack as a personal one against him. His universe closes to one point; himself. He feels no remorse, only vindication in the faces around him, for they do not truly know him, the self-named "omphalos, the center, of all this cata-clysmic disruption" (*Dr. B,* 6). But Bluthgeld is a false center who cannot organize an orderly existence.

Hoppy Harrington moves also to fill the power vacuum. While Dangerfield has innocently created an illusion of normality for a people hungry for it, Hoppy makes use of that illusion for egocen-tric purposes. Like a thief in the night, he steals the personality and role of Dangerfield, displacing him and assuming his influ-ence by imitating his voice and overriding the transmissions. Even when challenged by Bluthgeld, self-resurrected from anonymity, Hoppy wins; their conflict is symbolic of the battle between theoretical science and technological pragmatism.

Unhappily both characters are neglectful of humanistic con-cerns. In the politics of survival, the center of power must be humanistic. When the old, traditional power centers fail, then a new imaginative force must flow into the vacuum, a fresh man-infestation of the *élan vital.* At first, this may serve simply to reinforce the older, failing center, if that center has value; out of the reinforcing effort, the new force must gain the strength and experience to serve when the time comes. But, above all, it *must* be humanistic; it must want to see, to hear, to sense all that life has to offer. In *Dr. Bloodmoney* this new force finds expression in Bill Keller, a "sport" or mutant resulting from the radiation of the bombs. Actually a symbiote sharing his sister's body, but at first thought by others to be an "imaginary playmate" of hers, Bill finally separates himself to merge with different life forms, (first a snail, then a worm), learning from them until he finally ousts Hoppy from his bodily container and takes it over for himself. With that action he removes a false center, reestablishing the preeminence of Dangerfield. Weak and failing though Dangerfield is, he can provide a more authentic human focus for those in human bondage until the new spirit (Bill) can assume this responsibility.

In the quasi-utopian world of *Dr. Bloodmoney,* this reestablishment offers only a temporary relief which is undercut by a sense of perverseness. The people in this postcataclysmic society *know* that Dangerfield is Up There; after a hiatus, his voice emanates again with certainty from the radio receivers. His listeners have now accepted the fact that he is human and must die soon. With the hopes that he will continue the meaning in their lives, for a time at least, comes that brief reprieve for them. The powerless love which they hold for him is given the priceless second chance to expand and help to fill the vacuum that will occur when he does fall silent. The politics of group survival operates not only in terms of an economic community or of governmental autonomy but most importantly in a society of humanistic beings who are fully aware of the need for compassion and understanding.

There is yet another arena where Dick's political dreams can flourish and where his introverted brand of activism can work. In *The Three Stigmata of Palmer Eldritch,* we enter that arena—the metaphysical reality which forever eludes us, a reality of which we are forever a part, yet paradoxically from which we must remain forever estranged. *Palmer Eldritch* hurls us into the politics of existence. The ancient, unanswered, but forever asked questions arise: Is there a God? What does it mean to be human in the presence of the infinite and the eternal? Are good and evil merely opposing faces of the same coin? With William Blake, again, we must answer with uncertainty:

There is an Outside spread Without & an Outside spread Within,
Beyond the outline of Identity both ways, which meet in One,
An orbed Void of doubt, despair, hunger & thirst & sorrow.
—from *Jerusalem* 1, 18, 2–4

In *Palmer Eldritch* Dick suggests a vision similar to Blake's void of doubt, despair, and sorrow. His title character, Palmer Eldritch, carries always within him the three stigmata of alienation, blurred reality, and despair. This dark vision, however, does not appear with full clarity until the story has unfolded in all its complexity.

The novel contains many of the science-fictional devices and motifs found in Dick's previous works; its world has its quota of conapts, precogs, and runnels. It takes place in the distant future, for reference is made to the dying sun with its last, intense flarings. Like many of Dick's other imaginative worlds, this one contains business empires at war with each other while a powerful political entity views the struggle from a lofty distance, taking tribute from both sides. While we may not feel comfortable with the knowledge of E-Therapy, a process of stepped-up evolution, we do find other familiar points of reference. Men still fight to climb up corporate ladders, and slick salesmen sway a gullible buying public with their falsely optimistic pitches. The instinct for self-preservation at whatever cost remains very much alive in this new world. As one of the characters, Barney Mayerson, cynically notes, "That's the name of the comedy we're stuck in" (*3SPE*, 7).

Mayerson, a precog, works for Perky Pat Layouts, Inc., an industrial giant which manufactures miniature environments for sale to the colonists on Mars. These dollhouse constructs include a male and female doll, complete with all the possible material extensions of modern life. With the help of Can-D, a hallucinogenic substance also purveyed by the monopoly, people can enter into a new, illusory reality of complete material wish fulfillment. Though banned on Earth, the Perky Pat layouts and Can-D find great acceptance on Mars, where Earth's excess population is housed in hovels amidst the hostile environment.

Mayerson's boss, Leo Bulero, a superevolved human "bubblehead," has benefited from E-Therapy to such a point that he now outthinks and outmaneuvers his business opponents and associates alike. That is, he does so until he finds himself at odds with Palmer Eldritch. Eldritch, returning from a ten-year voyage in deep space, possesses a new drug, Chew-Z, which surpasses the performance of Can-D. Chew-Z, it is claimed, can stimulate a miraculous shift into a nontemporal state of being, bestowing immortality without the need for passage through death. Unlike Can-D, which changes the appearance of life only, the new drug changes its very essence. With the appearance of the new product, the battle lines are drawn between the two businessmen, but it is not long before we are aware that the struggle has moved to a more spiritual level, with Bulero as a champion of the truly human and Eldritch as a representative of the metahuman.

At this point Dick confronts us with the politics of existence and identity, for it becomes increasingly evident that Eldritch is both himself possessed and one who seeks to possess, in the occult sense of that term. His two names, at connotative odds with each other, suggest spiritual distortion; his appearance furthers that suggestion. Upon his return from the ten-year pilgrimage into the Without, his body reflects the state of the Within: eyes that are blind but replaced by artificial lenses; an artificial hand that lacks the delicate sensitivity of human fingertips; and a ravaged face with steel teeth, feral in their hard brilliance. This "eldritch" appearance foreshadows his eldritch ability to invade the very soul and ego of those who use his drug. He absorbs their very essence into his own. Yet he is weak in the face of determined human resistance. Free will is the only weapon against his invasion of the human spirit. But that free will must be coupled with an acceptance of the consequences of making a choice. As Mayerson says, "You know, we got ourselves into this" (*3SPE*, 11). And again, as he accepts the fact that the past is irrevocable in spite of the drug's effect, he acknowledges that he is a creature of time and circumstance: "I *made* this situation" (*3SPE*, 10).

Despite the aura of evil which surrounds Palmer Eldritch he paradoxically moves to correct unfortunate or harmful situations. Under the influence of the drug, Mayerson encounters Eldritch in a different reality where Eldritch seems motivated only by good impulses. What is good and what is evil? Is it good to try to undo the damage resulting from improper choices made in the past? Is it evil to reject the responsibility for having made those choices? Is it human to do both? Once we accept the consequences of our own actions, we have accepted the fact of our own existence. Even with knowledge of the fragility of human existence and the seeming intransigence of the universal forces beyond our control, there is still hope. Like Bulero in his interoffice memo, we can say that we "have faith that even in this lousy situation we're faced with we can make it" (*3SPE*, Preface). The politics of human existence, like the politics of business, of international relations, or of survival, operate around a power center. That center can be beyond us, in a realm of nonbeing. It can be in the midst of cosmic or metaphysical forces which we may label good or evil or God or fate or *Moira* (fate) or the Absolute or Nemesis. On that high level of abstraction, the individual human being cannot exist. When the politics of a situation harden into a government, then it is important that the center be far from the margin of nonbeing and rest in an inviolable core of authentic humanity.

In the novels discussed here, one is hard put to locate a hero or even a protagonist in the broader sense of that term. At any given moment, a character may gather the focus of attention around him; but the immediate reality is apt to dissove into an equally valid alternate reality in which he has no significance whatsoever. Yet within each of these novels there is one character operating as a "redeemer" or the symbol of, in the words of Black Elk, the "heart of human life."[11] In Tagomi, Bulero, Bill Keller, Manfred Steiner, and certain special others lie the seeds of a truly human existence, seeds that will grow and flower in spite of the ersatz institutions and artificial human beings around them. But these redeemers operate only at the plot level and, as has been mentioned before, Philip Dick's novels do have their own brand of forgettability. But they also have their own brand of memorability, for Dick is both a political visionary and a verbal magician. Like Black Elk, the visionary wise man of the Oglala Sioux, Philip Dick must be acutely aware that "anywhere is the center of the world."[12] So too is the center in the person reading one of Philip K. Dick's political dreams and the power is there to move us to awareness, to repel us from the margin of Non Entity.

7. In Pursuit of *Ubik**

MICHAEL BISHOP

IN ITS CAGEY insusceptibility to any absolute interpretation, and in its bleak, funny, and/or disorienting surrealism, reside a great deal of the fascination and most of the exasperating *slipperiness* of Philip K. Dick's *Ubik*, "that magnificent but flawed novel" whose allegorical import seems to be that humanity's essential heroism lies in our private, day-by-day attempts to defeat, or at least to counterbalance, the entrenched and abiding forces of entropy.

Because we all instinctively shun chaos, casual readers as well as critics frequently try to pin down a work of fiction. We immerse a story or a novel in chloroform, spread its diaphanous wings against a contrasting velvet backdrop of exegesis, and poke color-coded pins into its lobes and lights. We do this to keep our literary lepidopteron from fluttering ambiguously away. The creature now on display may seem to possess a symmetry never before so conspicuous or intellectually gratifying—but it certainly isn't going to fly again.

As raggedly regal as some weary monarch butterfly migrating

---

*This chapter appeared originally, in slightly different form, as the "Introduction" to a hardcover reprint of *Ubik* (Boston: Gregg Press, 1979). "Introduction" copyright © 1979 by Michael Bishop.

137

to God-knows-where, *Ubik* has attracted any number of readers—both high-powered literary critics and eager book-rack aficionados of Dick—who would like to determine what sort of creature it is and exactly where it's going.

The fascination, like the exasperation, sometimes seems universal. And although *Ubik* hasn't always escaped our lunging nets, for over ten years now it has manifested a far-from-fragile resistance to the chloroform of analysis and a downright uncanny refusal to submit to entomological crucifixion. Sometimes it has done so to our chagrin, disgruntlement, or contempt (a few have alleged that *Ubik* is a mechanical butterfly, crudely assembled and bound to fall apart); but often, particularly if we are at heart sympathetic to its flight, it has done so to our delight and even exhilaration.

Whatever our attitude toward it, *Ubik*—in ragged, beautiful gyrations confounding our ability to follow—keeps flying. It invites our continued pursuit by its very elusiveness. Further, I'm convinced that three-quarters of the fun of *Ubik* (as serious as that fun may often seem) just happens to lie in the pursuit.

Norman Spinrad, who believes that a century from now Dick may well be regarded as the most important American novelist of our time, has trenchantly explained why the pursuit of ultimate meaning in another of Dick's novels so often dazzles and perplexes:

> In a Dickian universe, there are many realities, most of them equally valid, but none of them an overview of the whole. If his plots sometimes seem contradictory, they are deliberately so. To keep all the loose ends tied up would violate verisimilitude in the service of consistency, for the Dickian universe has ambiguity and indeterminacy at its core.[2]

Spinrad eventually acknowledges that what does abide as a constant in Dick's complex metaphysical musings is "the overall concept of *relative* deity and the ultimate subjectivity of reality."[3] Applicable to such diverse and challenging novels as *The Man in the High Castle, Martian Time-Slip, The Three Stigmata of Palmer Eldritch, Flow My Tears, the Policeman Said,* and Dick's devastatingly intense *A Scanner Darkly,* this judgment also has a telling relevancy to the absurdist allegory embodied in *Ubik.*

Ubik dazzles and perplexes because the reader takes leave of its final line—"This was just the beginning"—with no certainty as to which reality, Joe Chip's or Glen Runciter's, more correctly or at least more powerfully deserves the imprimatur of our belief and allegiance. Those inclined to snippiness with writers who refuse to rubber-stamp the final page of their works with the invisible legend HAPPY ENDING or maybe HEART-RENDING FINALE will toss the book aside, thinking themselves the dupes of Dick's cruel indecisiveness. But, as Spinrad, Stanislaw Lem,[4] and others have pointed out, and as the works themselves so starkly demonstrate, the ambiguity and intentional irreality of Dick's fictional universes imbue them, paradoxically, with an off-center *life-likeness* either absent from or altogether alien to the novels of more conventional artists. *Ubik* is no exception.

Much critical debate, however, has focused on the matter of how successful the novel is, even on its own idiosyncratic terms. The consensus seems to be that *Ubik* represents at best an imperfect masterpiece.

Clearly, the novel gathers force, conviction, and, strangely, even verisimilitude after the explosion of the unlikely "humanoid bomb" in Chapter 6.[5] Immediately, Joe Chip and all the other antipsionic agents of Glen Runciter's "prudence organization" find that they have become subject to an accelerated process of decay and devolution. Entropy's pawns, they seek valiantly to discover and negate the sadistic game-player who deploys them toward their own defeat. Moreover, the details with which Dick authenticates these eerie post-Luna passages in which the lineaments of the past emerge skeletally and then altogether fullbodiedly from a dubious present contribute immeasurably to *Ubik's* impact. These details stagger and convince, disdaining to let us go until Dick, in his final chapter, releases us to a conundrum even more puzzling than a resurrected past.

Who, then, can quarrel with what Dick accomplishes in *Ubik*?

Darko Suvin, in another chapter of this volume, indicts Dick for "a serious loss of narrative control," alleging that the novel's denouement is "irresponsibly reminiscent of the rabbits-from-the-hat carelessness associated with rankest van Vogt if not 'Doc' Smith: the false infinities of explaining one improbability by a succession of ever greater ones."[6] I believe that Spinrad's indeterminacy argument, as well as my own approach to *Ubik,* totally invalidates this criticism.

I am more in sympathy with the intimations of Brian W. Aldiss and others that *Ubik,* especially in its first six or seven chapters, suffers from a kind of structural obfuscation and a comic-book quirkishness of style that have nothing to do with the novel's unifying theme and that consequently violate even the *playful* seriousness of its dominant tone.

Let me cite a few instances of this latter flaw. Here, for example, is Dick's description of the psionic double-agent G.G. Ashwood when Ashwood first enters Joe Chip's "conapt":

> Square and puffy, like an overweight brick, wearing his usual mohair poncho, apricot-colored felt hat, argyle ski socks and carpet slippers, he advanced toward Joe Chip. (*Ubik*, 3)

Two chapters later, having rushed offstage for a costume change, this same character pops up in the office of Joe Chip's boss, Glen Runciter:

> Over by the window G.G. Ashwood, wearing his customary natty birchbark pantaloons, hemp-rope belt, peekaboo see-through top and train engineer's tall hat, shrugged indifferently. (*Ubik*, 5)

Almost masochistically dissatisfied with these two overripe sartorial tableaux, Dick then proceeds to parade before our bewildered eyes the entire ragtag group of "inertials," or anti-Psi agents, whom Runciter eventually takes with him to the Moon.

As a result, we conjure from Dick's suddenly rococo prose a bald Greek in "old-fashioned, hip-hugging gold lamé trousers"; an "anti-animator" wearing "a polyester dirndl, his long hair in a snood, cowboy chaps with simulated silver stars"; and a fellow named Fred Zaffsky "clad, for this occasion, in a shift dress the color of a baboon's ass." Later, when the novel's unsettling "regression of forms" is just getting under way, promising complete deliverance from this distracting descriptive silliness, Dick intractably trots out his moratorium owner, Herbert Schoenheit von Vogelsang, in "tweed toga, loafers, crimson sash and a purple airplane-propeller beanie."

What compels Dick to demean his characters in these petty ways? Why, like some mad Warner Brothers wardrobe lady, does he occasionally succumb to the urge to drape his helpless charges in the hand-me-downs of a B-movie nightmare? Does he really expect us to believe that the attire of 1992 will so blatantly mock itself? Maybe this is satire. All I can do, however, is hazard that the exigencies of writing commercial fiction have here taken their toll, perhaps in the service of some incidental (no pun intended) padding—then step back and marvel that *Ubik* transcends this incongruous difficulty and eventually points to a genuine auctorial concern for every single one of its characters.

The triumph of *Ubik*, to return to my principal assessment of its meaning and worth, derives in large measure from Dick's handling of three distinct elements: (1) the concept of half-life, on which hinges our ambiguity about which of several subjective realities, if any, we ought to regard as reliable; (2) the characterization of Joe Chip, whose centrality to the novel, even when his energies and élan are at their lowest ebb, we never actually doubt; and (3) the allegorical import of Ubik, the enigmatic "reality support" that shouts its manifold virtues in Madison Avenue-like epigrams to every chapter and that comes to disclose itself in the guise of an aerosol bomb composed of, redundantly as Dick points out, "negative ions." Dick's careful integration of these three elements into a narrative not necessarily reducible to a single comprehensive diagnosis sparks *Ubik* to shimmering, palpitating life.

First, then, in a partial damming of the tidewaters of entropy and death, stands the metaphysical bulwark of half-life, which Dick posits as a futuristic answer to unappealable extinction. Suspended between life and death, available for brief microphone-amplified chats with friends and relatives, the inhabitants of Vogelsang's Beloved Brethren Moratorium—entombed in their "cold-pac bins"—drift toward a destiny embodying a rebirth at some unspecified time, meanwhile dreaming their own secret realities and in some instances sharing the subjective experiences of the more vigorous half-lifers with whom they are interwired. It's no accident, I feel sure, that Dick has dubbed this metaphysical condition with precisely the term employed by nuclear physicists to designate the "rate of decay of radioactive materials."[7] Half-life in this scientific sense is also known as either the "decay coefficient" or "disintegration constant," and these two terms also have a forceful thematic eloquence when we consider them in relation to Dick's novel.

Half-life in *Ubik* is entropy not at bay but temporarily in abeyance. When, early in the novel, Glen Runciter visits his wife Ella in Vogelsang's moratorium, he puts on the earphones through which he periodically communicates with her, then engages in some significant, private musing:

> How did it feel, he wondered, to be in half-life? He could never fathom it from what Ella told him; the basis of it, the experience of it, couldn't really be transmitted. Gravity, she had told him, once; it begins not to affect you and you float, more and more. When half-life is over, she had said, I think you float out of the System, out into the stars. But she did not know either; she only wondered and conjectured. She did not, however, seem afraid. Or unhappy. He felt glad of that. (*Ubik*, 2)

As one more soldier in our ongoing war against decay, disintegration, and devolution, Runciter indeed has cause to feel glad. Humanity has developed the blessing of half-life, and his wife, whom he sincerely loves, is one of the lucky beneficiaries. Runciter is already aware that each time he communicates with Ella she is brought ever so slightly closer to actual death. However, his ignorance, at this stage, of the pernicious subjective states into which half-lifers may drift or be driven establishes a dramatic irony whose full weight comes crashing down only when, along with Joe Chip, we get to a certain provincial hotel in Des Moines—which, not merely fortuitously, just happens to be the city of Runciter's birth. Early on, then, we believe with Runciter that there is no longer any need to "bury the dead for fear that they walk to the grave in labor"; that a babe in its birthday suit may not necessarily be "dressed to die."[8]

And this reprieve from death is the gift of half-life—even though, within it, the shadowy wasteland of Ultimate Ends still occasionally shows its contours to those who struggle against the malign and faceless Puppeteer manipulating their subjective experience. Here, for instance, in a beautiful but chilling passage detailing the horror of this force, Dick takes us into the mind of Joe Chip's friend and colleague, Al Hammond, a black "inertial" gradually losing ground to the glaciers in this wasteland:

> Now he became aware of an insidious, seeping, cooling-off which at some earlier and unremembered time had begun to explore him—

investigating him as well as the world around him. . . . The chill de-
based the surfaces of objects; it warped, expanded, showed itself as
bulblike swellings that sighed audibly and popped. Into the manifold
open wounds the cold drifted, all the way down into the heart of
things, the core which made them live. What he saw now seemed to be
a desert of ice from which stark boulders jutted. A wind spewed across
the plain which reality had become; the wind congealed into deeper
ice, and the boulders disappeared for the most part. And darkness
presented itself off at the edges of his vision; he caught only a meager
glimpse of it.

. . . Strange, he thought. Is the whole world inside me? Engulfed by
my body? When did that happen? It must be a manifestation of dying,
he said to himself. The uncertainty which I feel, the slowing down into
entropy—that's the process, and the ice which I see is the result of the
success of the process. When I blink out, he thought, the whole universe will disappear. But what about the various lights which I should
see, the entrances to new wombs? (*Ubik*, 9)

Hammond is right. His own subjective universe will soon disappear, and half-life will not have spared him an unknowable trans-
figuration. But the puzzling mention of "the entrances to new
wombs" in this passage hints that even if Hammond's and his
colleague's struggles to resist the dark are doomed, they nevertheless comprise an essential and heroic validation of the human
spirit. Rebirth is a promise that may well be broken, but, having
no other choice, one accepts it on faith.

Which brings me to Joe Chip, heroic *schlemiel* and tarnished
knight errant. Chip—a dedicated working stiff, a perennially
out-of-pocket Sisyphus, and the point-of-view character who
seems to matter most to Dick—is a shaving off the fallen family
tree of humanity: a chip off the old but sometimes praiseworthy
blockheadedness by which we and our progenitors have sought to
insist upon the meaningfulness of our lives. Joe Chip is Joe Blow,
Joan Foe, John Doe, or Jane Schmoe—in a word, Everyman.
Dick sends Joe into the fray as his personal representative—*our*
personal representative—and this poor, hard-beset, pertinacious
puppet does us all proud. In his efforts to cut or at least to tangle
the metaphysical strings by which the faceless Marionette Master
yanks him about, Joe Chip inevitably reinforces the apron strings
of his own humanity, binding himself to all of us by the heroism of
his persistence.

Nor do I believe it solely inadvertent that the surnames Chip
and Dick share a clipped, unifying assonance, by which similarity

I think the author intends to imply not that his protagonist is his mouthpiece but rather that even in his capacity as novelist and artificer he must acknowledge his blood-bond with Everyman. In this way, rather than through cloying exhortations to Love Thy Neighbor, Dick reveals his compassion for Joe Chip and, by simple extension, for every one of us.

Even Runciter recognizes that the air of surrender Joe sometimes seems to exude is only an intermittent spiritual pollutant:

> He [Joe Chip] had a peculiar defeated quality hanging over him, and yet, underneath, he did not seem to have given up. A vague and ragged hint of vitality lurked behind the resignation; it seemed to Runciter that Joe most nearly could be accused of feigning spiritual downfall . . . the real article, however, was not there. (*Ubik,* 4)

Later, when Joe has brought Runciter's corpse back to Zürich in an attempt to get it into a cold-pac bin before all encephalic activity has ceased, he gives evidence of his vitality by raging indignantly against a homeostatic coffee-shop speaker unit that has denied him credit:

> "One of these days," Joe said wrathfully, "people like me will rise up and overthrow you, and the end of tyranny by the homeostatic machine will have arrived. The day of human values and compassion and simple warmth will return, and when that happens someone like myself who genuinely needs hot coffee to pick him up and keep him functioning when he has to function will get the hot coffee whether he happens to have a poscred readily available or not." (*Ubik,* 7)

Joe's speech is funny as well as stirring because the denial of a cup of coffee has incited him to passionate Ciceronian rhetoric—but anyone who has lost a quarter in an impassive vending machine will understand the sources of his inspiration. And such machines are far more all-pervasive in Joe's society than in our own.

In Chapter 13, with the images of Wendy Wright's, Al Hammond's, Edie Dorn's, and even Glen Runciter's mummified corpses like burrs in his consciousness, Joe begins to feel the onset of decay and disintegration in himself. Believing that he is going to die, he undertakes to climb the hotel stairs, shunning the regressive mechanical trap of the elevator and virtually ignoring the psionic agent Pat Conley's mockingly disinterested commentaries on his step-by-step progress.

In this nightmarish scene, Joe Chip's Everyman nature manifests itself in a distinctly Sisyphean guise. Joe climbs not only to
find an isolated place to die, but to spite the "infantile, retarded
entity" enjoying the spectacle of his struggle and relishing the
inevitability of his defeat. Although Joe apparently can't win, he
might be able to lose in a mood of obstinate if largely self-delusive
indomitability; and, like Sisyphus, that is exactly what he attempts. In his awareness that he must ultimately surrender to his
fate, for a brief moment Joe Chip becomes a character of near-
tragic proportions, his heroism deriving from his scorn for the
infantile god persecuting him and from his astonishing dogged-
ness.

Albert Camus wrote on the tragic implications of the Sisyphus
myth and the superiority of Sisyphus to his fate, as follows:

> If this myth is tragic, that is because its hero is conscious. Where
> would his torture be, indeed, if at every step the hope of succeeding
> upheld him? The workman of today works every day of his life at the
> same task, and this fate is no less absurd. But it is tragic only at the
> rare moments when it becomes conscious. Sisyphus, proletarian of the
> gods, powerless and rebellious, knows the whole extent of his
> wretched condition. . . . The lucidity that was to constitute his torture
> at the same time crowns his victory. There is no fate that cannot be
> surmounted by scorn.[9]

I don't want to push this parallel too far (for fear it will roll back
on me), but I think it is safe to add that both Sisyphus and Joe
Chip achieve an existentialist victory over their fates by staying
scornfully on the go.

Finally, at least for my present purposes, I come to Ubik. With
this substance the mysteriously resurrected Runciter—whom Joe
has seen dead and dehydrated in a casket at the Simple Shepherd
Mortuary—generously sphritzes his dying employee, thereby
temporarily resurrecting Joe, too. What, then, is Ubik?

Near the end of the novel, Joe asks this question of a representative of the manufacturer of Ubik in its spray-can incarnation.
He receives an answer so overloaded with technical jargon that
he interrupts the young woman's recitation with a pointed objec-
tion. This untenable, pseudoscientific answer, along with the
chapter-heading ad parodies in which Ubik pops up as everything
from a salad dressing to a toastable aphrodisiac, suggests that
Dick is purposely employing a technique of subtle misdirection to

obscure a truth that our consumer- and technology-oriented society itself obscures in its obeisance to the profit motive and its trivialization of scientific research. We have prostrated ourselves before the Golden Calf, these jaunty ad jingles intimate, and our priests are those who make change to the intonation of either arcane polynomials or the meaningless acronyms of toothpaste and motor-oil additives.

In fact, the single most striking instance of devolution and decay in *Ubik* is Dick's oblique demonstration that, for many of us, a crass materialism has supplanted spiritual resilience as our chief "reality support." Private faith has fallen to a variety of different physical or social hungers. Because it has, entropy has overwhelmed another of our barricades, and we have retreated willy-nilly closer to the brink of chaos.

What is Ubik *really,* then?

It first appears in the narrative when Joe Chip finds himself watching a television commercial and listening to a "hard-eyed housewife" extolling its virtues: "'I came over to Ubik,'" she says, "'after trying weak, out-of-date reality supports.'" The name, as Chip himself realizes, comes from the word *ubiquity,* "omnipresence," by way of the Latin *ubique,* "everywhere." In the epigram to the novel's closing chapter Dick reemphasizes the universality of Ubik while elevating it from the status of a bra or a mouthwash to that of a life-giving, ineffable First Mover:

> *I am Ubik. Before the universe was, I am. I made the worlds. I created the lives and the places they inhabit; I move them here, I put them there. They go as I say, they do as I tell them. I am the word and my name is never spoken, the name which no one knows. I am called Ubik, but that is not my name. I am. I shall always be. (Ubik,* 17)

As Peter Fitting has observed, these words echo the phraseology of the opening of the New Testament's Book of John, thus metaphorically equating Ubik with several of the "attributes of the Christian God."[10] And, after sixteen epigraphs resonating with contemptible Madison Avenue slang and jargon, this sonorous final declaration swivels our heads around and shoves our noses into a truth we've been ignoring.

Namely, in whatever avatar or costume a person chooses to worship or drape it, Ubik is the affirmative principle. To put it another way, Ubik is whatever helps John Doe or Joan Foe make it through the Dark Night of the Soul.

If Ubik seemingly thwarts our each and every attempt to give it a more specific christening, it does so because Ubik is multitudinous as well as singular, private as well as universal. Moreover, as the entire thrust of Dick's novel implies, Ubik operates at full potency only when a person conjures its unique qualities as a "reality support" from inner, or spiritual, resources rather than from external, or material, ones. That Joe Chip succeeds in his Sisyphean ascent of a set of hotel stairs stems directly from the fact that he has long since *internalized* the secret, unnamable Ubik sustaining him. His victory is spiritual as well as physical, and it embodies an awesome hope for us all.

Whose reality is uppermost at the conclusion of *Ubik*?

Dick drops a fascinating clue when he allows Glen Runciter to forage from his pockets several fifty-cent pieces bearing the profile of Joe Chip. My own answer, then, is that Joe Chip's reality is the true one.

The maddening complexity of this interpretation will begin to dawn, however, only when you consider that Joe Chip—if indeed he deserves the title Everyman—subsumes in his person you, me, Glen Runciter, Herbert von Vogelsang, and maybe even the Manichean half-lifer opponents Jory Miller and Ella Runciter who are apparently warring to establish preeminence. At this possibility, I'm afraid, the mind not only reels but boggles.

For Joe Chip, like Ubik, is universal as well as private, multitudinous as well as singular. Quite literally, he is everywhere. And one of his hypostases is keeping house in your own heart and head.

Meanwhile, in ragged, beautiful gyrations confounding our ability to follow, *Ubik* keeps flying. Pursue it.

8. *Ubik:* The Deconstruction of Bourgeois SF*

PETER FITTING

PHILIP K. DICK'S *Ubik* (1969) is, for this reader, one of the most important science-fiction works of the 1960s, for it is both deconstruction and a hint at reconstruction: it lays bare the principal ways that science fiction can be used for ideological ends, in terms of science and of fiction, while tentatively looking towards a future freed from the restraints it has exposed. In this novel Dick has exploded and transcended the science-fiction genre and the "representational novel" of which it is a part.

Two general criteria are most commonly used to screen out the "trash" from those SF works which are deemed worthy of critical attention and inclusion in the university curriculum. The first refers to a work's scientific or philosophic intentions and content, by virtue of which it is described as fictionalized science (vulgarization), or as a pardigm of the scientific method (extrapolation) which may be used to probe our contemporary problems—for instance, science fiction as Utopian Literature. A pedigree of academic worth may also be granted on the basis of formal criteria, involving the discovery of aesthetic or literary qualities: attention to style, imagery, and metaphor, and to the work's striv-

---

*This article appeared, in slightly different form, in *Science-Fiction Studies* 5 (March 1975).

ing towards the status of High Art.[1] These attempts to make the genre respectable through its assimilation into some larger literary tradition effectively strip it of its specific or generic qualities. Thus they also fulfill an important role in the preservation of the literary status quo and, in corollary fashion, of the society it is the university's function to support. But such conformist critical recuperation cannot make sense of much that is best within the genre, and in particular, of the writing of Philip K. Dick.

Dick's writing is not easily included within traditional academic limits, for his novels often seem to be badly and carelessly written, with superficial characterization, confusing plots, and similar deviations from recognized principles of "good writing." This apparent inattention to writing, along with an overabundance of traditional science-fictional motifs and conventions have earned him the neglect of the proponents both of High Art and of the New Wave; while his sprawling, chaotic near-futures and his total disregard for the traditional science-fictional virtues of rationality and futurological plausibility have caused him to be overlooked by the proponents of the more traditional extrapolative science fiction.[2] However, this chapter will attempt to set out, through the example of *Ubik*, how Dick's work presents a model of a more subversive form of writing which undermines rather than reconfirms the repressive system in which it has been produced, and acts as a critique of the ideological presuppositions of the science-fiction genre and of the traditional novel in general.

As with his other fictions, from *Eye in the Sky* (1957) and *The Man in the High Castle* (1962) through *The Three Stigmata of Palmer Eldritch* (1964) and *Maze of Death* (1970), *Ubik* is centered on the "reality problem"—on the efforts of a group of people to grasp an elusive, changing, sometimes hallucinatory, and often hostile reality. The novel divides readily into two parts. The events which lead up to the explosive climax take place primarily on a single plane of reality involving the business rivalry between Hollis Talents' psi agents and Runciter Associates' "inertials" (anti-Psis). Then, following the explosion and death of Runciter, reality begins to lose its consistency and integrity. Although Joe Chip and the other inertials succeed in transporting Runciter to the Blessed Brethren Moratorium where the dead are preserved in "half-life"—a state between "full-life and the grave" (*Ubik*, 2) in which the subject may be revived and communicated with as long as the waning "cephalic activity" is retained—attempts to revive Runciter fail and are superseded by the inertials' own anxious efforts to understand what is happening to them. Faced with a disintegrating, hostile reality, they surmise that there are two opposing forces at work: a "process of deterioration" in which their reality ages and decays, and another force which counteracts the first and involves inexplicable manifestations of the dead Runciter.

Their attempts at comprehension can be seen in the different hypotheses which they develop and which occupy much of the novel: they think that Runciter has prerecorded messages to them before his death; that Runciter is alive trying to contact them in half-life; or that Pat (Joe Chip's wife) is an agent of Hollis and has succeeded in trapping them in a mental illusion. But, as Joe Chip concedes, they can't make it all add up; finally, he "meets" Runciter, who assures him that they—not he—were killed in the explosion and are now linked together in half-life where he has been trying to communicate with them. And the inertials' shared awareness of Des Moines in 1939 is the mental construct of the boy Jory who maintains his own half-life by feeding on the vitality of other half-lifers. Yet this final explanation is first modified when Chip inadvertently summons into this illusion a living person from the future who replenishes his supply of Ubik, the "reality support" which protects him from Jory; the explanation is then destroyed when Runciter, upon leaving the Moratorium, discovers that all his coins and bills bear the likeness of Joe Chip.

From the first mention of half-life—a phenomenon which, according to Runciter, has "made theologians out of them all" (*Ubik*, 2)—to the inertials' quest for the meaning of their existence and their awareness of the forces of life and death, the narrative of *Ubik* continuously plays with a metaphysical dimension. Half-life is not presented as a realistic future possibility— that is to say, the novel does not explain how half-life might be possible, nor does it explore the possible moral, ethical, or scientific problems raised. Thus the reader might begin by envisaging half-life as the fictional transposition of the world of ghosts and spirits into a science-fiction novel, where the explanation is provided by pseudo-scientific assertions rather than by reference to the supernatural. Within this context both the quest for meaning and the never-ending struggle between the forces of life and death have traditionally a metaphysical significance. The quest would usually rouse the reader to expect not only that there is some discernible meaning in reality, but that this meaning lies beyond or behind observable reality (teleology) and that man sometimes receives messages from the beyond about the meaning of reality (divine revelation). Jory, the negative force of illusion and death, is the devil in this Manichean allegory, while the Runciters are the agents of Ubik, the life-preserving force which is clearly analogous to God: by its name (from the Latin *ubique,* the root of *ubiquity,* one of the attributes of the Christian God), by its functions and, most explicitly, by the epigraph to the last chapter which recalls John's "In the beginning was the Word . . .":

> I am Ubik. Before the universe was, I am. I made the suns. I made the worlds. I created the lives and the places they inhabit; I move them here, I put them there. They go as I say, they do as I tell them. I am the word and my name is never spoken, the name which no one knows. I am called Ubik, but that is not my name. I am. I shall always be. (*Ubik,* 17)

Although the reality problem is thus posed in metaphysical terms, such expectations by the reader are ultimately frustrated, and metaphysics is rejected. The characters are unable to discover any final, comprehensive meaning, and Joe Chip realizes, when he meets Jory, that there is nothing *behind* that reality: "Well, he thought, that's one of the two agencies who're at work; Jory is the one who's destroying us—has destroyed us, except for me. Behind Jory there is nothing: he is the end" (*Ubik,* 15). And again, when he meets Ella, he exclaims *"You're the other one,* Jory destroying us, you trying to help us. Behind you there's no one. I've reached the last entities involved" (*Ubik,* 16).

Yet Joe Chip's discovery of the "last entities involved" is not the finding of a final or first cause. Jory and Ubik, although they may be seen as allegorical representations of God and the Devil, are limited, nonetheless, in several crucial ways which weaken this allegory; or rather, which suggests a criticism of such idealistic concepts as "God" or "the Devil." In fact, Jory only "speeds up" the "normal cooling off" and death of things which is the "destiny of the universe" (*Ubik,* 13). Nor does Jory think of himself as evil: his own half-life, he tells Chip, depends on his ability to prey on weaker half-lifers, a dependence which is very similar to Joe Chip's "ecological" argument in defense of Runciter Associates' and the anti-Psis' "neutralizing" of Psis: "[anti-Psis] are life forms preying on the Psis, and the Psis are life forms that prey on the Norms . . . Balance, the full circle, predator and prey. It appears to be an eternal system; and frankly I don't see how it could be improved" (*Ubik,* 3).

In metaphysical terms, the concept of Ubik is also an analogue to Christian "grace," the divine assistance given man to help him through the earthly vale of tears into which he is fallen, towards the afterlife and his heavenly reward. Joe Chip's quest becomes, in large part, a search for Ubik (as Perceval's quest was for the Grail, symbol of Christian grace and redemption), which will protect him from the forces of evil and death (Jory). However, Ubik's significance as a mediating agency or signpost of metaphysical reality is undermined in several critical ways. First, it protects Chip by maintaining an illusory reality for him, while covering up the "real" reality of the Moratorium. In similar fashion the established Christian religions have glossed over the human problems and injustices of reality while affirming that this existence is but the shadow of and preparation for an immaterial, ideal reality. Second, Ubik is desacralized through the ironic use of epigraphs, which I shall discuss in a moment, and within the narrative itself. For as Chip learns in Chapter 16, Ubik is a *human* invention, an image of humankind's own struggle against entropy, rather than an image of divine assistance or guidance in that struggle. And the final reference to Ubik in the narrative is an ironic comment on divine intervention: after the attractive young woman who has materialized from the future to bring Joe Chip a spray can of Ubik disappears, leaving him in the middle of trying to invite her to dinner, he discovers a message on the can: "I THINK HER NAME IS MYRA LANLEY. LOOK ON REVERSE SIDE OF CONTAINER FOR ADDRESS AND PHONE NUMBER" (*Ubik,* 16).

An epigraph in the form of an advertising jingle opens each chapter of *Ubik,* except that the last chapter has the epigraph quoted above, which can, however, be read as a theological "super-ad," confirming the novel's strange juxtaposition of religion with capitalist consumerism. These commercials, which have little or nothing to do with the narrative, sell Ubik as the best beer, the best instant coffee, the best shampoo, etc.

Friends this is clean-up time and we're discounting all our silent, electric Ubiks by this much money. Yes we're throwing away the blue-book. And remember: every Ubik on our lot has been used only as directed. (*Ubik,* 1)

The best way to ask for beer is to sing out for Ubik. Made from select hops, choice water, slow aged for perfect flavor, Ubik is the nation's number one choice in beer. Made only in Cleveland. (*Ubik,* 2)

If money worries have you in the cellar, go visit the lady at Ubik Savings & Loan. She'll take the frets out of your debts. Suppose, for example, you borrow fifty-nine poscreds on an interest-only loan. Let's see, that adds up to—(*Ubik,* 8)

These "commercial messages" provide a restatement of Karl Marx's description of value, for Ubik is a *universal equivalent* (the embodiment of exchange value), which can represent or replace any other commodity: under capitalism everything has its price; while the presentation of Ubik through these ads stresses the obligation of capitalism to produce needs (use-values) in the consumer.

Furthermore, the epigraphs, by their lack of pertinence to the narrative (where Ubik is a "reality-support" which comes in a spray can and is not mentioned until Chapter 10), may also be seen as a further subversion of the metaphysical concept of representation. An epigraph, like a title, is expected to serve as a comment and/or digest of the contents of a chapter, as if meaning were *contained* in the writing and could be summed up in the way that labels tell us what is inside a can at the supermarket. Impertinent or facetious epigraphs (or chapter headings, as in *Maze of Death*) are a deliberate mislabeling which violates the commercial contract at the basis of the traditional novel.

The ironically inappropriate epigraphs to each chapter are thus a prelude to a more complex refutation of teleology and metaphysics in *Ubik* which depends upon recognizing the metaphysical presuppositions of the novel-form itself. The classical bourgeois novel has been described by recent French literary theorists as itself a metaphysical construct: traditionally, the novel has been a representative medium, and the concept of representation implies that the text is a restatement of some pre-existent meaning.[3] This attitude reduces reading to a *looking through* the text to the "real" meaning, whether that meaning is rooted in empirical reality, the author's conscious design, or unconscious auctorial intentions. Such a transcendental bias enhances the meaning (the *signified*) while reducing the *signifier* to a means; it thereby masks and mystifies the text itself, both in its materiality (its texture) and in its production (the act of writing), in much the same way that—as Marx has shown—exchange-value effects a masking and mystification of an object's use-value as well as of the concrete human labor invested in it.[4]

The traditional "representational novel" functions in this way as an ideological support for capitalism: it reinforces a transcendental conception of reality which mystifies the actual reality of the capitalist mode of production and the resultant repression and alienation. And although science fiction stories depict an imaginary reality, they have traditionally been concerned with the representation of a "fictional alternative to the author's empirical environment" which is usually internally consistent and regulated by knowable laws.[5] As in other types of novels, there is a discernible, comprehensible meaning which informs the science-fiction novel. (And this quite apart from any criticism one could make of the "contents" of the traditional science-fiction novel.) But the reader of *Ubik* is refused any such final, definitive interpretation. At the end of the novel, the reader seems at last to have been given a complete explanation of the events according to which Joe Chip and the others are in half-life while Runciter is alive trying to contact them. The reader's usual satisfaction in finishing a novel and looking back over how everything fits together derives from the formal confirmation of his conception of reality and, in the case of *Ubik*, from his relief at having finally resolved the disquieting tension between fictional reality and illusion. But this satisfaction is short-lived, for as Runciter leaves the Moratorium he discovers that the coins and bills in his pocket all bear the likeness of Joe Chip (as, at the beginning of the second part of the novel, Joe Chip and the other inertials' money bore the likeness of Runciter)—an indication that this reality is also an illusion. And the novel concludes as Runciter looks disbelievingly at his money: "This was just the beginning": the beginning of an endless series of illusory realities, but for the careful reader, also the beginning of an end to a number of illusions about both reality and the novel. There is no satisfactory single interpretation of *Ubik*, my own included; and the thoughtful reader's traditional goal—the discovery of that interpretation—is frustrated. However, that frustration was planned; this kind of text is no longer a window opening into transcendental meaning, but a mirror which reflects the reader's perspective, forcing him out of his familiar reading habits while drawing his attention to the role of the novel as a form of manipulation.

Ubik is not only a deconstruction of the "metaphysical ideologies and the metaphysical formal implications of the classical bourgeois novel," but also of what (in *Solaris*) Stanislaw Lem has described as the "anthropomorphic presuppositions of science and of science fiction." Science is expressly demystified, first of all, through the disregard for scientific plausibility and through the single "scientific" description of a technological device in the novel:

A spray can of Ubik is a portable negative ionizer, with a self-contained, high-voltage, low-amp unit powered by a peak-gain helium battery of 25 kv. The negative ions are given a counterclockwise spin by a radically biased acceleration chamber, which creates a centripetal tendency to them so that they cohere rather than dissipate. A negative ion field diminishes the velocity of anti-protophasons normally present in the atmosphere; as soon as their velocity falls they cease to be anti-protophasons and, under the principle of parity, no longer can unite with protophasons radiated from persons frozen in cold-pac; that is, those in half-life. The end result is that the proportion of protophasons not canceled by anti-protophasons increases, which means—for a specific time, anyhow—an increment in the net put-forth field of protophasonic activity . . . which the affected half-lifer experiences as greater vitality plus a lowering of the experience of low cold-pac temperatures. (*Ubik*, 16)

This passage parodies the sort of scientific jargon which is often used, by scientists *and* science fiction writers alike, to conceal ignorance rather then to convey information or knowledge (try reading a textbook description of cancer, for instance, a "disease" which science can "describe" without understanding it).

More importantly, *Ubik* is a critique of the *a priori* modes of perception which inform scientific thinking and which science often claims as objective empirical principles.[6] Dick undertakes this critique of scientific imperialism and tunnel-vision by carrying subjectivity to an extreme, by reminding us—as he has done perhaps most effectively in *Clans of the Alphane Moon* and *Maze of Death*—that the position of the observer is an extremely subjective perspective from which to deduce universal laws; that "reality" is a mental construct which may be undermined at any time.

Dick's writing has often been labeled schizophrenic, but it is time to recognize that this is not necessarily a criticism, that schizophrenia may be, in R.D. Laing's words from *The Politics of Experience,* a "breakthrough" rather than a "breakdown." Philip K. Dick's writing is an example of such a breakthrough, not only in the sense of a deconstruction of the science-fiction novel, but also of a breaking through the psychological and perceptual confines imposed on us by capitalism.

The repression of the individual under capitalism goes beyond the obvious economic and military machinery of imperialism or the internal police control which Dick has frequently denounced in his public letters and speeches. It also functions in a more subtle and dangerous way through the control and direction of our forms of perception and thought, making a radically different reality either unthinkable or horribly monstrous. The well-known film *Forbidden Planet* (1956), for instance, is a classic presentation of the theme of the "monsters of the id," those libidinal energies which (from the notion of "original sin" to the contemporary theories of man's innate aggressiveness), we have been taught to fear and distrust, which society seeks to dominate and control, and which are unleashed from the unconscious whenever the individual's conscious vigilance is relaxed. Unlike this film, which contains an explicit warning against the unbinding of those forces, A. E. van Vogt's *Voyage of the Space Beagle* (1950) reveals a more ambiguous attitude towards that repression. For what is striking about van Vogt's novel (especially in view of his expressed political philosophy) is not so much the voyage, which is both a voyage of self-discovery and an expression of the familiar science-fiction theme of the need for synthesis and integration of different scientific methods and disciplines in order to meet the challenges of a changing world, but the narrative of a series of contacts between humans and hostile space creatures. Like the monsters of *Forbidden Planet*, these creatures are symbols of the raw, unrepressed libidinal energies which threaten the fabric and smooth functioning of capitalism. Yet in his presentation of these monsters, we can detect as well an implicit (or illicit) desire for their force and power which contradicts the novel's explicit message of science containing those threats. During each confrontation in van Vogt's novel, the reader looks for a time through the monster's eyes, feeling and perceiving reality as the monster experiences it. This identification, however brief, provokes our admiration and envy. To an even higher degree, this is the case in the emphatic understanding of what it would be like to be a Loper in Clifford Simak's *City,* (1952), where almost the entire population of Earth emigrates to Jupiter when offered the chance of becoming such a monster.

The science fiction of Philip K. Dick concentrates less on the actual unbinding of these forces (Dick's use of parallel worlds, his exteriorization of internal reality) or on the "real" shape they might take than on attacking the forms of control which I have discussed—the presuppositions of the novel form and of science. Although a metaphysical solution is rejected, although there seems to be no final answer then to the question of what reality is, and although for Dick there can be no single, final reality, there is little pessimism in the endings of Dick's novels when compared to the facile pessimism of the currently fashionable literature of despair. Although *Ubik* does mark the end of some of our illusions, it is hopeful in its refusal to close the conflicts by a pat happy or unhappy ending in much the same way as another important science-fiction novel of the 1960s, Samuel Delany's *The Einstein Intersection* (1967). In Delany's postcataclysmic world, strange mutated beings roam the Earth and speak of a different and unknowable future, but one towards which they move deliberately, with hope and longing. *Ubik,* through the figure of Ella Runciter, also holds out the promise of a different, unknowable future. Ella is leaving half-life for a "new womb" to be "reborn." This rebirth begins with the dissolution of the personality, as can be seen in Ella's description of the intermingling and "growing together" of different personalities in half-life. But this rebirth is not described as reincarnation; it does not involve becoming something specific, something which has been designed or programmed: rather it is an opening towards new forms and new collective possibilities.

9. The Search for Absolutes

EUGENE WARREN

PHILIP K. DICK'S fiction is based upon a vision of reality that gives his novels and stories tremendous force and that has undergone a clear pattern of development through his career. His fiction focuses on an intense, frightening view of our society—its mass population, its artificial environment, its confusion of the real and the fake, its loss of absolute values. In the distorting mirror of Dick's work, our commonplace illusions are paradoxically warped into the shape of truth.

This chapter will deal with the desire of Dick's characters to know an Absolute Reality, with his portrayal of the figures of the Father, the Leader, and God as examples of the absolute, and with the ambiguities caused by the dependence of "reality" on the minds which perceive it. Dick's protagonists generally begin as naive realists, firmly convinced that their perceptions provide them with knowledge about what is actually present in the world around them. But then an encounter with the radical uncertainty of reality throws the protagonists into a world where both external reality and their own identities are drastically questioned. The most basic question raised by such an experience is this: Is there an ultimate, absolute reality, and can we know it? As Dick forces his characters to confront this question in a variety of contexts, he portrays the basic dilemma of our technological society: we can

161

no longer tell the real from the fake, the illusory from the substantial; we no longer have an absolute basis for knowing what is real. In the seventeenth century, Descartes drove a fatal wedge between mental and physical reality; and then Berkeley, Hume, and Kant showed in their various ways that "mind makes nature."[1] Now that these philosophical speculations have become a part of our common experience, we are confronted with the widespread conviction that there is no objective reality—yet we still have a desire for the ultimate and absolute that causes us to seek satisfaction through a variety of drugs, religions, and therapies.

A further aspect of the dilemma of our culture is that we have lost confidence in what one might call *intrinsic* authority— authority that is authoritative by reason of its fundamental nature. Aware of this lack, we seek for all sorts of substitutes, substitutes which usually turn out to be worse than no authority at all.

In our society, the primal, or initial, experience of authority is the child's experience of parental control. In an early story, "The Father-Thing" (1954), Dick explores a young boy's discovery that a "thing"—a funguslike intelligent being—has consumed his father. The boy, Charles Walton, has seen his father talking to the fungus in the garage, and is naturally perturbed when it, rather than his father, comes in to supper. The young boy's confused responses to adult authority are established by the whole atmosphere of his search to find out what has happened to his father, and his efforts, with his young friends, to destroy the "father-thing," as they have come to call it. Charles and his friends are in awe of adults at the same time that they are terrified by the father-thing and are determined to destroy it. The father-thing's words and actions—he vows to teach the boy a lesson—are almost perfect imitations of the lower-middle-class American father. As the father-thing is attempting to feed Charles to the "Charles-thing" (another fungus, which is not yet mature), he tells Charles, "This is for your own good. I know best, Charles." The words are mundane; the chilling situation in which they are spoken is an image of the child's terror at the hands of what he perceives as absolute adult authority, seemingly arbitrary authority acting in response to motives beyond his comprehension.

In Dick's subsequent fiction, political authority figures and God are clearly parallel to the father figure in "The Father-Thing."

Just as Charles and his friends suffer shock and terror when they discover the truth about what has happened to Charles's father, so do the adult characters react when they discover that their own authority figures are not what they seemed to be. In his early novel, *The Man Who Japed* (1956), Dick deals with the important role of the mass media in establishing and maintaining authority in a technological society. Here Dick creates a puritanical society, governed on the principles of Morec (Moral Reclamation)—a religio-political movement founded by a Major Streiter, which resembles Frank Buchman's Moral Rearmament. The main character, Allen Purcell, is the head of an agency which provides propaganda packets to Telemedia, the worldwide institution which controls the media and uses propaganda to establish and maintain the principles of Morec.

The Man Who Japed touches upon the theme of the ambiguity of reality in two ways. First, Purcell, who is a committed member of the Morec society, undergoes fugues, or fuguelike episodes, in which he vandalizes—"japes"—a statue of Major Streiter. What he usually thinks of as his real self is undermined by another self that is capable of acting against his consciously held principles. Purcell's japery is motivated by his resentment of the extreme puritanism and restrictiveness of Morec society. Yet his rejection of Morec is not total: after he is kidnapped to a resort planet and has the opportunity to live a hedonistic life, he chooses to return to Earth where he can live a more purposeful existence.

Second, *The Man Who Japed* deals with the manner in which the mass media deliberately structure reality, with what Daniel J. Boorstin calls the "pseudo-event."[5] Purcell's pseudo-event is a media campaign aimed at breaking down the restrictiveness of Morec. In it, he portrays Major Streiter as having actually practiced cannibalism (termed "active assimilation") as a technique for social reconstruction. Particularly revealing is the response of Mrs. Georgina Birmingham to the media campaign. Mrs. Birmingham is a "block warden": her role is to coordinate the use of technical devices and people in spying on those who live in her apartment block. She is a bigoted and tyrannical person, who takes the prude's delight in uncovering wrongdoing, especially if it is of a sexual nature. When Mrs. Birmingham turns on the television to watch the program in which active assimilation will be discussed, she is "delighted. She had been hearing about active assimilation for some time, [through teasers in the media] and this was her opportunity to learn once and for all what it was" (*MWJ*, 22). Here is the perfect picture of the informed and knowledgeable citizen of a mass society—an opinion leader—setting herself up self-righteously to be "informed" by a completely concocted event. The panelists are all employees of Telemedia, or friends of Purcell; all of the media are being coordinated in a campaign to undermine Morec by portraying Major Streiter as a cannibal.

The lie becomes reality in the mind of society by being broadcast; and then, being recognized as a reality, it has real effects. In this case, the propaganda techniques of the mass media are being used for a "good" purpose: the freeing of society from crippling restrictions. But a question remains: can Mrs. Birmingham be freed by having her sense of reality manipulated in one direction rather than another? Can the subjects of mass media really be free while remaining subjects of that media? I do not fault Dick for not answering this question (which he did not directly or consciously raise) in *The Man Who Japed*; but I do think that his failure to raise it shows that, at this point in his career, he had not pushed the stripping away of illusions as far as he does in later works, such as the novella "Faith of Our Fathers," which I will discuss later.

Dick also deals with the creation of false realities through mass media in "If There Were No Benny Cemoli" (1963). The title of this story implies that the political leader is an analogue of God. Just as "if there were no God, it would be necessary to invent him," so it is necessary for the media to invent Benny Cemoli. His role is to take the blame for an atomic holocaust that has devastated Earth. Colonists from Mars and Venus are rebuilding Earth when a mission from the Centaurus Urban Renewal Bureau (CURB) arrives. CURB includes a rather zealous police force which wants to punish those who were responsible for the war. The guilty parties invent Benny Cemoli, a rabble-rouser who supposedly ascended to power and set off the holocaust. They do this by programming the "cephalon" (brain) of the *New York Times*, which is a "homeopape"—a self-generating homeostatic newspaper. When the homeopape begins printing stories about Cemoli's prewar exploits, the CURB officials are beguiled by them and begin a manhunt for Cemoli, hoping to find him alive.

Meanwhile, the real people behind the war are safe from police investigation. This story combines the illusory leader—in this case, literally, since there *is* no Benny Cemoli—with the theme of the power of the media to create ersatz realities. Just as the viewers of Allen Purcell's media jape, in *The Man Who Japed*, are convinced that Major Streiter was a cannibal, so are the CURB officials convinced of the reality of Cemoli's existence. And, since they actually believe in his reality, he has effects in the real world; though there is no Benny Cemoli in a literal sense, there is the Benny Cemoli in whom the CURB officials believe and to whom they assign the guilt for the war. Benny Cemoli is the epitome of the pseudo-event, since he is indisputably the illusory cause of real events.

To carry through the unstated analogy between Benny Cemoli and God: if there is no God but some people *think* there is, and if they act on that belief, then their reality will be much as it would be if there actually *were* a God existing independently of their belief. Certainly, the CURB officials have good, if circumstantial, evidence to support their belief in Benny Cemoli's existence. There is not only the documentation provided by the homeopape, but also a secret meeting room with a picture of Cemoli, and a fabricated textbook from his era. The CURB officials are only being rational by acting on the evidence which they have.

The importance of the political leader is also a theme of Dick's novel *Now Wait for Last Year* (1966). Gino Molinari is the UN Secretary General leading Terra in an interstellar war. Terra's allies, the Lilistar empire, are human but treacherous; their enemies, huge insects called Reegs, are repulsive but good. Earth is the weaker partner in the alliance with Lilistar; therefore, to keep Terra from being entirely taken over, Molinari resorts to various strategems, including ill-health and even death. In contrast to Benny Cemoli, who is an illusionary "sufferer" created to deflect punishment from guilty leaders, Molinari is the leader who suffers selflessly for his people.

However selfless Molinari might be, though, he is also very human: the chief of his medical staff gives this description of Molinari:

"one overweight, middle-aged Italian, who lives in Cheyenne Wyoming, with his enormous family and his eighteen-year-old mistress, who has stomach pains and enjoys eating a late night snack of batter-fried giant prawns with mustard and horse-radish." (*NWLY*, 5)

Thus described, Molinari sounds like a stereotype, a caricature of Benito Mussolini, down to the resemblance of names. And yet, Molinari's goals and actions are in large part altruistic and self-sacrificing. As such, in his self-sacrifice, Molinari is really an anti-Leader, the opposite of a dictator. Even his nickname, the Mole, indicates this, suggesting blindness and bumbling, as well as an ironic parody of Asimov's the Mule in the *Foundation* series.

The protagonist of *Last Year*, Eric Sweetscent, sees Molinari as having "a swiftness of reflex," "an intensity" that is not "normal or human," and as having a response to reality faster and surer than that of the ordinary person; to Sweetscent, Molinari's intensity pivots on an awareness of "the imminence of harm" (*NWLY*, 3). Thus the Mole's survival traits embody Paul Williams' maxim about Dick's work: "Paranoia is true perception."[3] For example, when under pressure from the Lilistar leader in a conference, Molinari's defensive response is simply to die. He is not cleverer than the Lilistarmen, nor more powerful, but his death defeats their efforts to gain control of Terra.

It is established early in the novel that Molinari has a death-wish. The Mole wants to die, as the ultimate release from his suffering. Sweetscent, reviewing Molinari's medical records, realizes that Molinari wants to be ill; at some level of his being, the Mole's symptoms are chosen by him. Towards the end of the book, Sweetscent encounters himself in the future, and his future self tells him that Molinari, when he dies beyond recovery, will be replaced by another Molinari from a parallel world. Then the future Sweetscent tells his past self, "Molinari's *whole psychology, his whole point of orientation is to dabble with death and yet somehow surmount it*" (*NWLY*, 12). This daring of death, and surmounting it "somehow," suggest Jesus' confrontation with and victory over death. Even the ability to die and return to life is a parallel, in being the weapon which defeats the enemies both of Christ and of the Mole.

Lest this parallel seem too far-fetched, or the chimera of a critic's obsession with Christ-figures, there is a passage where an explicit equation is made between the Mole and Christ. In a discussion between Teagarden and Sweetscent, Teagarden first points out that the Mole is an anomalous dictator in that he takes the blame for his own mistakes, and this taking his own guilt causes him to suffer; further, the Mole is acting out of love: "He loves Terra. He loves the people, all of them, washed and unwashed; he loves his pack of sponging relatives" (*NWLY,* 5). Teagarden stresses Molinari's actual acceptance of the blame for his mistakes and concludes by explicitly comparing Molinari to Christ, implying a somewhat unorthodox reading of the Passion of Christ. Christian theology has not usually seen the Crucifixion as the act by which God assumed the burden for His own mistakes, even though Christ's sacrifice has always been seen as voluntary and loving. Certainly, the Mole goes beyond the usual human response in so freely taking the responsibility for what he has done, and in suffering for others.

One must remember, however, that this parallel between the Mole and Christ is only Teagarden's perception; another character, Dorf, immediately challenges it, reminding Teagarden that Molinari's mistress, Mary, would tell him that Molinari is "a pig in bed and at the table, a lewd middle-aged man with rape in his eye, who ought to be in jail" (*NWLY,* 5). To which Teagarden's response is that Mary loves and accepts the Mole. In a later scene, Mary herself tells Sweetscent that Molinari has his illnesses because "he wants to be a baby again so he won't have grownup responsibilities" (*NWLY,* 7). Mary's understanding of Molinari seems directly contradictory to Teagarden's. A resolution of this contradiction may be found in a passage near the end of the book. Molinari has just died irrecoverably. Another Molinari is standing by, in coldpac, waiting for this situation. In reflecting on the motivations of these various Molinaris, Sweetscent thinks, "He was not trying to be immortal, a god" (*NWLY,* 13). Instead, Sweetscent decides that Molinari was simply trying to carry out his responsibilities as Secretary General and as a human being. Thus Molinari is Christlike both in his suffering for all people, washed and unwashed, and his willing acceptance of guilt and suffering; but he is unlike Christ in that he is not divine and in that the guilt Molinari bears is his and only his. A further, more subtle relation between Christ and the Mole is suggested by Sweetscent's reflection that the Mole was not seeking to be a god; in his epistle to the Philippians, Saint Paul wrote that Jesus "did not count equality with God a thing to be grasped, but emptied himself, taking the form of a servant. . . . he humbled himself and became obedient unto death. . . ."[4] Just as the man Jesus did not grasp after the prerogatives of divinity, but accepted human suffering, so Molinari, in his role as UN Secretary-General, does not seek glorification—whether the semiliteral deification of emperors, or the practical deification of modern tyrants in the secular state. That is, Molinari is also like Christ in renouncing any personal glory or adulation. I cannot argue that Dick had Paul's letter to the Philippians in mind, although he may have been aware of that particular passage's significance in recent theology through his friendship with the late Bishop James A. Pike. In any case, the relation between Christ and Molinari on that point seems well established.

In *The Simulacra* (1964), Dick deals with a complex political illusion centering on the authority figure—figures, rather, since the USEA (the United States of Europe and America) is governed by a President, who is elected every four years, and a First Lady, who seems to be deathless. The First Lady, Nicole Thibodeaux, has been in office for seventy-three years and seems to wield the real power. She actually is an actress, a series of actresses having taken the role since the death of the original Nicole. And the President is actually a simulacrum, replaced every so often in a phony election. Thus there are several layers of illusion around the authority: first, the President is ruler only by a legal fiction, his wife really ruling; second, the wife is an actress and the President a simulacrum. Third, Nicole really does not govern, but takes orders from a shadowy council of nine which very few people know about.

The attitude of an ordinary citizen to Nicole illuminates the relation between illusion and reality: Ian Duncan deliberately chooses to believe in an illusion, rather than accept a discomforting reality. He and a friend are planning to perform their musical act before Nicole in the White House, and the friend points out that Nicole, who appears youthful and beautiful on television, must be at least ninety years old since she has been the First Lady for seventy-three years. Duncan protests with horror that he prefers the illusion to the reality: "What's real and unreal? To me she's more real than anything else. Even than myself, my own life" (*Sim.*, 9). Duncan's choice is unequivocal: he hugs the illusion to himself. The reason for his choice is made explicit in a scene where Duncan imagines Nicole going over the entertainment schedules with his and his friend's names; the thought that Nicole knows of his, Ian Duncan's, existence elates Duncan, because he feels that only so can he really be sure of his existence:

> *She knows of our existence.* In that case, we really do exist. Like a child that has to have its mother watching what it does, we're brought into being, validated consensually, by Nicole's gaze. (*Sim.*, 9)

In the absence of Bishop Berkeley's God, Who brings the world into existence simply through knowing it, and Who therefore would validate even the existence of insignificant Ian Duncan by knowing *him*, Duncan must turn to a political authority for validation of his existence. And since the USEA is supposedly a democracy, the reality Duncan attains in being known by Nicole is appropriately a consensual reality, a public knowledge which will presumably be established finally through the media, since the White House concerts are broadcast.

Duncan's dilemma is reflected in the study *Propaganda* by the French thinker Jacques Ellul. In discussing the psychological effects of propaganda, Ellul points out that the alienation caused by propaganda can cause the propagandee—the victim of propaganda—to indentify with the leader; the propagandee thus loses control of his own life and is now controlled by external forces. According to Ellul, the propagandee "lives vicariously through the hero. He feels, thinks, and acts through the hero . . . he accepts being a child. . . ."[5] Ellul also emphasizes the false sense of intimacy created by television as a medium of propaganda.[6] These (and other) characteristics of propaganda described by Ellul are found in Dick's fiction, and figure very much in Ian Duncan's life as described in *The Simulacra*. Duncan's reliance on Nicole for his sense of his own reality and his dogged preference for the comforting illusion over the disheartening reality are traits of the willing, complicit victim of propaganda.

When their musical performance fails, Nicole tells Duncan and his friend the truth—that she is an actress, the fourth to play Nicole's role, and that a secret council of nine members actually governs the USEA. Ian Duncan is stunned. The inside knowledge which he has just received from Nicole means that he will either be put to death or will have his memories eradicated, to prevent him from revealing what he knows. In frustration Duncan perceives that he and Al Miller have come close to penetrating "the actuality behind the illusion, the secrets kept from us all our lives" (*Sim*, 12). He is finally able to admit to himself that he, like most other citizens of his society, does not know what is really going on, does not know what forces really control his life. All the comforting illusions of propaganda are washed away in the presence of his own impending death. In the end, though, he does not die but loses his memories.

After the eradication of his memories, Duncan is returned to his apartment, where he watches Nicole on television: her "warm, familiar" presence and her direct speech to the audience exemplify Ellul's remark about the false sense of intimacy created by television. Even more, the power of modern techniques of control is shown: with his memories of the incident in the White House erased, Duncan, who once was on the verge of knowing the truth behind appearances, accepts the false appearance of Nicole on television as being what it purports to be.

In contrast, the characters in *A Maze of Death* (1971) successfully penetrate to the reality behind their illusory experience. All but the last two chapters of *A Maze of Death* are set in an experimental colony on a planet called Delmak-O. As the colonists arrive, they discover that they do not know the purpose of their colony, and the taped instructions are (it seems) accidentally erased. Then mysterious murders begin to occur. The characters discover at the end of the book that they are actually the crew of a stranded spaceship, the *Persus 9*. Through their computer, they experience, in "polyencephalic fusion," a variety of constructed realities, both to alleviate boredom and to drain away interpersonal hostilities. The realities they experience are technological realizations of the insight in another story, "The Electric Ant," that objective reality is a synthesis of many subjective realities. The concept that reality is an artifact is stressed throughout *A Maze of Death*.

At one point, Seth Morley, the protagonist, remarks that his fellow colonists exhibit "A kind of idiocy. Each of you seems to be living in his own private world" (*MD*, 7). Dick here is certainly playing on the Greek root for *idiocy*—*idios*, meaning "private." Morley's point, truer than he realizes, is that the colonists are caught in a fatal conflict between their private and their public realities. The colonists are really living in a world private to them as a group, experiencing an arbitrarily devised world; and each character's private personality seems to have a strong effect on the nature of that world and the events that occur there. Early in the book, Glen Belsnor, who is an engineer, says, "We live in a world created and manufactured from the results of the work of millions of men . . ." (*MD*, 7). Although at this point, Belsnor does not realize it, his words are literally true of Delmak-O, the world where he and the others are "living." Delmak-O is constructed from all the technological and cultural capabilities of the human race, as found on the stranded ship, *Persus 9*.

Further, the "objective" substructure of this world is opaque to the human mind—at least the ordinary human personality as it tries to apprehend the significance of its experience; what is objectively *real* about Delmak-O can only be rendered in terms of numbers that have no meaningful relationship to the actual, human experience of that world. When Seth Morley is fleeing in a squib—an aircraft—the squib's information computer, in answer to Morley's asking where he came from, replies in numbers. Morley, in turn, says that the "ident notation" is meaningless to him, to which the computer replies that there are no words to describe—name and locate—his point of origin. In other words, the computer knows where Morley began his flight, but it cannot communicate that information in terms meaningful to Morley. The crew, having come out of the polyencephalic fusion which creates their experience of Delmak-O, enters another such state just as the book is ending. Morley's wife, Mary, who has been looking for him, is left behind. When she returns to the control cabin of the ship, Mary sees her fellow crew members lying on their couches with the contacts in place, hooking their minds together so that they experience the same common reality. (It must be emphasized that their experience under polyencephalic fusion is entirely real to them, so that they suffer all the conditions of actual life. When they die there, they really experience death, coming back to life aboard the *Persus 9*.) As Mary observes them, her only clue to what they are experiencing is the output tape of the ship's computer, which is meaningless to her. The only objective, externally observable correlative to the crew's experience under polyencephalic fusion is a punched tape.

The situation of the colonists—their realization that their world is an artifact and that they are in a crippled ship circling a dead star—is an image of the situation of modern man, whose world of experience is real but deceptive, and whose rational knowledge (the punched tape) cannot be directly experienced as part of the world. What we need is a reference point, an objective but knowable and experienceable reference point outside our immediate experience in terms of which we could then explain the meaning of our experience. In earlier times such a reference point was provided by divine revelation or cultural tradition. In more recent times, it has been provided by the belief that science can provide us with objective knowledge of existence. However, science has even more recently become increasingly ambiguous and remote from ordinary experience with the overthrow of Newtonian physics. Some people, including characters in Dick's fiction, have attempted to find a meaningful level of experience through drugs. In *A Maze of Death*, the apparent impossibility of a transcendent reference point is powerfully embodied in the character of the Tench.

The Tench is a large cube of sentient gelatin, which the colonists on Delmak-O consult as an oracle. In Chapter 14, when they ask the Tench, "What is Persus 9?" (the ship's name, tattooed on each colonist), the Tench explodes and the world they have known in Delmak-O disintegrates. Fortunately for them, the *Persus 9* does not disintegrate. It is at this point that the crew "returns" to their ship. The Tench turns out to be the ship's computer which they have been using to generate polyencephalic fusion. The point is obvious: the question of the meaning of existence cannot be answered from a viewpoint entirely *within* existence; further, the question is a shattering one which, while it may be unanswerable, does reveal the shaky and contingent quality of existence, just as the Tench's inability to answer caused it to explode and dissolve Delmak-O. Ultimate questions may be devastating in their impact.

Nicole Thibodeaux is a "transcendent reference point" for Ian Duncan, since he finds the validation of his existence in the very act of being known to her. In this way, a political leader may serve the same function as God or divine revelation, in supplying an absolute locus for meaning. However, this political locus is only falsely regarded as being transcendent, and its effect may be either benevolent or malevolent, depending on the nature or whim of the leader. Gino Molinari is benevolent, both in suffering selflessly and also in that he does not claim an absolute status. In contrast the effect of Morec as a reference point, in *The Man Who Japed,* is almost completely malevolent; Nicole, however, seems to fall between the two poles in being as much a tool of the ruling council of nine as she is a free agent.

In *A Maze of Death,* the crew of the *Persus 9* creates a religion for the world of Delmak-O; while they are in polyencephalic fusion, this religion functions as a true source of transcendence, as an actual part of their experience. Based on an imaginary book, *How I Rose from the Dead in My Spare Time and So Can You,* this arbitrarily constructed religion would also appear to be a false source of transcendence, since it is real only in the context of the experience of polyencephalic fusion, and the crew does not expect it to remain real when their collective consciousness defuses and their awareness returns to the limited perspective of life on the *Persus 9.*

The apparent subjectivity of the religion is altered by the fate of Seth Morley at the end of the book. Morley is like many other Dickian protagonists—he is a scientist, not very happily married, conventional in his outlook and responses, but with a strong reserve of compassion. Like most of the other characters in the novel, Morley looks to God to help him with his troubles on Delmak-O. After coming out of the polyencephalic fusion, Morley has a hard time readjusting to the reality of the *Persus 9.* He seems to be "still entranced" (*MD,* 15), he cannot correlate the separate world lines of Delmak-O and the ship; and, most of all, he finds it difficult to believe that the religion, the experience of polyencephalic fusion, is not real. He is strongly affected by the realization that the God that he had direct contact with on Delmak-O was made up:

> "I wish to God," Seth Morley said, "that there was really an Intercessor." He still had trouble believing that they had made up Specktowsky's theology. "At Tekel Upharsin," he said, "When the Walker-on-Earth came to me it was so real; even now it seems real. I can't shake it off." (*MD*, 15)

Morley then goes off by himself. The Intercessor appears to him, asks him where he would really like to go (Morley would like to be a cactus on a desert planet) and apparently takes him there.

Up to this point the reader is prepared to accept what happens to Morley as a remnant of the Delmak-O experience, a sort of flashback in which he continues to experience elements of the polyencephalic fusion as real. But Morley is aware that the Intercessor could not be aboard the *Persus 9*; he tells the Intercessor, "But we invented you!" (*MD*, 16). The Intercessor ignores this, however. Further evidence that Morley's experience is somehow real is that his wife, Mary, cannot find him afterwards. Presumably, if his encounter with the Intercessor were an hallucination, she would have found his body, just as she sees the crew's bodies while they are in fusion and she is not.

The plot and images of *Galactic Pot-Healer* (1970) are more overtly mythopoeic and archetypal than is usual in Dick's fiction. For some readers, this may be a weakness, since it is a departure from the more recognizable science-fictional mode in which he usually works. However, *Pot-Healer* throws light on a number of Dick's major themes, perhaps just because of its archetypal nature. It will be considered here in relation to the theme of the uncertain nature of reality and the human search for an absolute reference point on which to base life.

The title seems to be a deliberate allusion to the biblical metaphor of God as a potter and the creation as His pottery; this metaphor is found twice in the prophecies of Isaiah and also in Paul's letter to the Romans.[7] In these contexts, it emphasizes divine sovereignty. More to the point of *Pot-Healer* is the reference in Isaiah to potsherds, fragments of pots. Joe Fernwright, the protagonist, is a pot-healer, a mender of pots; the ultimate significance of this is that creation itself, including humanity, is shattered, in pieces, and needs to be healed, to be welded into a whole again. There are several other biblical allusions which will be discussed later, in connection with the Glimmung, the quasi-deity of *Pot-Healer.*

A further religious analogue to the imagery in *Pot-Healer* may be found in the Kabbalah, the Jewish mystical and theosophical tradition, and especially in the version of the Kabbalah as elaborated by Isaac Luria and his followers.[8] Luria lived in sixteenth-century Egypt and Palestine; the aspects of his complex mystical system which relate to *Pot-Healer* may be summarized as follows: When God created the cosmos, He created a series of vessels to contain the divine light which emanated from His being. However, the light was too strong for the vessels, so they shattered, and the shards fell into the *sitra ahra*—the "other side," a demonic realm of darkness that is the inversion of the divine realm. These sparks of divine light give substance to the forces of the *sitra ahra*. In the Lurianic Kabbalah, humanity plays a part in the restoration of these sparks to their proper sphere, and therefore a part in the redemption of the cosmos, as it gradually is transformed into what God originally had intended it to be.

The plot of this Kabbalistic myth parallels in its essentials the plot of *Pot-Healer.* Joe Fernwright, a pot-healer, is summoned by very unusual means to take part in the raising of a cathedral from the depths of the sea on another planet, Plowman's Planet. All sorts of intelligent species have been gathered for this purpose by the Glimmung, a suprahuman entity that has some divine characteristics. Once on Plowman's Planet, Joe Fernwright discovers that there is also a *black* cathedral and a *Black* Glimmung, entities opposing the Glimmung who desires to raise the cathedral. There is also significance in the Glimmung's name for the place where the sunken cathedral is: he calls it "the aquatic sub-world," a phrase suggesting the *sitra ahra* of the Kabbalah, the tomb world of the Tibetan Book of the Dead, and the Jungian collective unconscious. Joe Fernwright and the other sentient organisms are to take part in a symbolic restoration and healing of a fallen and disordered creation, as they raise it from a sub-world of chaos.

Before discussing the character of the Glimmung, I will consider the significance of pot-healing in some detail. When Joe is summoned from Terra to Plowman's Planet by the Glimmung, they have a conversation in the Cleveland spaceport (the Glimmung being present there in human form). Joe has a potsherd from the sunken cathedral which the Glimmung has given him; it is referred to in this scene as "the small divine fragment" (*GPH*, 4). The adjective *divine* may be taken casually as simply stating Joe's aesthetic response to the shard; or it may be taken more seriously and literally as a statement of the intrinsic nature of the shard itself. The latter reading would seem the most true to the development of the book. The fragment of pottery is divine because it is a shard of the original creation which has now fallen into disarray but which still bears the possibility of becoming whole again. A few pages later, aboard the ship en route to Plowman's Planet, Joe tells a fellow passenger, Mali Yojez, that:

> "A healed ceramic piece is in the exact condition as before it broke. Everything fuses; everything flows. Of course, I have to have all the pieces; I can't do it with a fraction of the pot not present." (*GPH*, 6)

Joe makes the point explicitly: the healed pot is not just mended or patched back together, but is truly restored to its full original wholeness. The Glimmung makes the parallel between healer and creator explicit when he tells Joe that the "ceramic surfaces of the cathedral . . . are the clay and you are the potter" (*GPH*, 15). This transferral of the biblical metaphor to Joe Fernwright suggests a resolution to the human dilemma: that it is the common, ordinary human being—who nevertheless has a real talent—that must restore our existence to wholeness. And yet Joe cannot do this by himself; he needs not only the aid of the Glimmung but of the many other species gathered to participate in the raising of the cathedral.

In the conversation at the Cleveland spaceport, Glimmung tells Joe that the raising of the cathedral will mean the raising of all the latent or potential aspects of Joe's personality; that the successful raising of the cathedral will also mean the fulfillment of a wholeness of being not just for Joe Fernwright, but for all of the entities involved. The Glimmung, in effect, tells Joe that, as he is presently constituted, he has no real significance, but that he can acquire a genuine significance by taking part in the Glimmung's project (*GPH*, 5). This fulfillment of potential suggests not only the restoration of the sparks in the Kabbalah, but also the integration of the personality which is the goal of Jungian therapy. Dick is not providing an allegory of either Kabbalistic or Jungian significance; instead, these doctrines form part of his image for the restoration of human existence to wholeness from fragmentation, to reality from mere appearance.

The Glimmung (or Glimmung, his species name being also his personal name, just as *Adam* means both Adam as individual and as mankind) manifests himself in a variety of ways. His first appearance to Joe Fernwright suggests the cherubim of Ezekiel's vision, the wheel within a wheel: Joe sees "a great hoop of water spinning on a horizontal axis, and, within it, on a vertical axis, a transversal hoop of fire" (*GPH*, 4). The elemental significance of fire and water is obvious; and also the figure which Joe sees is a mandala, an archetypal image of wholeness; thus this apparition of Glimmung suggests the theophany of Ezekiel, and the wholeness resulting from the union of opposite elements (fire and water) is suggested by the circular imagery. Dick, however, adds a couple of touches of his own: there is a paisley shawl "over and behind" the two hoops, and at the center of the hoops is the face of an ordinary, pretty adolescent girl (*GPH*, 4). Joe quickly grasps the symbolic meaning of the hoops but is baffled by the shawl and the girl. I will only suggest that the girl, whatever else she may signify, is an *anima,* in Jung's sense of the feminine element that is part of a male's psyche.[9] Joe himself consciously regards Mali Yojez as an *anima* figure. Perhaps the Glimmung's youthful face is an apparition of Joe's *anima* at an even deeper level than Mali, an anticipation of the integration of the Glimmung's *anima* which occurs at the end of the book.

In his conversation with Glimmung at this first encounter, Joe asks him what he *really* looks like; Glimmung responds by asking Joe the same question, which Joe ducks by referring to Kant's distinction between *noumena* and *phenomena.* But Glimmung is not interested in Joe's philosophizing and becomes enraged when Joe presses him for an advance payment, manifesting a fierce face and causing the basement where they are to fall apart. Glimmung thus shows a temper, a capacity for violent anger not unlike God as portrayed in the Bible. The scene also recalls the disintegration of Delmak-O when the Tench is asked the unanswerable; Glimmung evidently transcends, at least partially, normal reality.

When Joe is at the Cleveland spaceport, Glimmung appears to him in human form. This appearance is not to be understood as an incarnation in the Christian sense of a total union of the divine and human, but more as an avatar in the Hindu sense of the divine temporarily appearing in human shape for a limited purpose. Elsewhere in the book, Glimmung appears as a giant albatross, as well as repeating his appearance as hoops of fire and water. Mali Yojez comments that "Glimmung isn't above lowly things" (*GPH*, 8). In this statement there is a hint that Glimmung simultaneously displays a divine humility and human imperfection, in that he is willing to use whatever means, however lowly, to achieve his goal.

Only once in the book does Glimmung seem to appear in his real form. When all of his crew of sentient organisms has gathered in a hotel on Plowman's Planet, Glimmung comes to address them. Joe regards this manifestation as Glimmung "as he actually was." It is an impressive appearance:

> Like the sound of ten thousand junked, rusty automobiles being stirred by one giant wooden spoon, Glimmung heaved himself up and onto the raised stage at the far end of the conference room. (*GPH*, 8)

When the real Glimmung shows up, the reality is too much for human senses to comprehend; the appearances of Glimmung as less than he is are more comprehensible to Joe and the others; are they, therefore, truer? If one cannot grasp a true manifestation of deity, but can grasp something of a mere appearance, one is left with the dilemma of whether to prefer the incomprehensible reality or the comprehensible appearance. As it relates to the divine, the tension between appearance and reality which runs throughout Dick's work, places the human being in a terrible predicament: if the divine is so much different from us, if the deity is so incomprehensible, what common ground can there be between man and God? This perplexity is a major part of the problem of Job, the good and pious man who suffers disaster. Job insists that there is no common ground between him and God (e.g., Job 9:32–33); and when God finally answers Job, He simply asserts the distance separating Man and God, in terms similar to those Glimmung uses to put Joe Fernwright in his place. God challenges

Job, "Where wast thou when I laid the foundations of the earth? Declare, if thou hast understanding. Who hath laid the measures thereof, if thou knowest?"[10]

And Glimmung similarly challenges Joe (note the similarity in names) when he shows impatience: "Are you timing the universe," Glimmung asked, "to see if it is late? Are you giving breadth and measure to the stars?" (*GPH*, 16). Glimmung here reminds Joe that he does not control the conditions of his life, and that therefore his impatience and self-importance are somewhat ludicrous. Joe Fernwright is certainly not an allegorical represent-ative for Job; his character and fate are much different. How-ever, Glimmung's remark to Joe is similar in tone to Jehovah's speech to Job, and helps both to characterize Glimmung as a quasi-deity and to establish the theme of human limitations.

Are we to take Glimmung as God? Or a god? The answer to the first question is apparently no. To the second question, Dick pro-vides a subtle, even ambiguous, answer. The characters of the book express several opinions about the Glimmung's nature. On the ship bound to Plowman's Planet, there is a discussion of this point. A timid man says that Glimmung is not a deity because he (the timid man) does not believe in deities. The red-faced man who asserted that Glimmung is a deity replies by pointing out that, in comparison to themselves, Glimmung has the powers of a god: he can manifest himself simultaneously at many different points, can perform "miraculous" actions, and has manipulated the lives of those he has called to the raising of the cathedral. On the other hand, Glimmung has definite limitations of power and knowledge, and seems to be in real danger from his opposite, the Black Glimmung. Furthermore, Glimmung speaks of himself as a "living entity," subject to rhythms of life, fluctuations of energy and power, with a certain dependence on his environment. He tells his followers, "I am larger; I am older; I can do many things that none of you, even collectively, can. But there are times when the sun is low in the sky, toward evening, before true night" (*GPH*, 9). And it is at those times that Glimmung suffers a di-minution of energy and even a sense of loneliness.

A further clue to Glimmung's nature is that he is compared to Faust throughout the book; once by Joe, who says, "God, in Genesis, was very Faustian" (*GPH*, 9). The particular point of comparison is the passage in Goethe's *Faust* in which Faust determines to drain a swamp in order to make the land healthful and useful. The relation both to Genesis and Glimmung is clear: God in Genesis made chaos into a cosmos of health and fertility; the Glimmung in raising the cathedral hopes to achieve restoration and healing on a large scale. The specific Faustian seems to be the element of recklessness or risk involved, an element which is not found in those conventional views of God which stress His power. Glimmung himself says that he is trying to discover the limits of his strength by pushing his strength to its limits. But to do this is to risk failure, is in fact to make failure inevitable if the strength being tested is limited, as Glimmung's is. As Mali says, "Faust always fails and Glimmung is an incarnation of Faust" (*GPH*, 14).

However, there is more to Glimmung than the parallel with Faust; he is also compared with Christ, and specifically with Christ as suffering. Glimmung becomes locked in a struggle with his counterpart, the Black Glimmung. (Each Glimmung has a personal black double, and he must eventually kill it or it will kill him.) This struggle superficially resembles that between Christ and Satan, but, in making the antagonists equal in power, it is more dualistic, more like Zoroastrianism than orthodox Christianity. The parallelism with Christ is made explicit in the scene where the Glimmung is injured and nearly defeated. The struggle takes place in the ocean—the aquatic sub-world. In other words, Glimmung fights his opponent in his opponent's realm, a realm of chaos and death. As Joe Fernwright observes the wounded Glimmung floating on the surface, he thinks thoughts that would have been appropriate for Christ's disciples at the Crucifixion (it is significant that Glimmung has called his followers from a variety of life situations, as did Christ). Joe thinks, "Why does it have to end this way?" He perceives the defeat of Glimmung as an ultimate defeat, just as Jesus' disciples saw Jesus' death on the cross as a final defeat. Then Joe feels "as if death were assailing him, too. As if he and Glimmung—" Dick breaks off Joe's perception of his own identity with the dying Glimmung. In doing so he is certainly suggesting strongly that Joe somehow shares in the Glimmung's sufferings and death, just as the early Christians came to understand that they shared in Christ's suffering and death. Strengthening this parallel, Joe then perceives the Glimmung in explicitly Christological terms: "like Christ on the cross it bled eternally, as if its blood supply were infinite" (*GPH*, 15). Water and blood swamp into Joe's boat, recalling the water and blood which flow from the crucified Jesus' side in the gospel of John.

A difference between the Passion of Glimmung and the Passion of Christ occurs, however, when the Glimmung tells his sorrowful followers that he has need of them, whereas Christ undergoes his Passion abandoned not only by his followers but also by God.

The wounded Glimmung incorporates his followers into his body, and, as a single polyencephalic entity, they descend into the aquatic sub-world and successfully raise the cathedral. The descent of Christ into Hell, as well as his followers becoming his body, are clearly alluded to here. Actually, the first attempt fails: two further conditions have to be fulfilled before the cathedral can be raised. First, the Glimmung must allow the passage of time, over which he has no control; second, the Glimmung must manifest a hitherto concealed female aspect of his identity—an aspect that is equally as important as the male aspect. Then, the cathedral becomes her (Glimmung's) infant. Glimmung has his own anima which must be integrated before he can become a completed being: the deity (if we regard Glimmung as such) also has an inner drama of character, an inner healing, which must occur.

If Glimmung is to be considered a deity, it is not because of his suprahuman powers, but because of his determination to bring healing and restoration to the world. A parallel is made between worry and *agape,* or divine love. Just as Christ was intensely concerned, so does Glimmung worry, and risk failure and death in order to benefit others. I am not arguing that *Pot-Healer* is a Christian novel in any strict sense. But as Dick's imagination struggles with the basic perplexities of human life, he draws upon many systems of belief and symbolism in order to embody his particular vision of human life. According to this vision, meaning is the result of a dogged struggle with fate and the forces of entropy, and is won at the cost of one's illusions, beginning with the illusion that ordinary reality is nothing more than what it appears on the surface to be.

At the end of *Pot-Healer,* Glimmung permanently incorporates all of his followers except Joe Fernwright and a multilegged gastropod (snaillike creature). Joe is apparently unwilling to sacrifice his personal identity in exchange for being spared the risk of failure, as those who entered Glimmung have been. On the advice of the gastropod, Joe tries to create his own, entirely new pot rather than simply to heal someone else's creations. The result is failure. While this denouement might seem rather bleak, it is in fact an assertion that one must choose the risks and failures of ordinary life over the promises of a deadening security.

There are other aspects of *Pot-Healer* which I cannot discuss here, but I do wish to allude to the use it makes of the Grail legends. The sunken cathedral parallels the Grail, the restoration of which will restore fertility to the mythical Fisher-King's lands. Not only Glimmung but also Joe Fernwright seem to be related to the Fisher-King. Glimmung twice uses a beautiful parable in which he refers to the spider in its web as "the little fisherman of the night" (*GPH,* 5), waiting for something to be snared so he can live; and when nothing comes, the little fisherman dies waiting. In this context, Glimmung tells Joe that there is no life that is insignificant, the implication being that Joe is the little fisherman of the night; Glimmung is reassuring Joe of the worth of his life, a reassurance Joe needs in the face of a technological society which denies the worth of any small life such as Joe's.

Then, when the cathedral is raised, Glimmung thinks, "It is done. . . . Now I can rest. The great fisherman of the night has received its victory. Everything has been set in order once again" (*GPH,* 16). As Joe is the small fisherman, so the Glimmung is the great one. Even such a quasi-divine entity as the Glimmung lives with uncertainties, risks, and possibilities of failure that parallel Joe's, but on a higher level. And only where there is a true risk of failure can there be true achievement, even for gods.

One of Dick's most shocking novellas is "Faith of Our Fathers" (1967). He says, in a note to the story, that in it he "managed to offend everybody," which he later regretted.[11] However, there is no need to apologize for this story, which succinctly carries the dark side of Dick's vision of life to its ultimate extreme end. Here, political and religious authority fuse with the illusions created by mass media, mass society, and modern technology and potent modern drugs.

The main character is a Mr. Tung Chien of Hanoi, a minor functionary in a totalitarian society ruled by the Absolute Benefactor of the People, head of a People's Republic of China which has conquered the western part of the United States. Mr. Chien confronts the appearance/reality dilemma on a variety of levels: the snuff which a street peddler forces him to buy turns out to be a potent drug; the papers he is given, ostensibly to judge their ideological correctness, are actually a test of Chien's own correctness; the Leader, who appears on television as an Oriental, in reality has the appearance of a Caucasian; even worse, the image of the Leader seen on television is produced by a hallucinogen with which the whole population has been dosed; finally, the Leader is not even human.

Chien's reality begins to crumble when he unwittingly takes the drug disguised as snuff which was forced on him by the peddler. He is at home, reading two papers which he is supposed to grade for ideological orthodoxy, when the Leader appears on television. Chien then takes the snuff, and sees on the screen not the Leader, but a hideous mechanical construction. Chien decides the snuff must be a hallucinogen and becomes disgusted. However, when the police analyze the snuff, it actually turns out to be an *antihallucinogen*. The logic of the situation is irrefutable: If, when Chien takes an antihallucinogen, he sees a "dead mechanical construct," then what he has been used to seeing is a hallucination. The real Leader is not the human image which everyone sees, but the monstrous image which Chien sees when he takes the snuff.

Chien receives a visitor who further complicates matters. She is Tanya Lee, part of an underground organization which includes the peddler from whom Chien got the snuff. She tells Chien that those who take the snuff see different images, twelve in fact; some which she lists for him are "the Clanker," the Gulper," "the Bird," "the Climbing Tube," and "the Crusher." The paradox is devastating: the people's drinking water is saturated with hallucinogens, but they see only one illusion; those who take the antihallucinogen see twelve different realities. Tanya Lee explains to Chien, "Twelve mutually exclusive hallucinations—that would be easily understood. But not one hallucination and twelve realities" ("FOF").

Tanya Lee helps Chien with his ideological test and he is invited to a stag party at the Leader's villa. The peddler again supplies him with an antihallucinogen, which Chien reluctantly takes. Now, he will see the Leader as he "really" is. From his arrival at the Leader's villa, Chien is confronted with deceptive appearances. The protocol officer mocks him; a girl with illuminated breasts turns out to be a boy; "a heavy-set, elderly man" tells Chien, "You have to be cautious around here" ("FOF"). Having arrived at the very center of the systematic illusion which rules his society, Chien is not only in a position to discover reality but to be destroyed by it.

When the Leader makes his appearance, Chien is devastated: it has no shape, being none of the twelve images which Tanya Lee described to him. When Chien looks directly at it, he cannot see it: "it was, in a sense, not there at all. . . ." ("FOF"). He sees it as passing through the villa, draining the life from each of the people there, feeding on an endless hatred. Chien recognizes the entity as God. It speaks to Chien telepathically in terms that recall the theophany at the end of Job—"I spread sharp-pointed things upon the mire. I make the hiding places, the deep places, to boil like a pot. . . ." Then it adds a monistic touch: "You are me. I am you. It makes no difference. . . ." And it further uses terms that recall the Sermon of the Mount: "No one is too small; each falls and dies and I am there to watch" ("FOF"). But whereas Jesus' reference to the Father who sees the sparrow's fall is comforting, this entity's use of a similar image is chilling. This is a vision of God as the eternal watcher, coldly observing the sufferings and deaths of His creatures, deluding and tricking them for his own obscure purposes. Chien's response links God with death and entropy, which destroy not only life but the physical universe itself.

In a last effort to preserve his dignity, Chien attempts to kill himself by leaping off the balcony. However, God stops him, grasping his shoulder with a pseudo-hand. Having kept Chien from committing suicide, God then asks Chien to see Him as He is and then to trust Him. Chien is naturally horrified. God goes on to tell Chien that "when you are crushed to death I will unfold a mystery" ("FOF"). This is a phrase from Saint Paul's first letter to the Corinthians, in which he discusses the resurrection: "Behold, I show you a mystery; . . . for the trumpet shall sound and the dead be raised incorruptible. . . ."[12] Even so, God explains the mystery to Chien,

> "The dead shall live, the living die. I kill what lives, I save what has died. And I will tell you this: there are worse things than I. But you won't meet them because by then I will have killed you." ("FOF")

The Leader/God then leaves Chien, advising him to await quietly his fate. When Chien strikes at the Leader, he experiences a violent pain in his head. Chien then vows that God also will suffer:

> I will get you. I will see that you die too. That you suffer; you're going to suffer, just like us, exactly in every way we do. I'll nail you; I swear to god I'll nail you up somewhere. And it will hurt. As much as I hurt now." ("FOF")

In a very real sense, this is a pre-Christian story; it might well be a fictionalized version of Jung's *Answer to Job*. God here is portrayed as the omnipotent determiner of all things—life and death, good fortune and disaster. Chien's determination to "get" God, to "nail" him, is an ironic reflection of the necessity in Christian theology that God suffer and die. Certainly, Chien would not knowingly make Christian statements; that is the irony. And yet, this is the only possible human response in the face of apparent divine indifference to, or approval of, human suffering and death. God *must* pay the price. Just as Gino Molinari suffers in behalf of the people of Terra, so must God suffer in behalf of his creatures.

In the fiction discussed in this chapter, authority, if it is not to be tyrannical, must be like that of Gino Molinari or the Glimmung: the leader must identify himself with his subjects, the deity must identify himself with his creatures, and both deity and leader must suffer in order to provide life and order.

However, when Chien returns to Hanoi, he has forgotten his determination to get God. Instead, he seeks solace in sex with Tanya Lee, advising her to forget all about opposing the Leader. He does not tell her directly that the Leader is God; but they discuss God, Chien asking her, "Did it ever occur to you . . . that good and evil are names for the same thing? That God could be both good and evil at the same time" ("FOF"). When Tanya asks him what to do about the entity he has seen, Chien replies, "Believe in it," though he admits that that will do no good. And when Chien undresses for bed, he discovers the stigma on his shoulder, the place where it grabbed him to keep him from jumping to his death. Later he sees the mark is bleeding.

What is the reader to make of this ending? Chien has been devastated by his encounter with God, a god who is beyond good and evil as they are understood by human beings. His whole world is crumbling, as is indicated in Tanya Lee's explanation of a Dryden poem quoted in the story: "All the celestial order of the universe ends" ("FOF"). All the rational, comprehensible order of Chien's universe has ended, and he is left in a terrifying universe, in which he is bleeding to death from the imprint of God's hand. Obviously, direct contact with the divine is fatal. And the touch of God's hand, although it saves Chien's life, is far from comforting. And yet there are perhaps a couple of clues which preserve the story from a total nihilism. There is God's promise that death will save him from worse things; there is also the hint, in Chien's determination to nail God, that, if God could suffer as humans do, then a new relation, a more comforting one, would be established between the human and the divine; there is, finally, that bloody stigma, which establishes a relation of suffering between Chien and God—although described as a "pseudo-hand," it is a hand with which God grasps Chien; thus, perhaps, the stigma is the obscure and painful promise of God's potential humanity, of His yet-to-be identification with human beings in the suffering which He caused by creating them.

Seen in the larger context of Dick's fiction as surveyed in this chapter, "Faith of Our Fathers" is the epitome of the dark and terrifying side of his effort to penetrate appearances and come to reality. The conclusions of *Galactic Pot-Healer, Now Wait for Last Year, A Maze of Death, The Man Who Japed*, and *The Simulacra* are more optimistic because they are open-ended. Allen Purcell does not flee Terra, but stays to help establish a freer society; Joe Fernwright learns to risk and accept the failure of his own efforts (the pot he makes); Eric Sweetscent accepts and prepares to deal with the pain of his marriage; Seth Morley enters a millennium of healing as a cactus; and the society ruled by simulacra enters into a period of chaos which promises freedom; in the same way, the actress who has played Nicole Thibodeaux is freed from her role and can now enter an authentic, though dangerous phase of life. In each of these cases, the conclusion leaves at least some of the characters with promising possibilities. Perhaps Mr. Chien has possibility also, depending on what one makes of God's assertion that He will give the dead life; perhaps by accepting the death laid on him, Chien will find unexpected life.

For the characters in Philip K. Dick's fiction, the beginning of wisdom is the realization that things are not what they seem. This realization is threatening and may destroy them; but there is always a possibility that, if they persevere, if they accept the risks of seeking to know what is real, and *especially* if they accept their own suffering, they will find reality, even though it may devastate them, as it did Mr. Chien. But even though Dick's vision stresses the precariousness of human life—and even its fallenness—Mali Yojez says, "Death and sin are connected"[13]—it does not seem totally pessimistic. Allen Purcell, Eric Sweetscent, and Joe Fernwright, among others, end stronger and freer than they began. Fragments, potsherds, of a shattered cosmos, they have begun to be healed.

10. The Labyrinthian Process of the Artificial: Philip K. Dick's Androids and Mechanical Constructs

PATRICIA S. WARRICK

WHAT IS THE authentically human? What is the nature of the alien elements that are threatening and vitiating living, intelligent human beings? These questions are deeply rooted in Philip K. Dick's work, and to them he has provided a bizarre variety of answers, answers that are constantly being pushed aside and replaced by new possibilities. Finding an answer to the question of what is truly human and what only masquerades as human is, for Dick, the most important difficulty facing us. Some of Dick's richest metaphors stem from the profusion of electronic devices which populate his near-future wasteland landscapes—electronic constructs that in his early fiction menace the few humans surviving a nuclear holocaust; constructs that, evolving over the years toward ever more human forms, become instructors to man in the search for authenticity and wholeness.

The setting of Dick's near-future fiction is often a twilight world shrouded in smog and dust, decaying into rusty bits and useless debris. "Kipple" accumulates as the process of entropy advances. The wasteland may be a battlefield smouldering in radioactive ash, a vast "junkyard" containing the rotting remnants of West Coast suburbia, or a Martian landscape, virtually lifeless except for the Earth colonists whose electronic constructs assist in nearly fruitless gardening attempts. Manfred Steiner, the autistic but precognitive schizoid child in *Martian Time-Slip* (1964), agonizingly utters a single word to describe the horror of the accelerating entropic process: gubble (*MTS*, 9). How is man to survive and remain human in this desert of decay?

Dick's visionary landscape is dark, but not devoid of hope. He shares the arid wasteland view of contemporary culture held by other dystopian writers, but he struggles against capitulation to despair. He throws torches of possibility into the darkness of the future as he sees it. These torches reveal that survival can be achieved not by returning simplistically to an earlier pastoral world view, nor by a destructive repudiation of technology. Instead, technology must be transformed, and in turn man will be transformed. The future —if we survive—will be new, radical, unexpected. It will be a world where, as man and his electronic technology seed each other with possibilities, new forms will begin to appear.

Dick's Vancouver speech, "The Android and the Human" (1972), and his more recent "Man, Android, and Machine" (1976), emphasize the significance he assigns to the relationship between man and his machines. This chapter will trace the process of Dick's artificial constructs from their first appearances in his short stories of the 1950s, through the mid-1960s, and finally, through the last period, the late 1960s and 70s, when he becomes increasingly obsessed with metaphorical androids—humans who have lost their humanness and become mere mechanical constructs unable to respond with creativity and feeling. This journey through his fiction is indeed a process and not a progression. Dick's world is a world in motion where destinations are never reached, where utopia is never achieved. Like his Martian colonists in *The Three Stigmata of Palmer Eldritch*, (1965), we (Dick's readers) are pilgrims without progress. But he will provide flashes of possibility to illuminate our way.

"The Preserving Machine" (1953), an example of Dick's early fiction, creates a metaphor for this process of the artificial. "Doc" Labyrinth, a present-day Los Angeles suburbanite, broods over the impending collapse of our civilization and all the fine, lovely things that will be lost. Music, especially classical music, the most fragile artifact, will be destroyed as bombs fall and musical scores are incinerated. To avert this loss, he contracts the building of a Machine to preserve the great musical scores by processing them into living forms. The Preserving Machine produces a peacocklike mozart bird, a schubert sheep, a brahms centipede, a stravinsky bird, a bach bug, and a wagner animal. But unexpected problems arise from Doc Labyrinth's act. He discovers that he has no control over the result. "It was out of his hands, subject to some strong, invisible law that had subtly taken over, and this worried him greatly. The creatures were bending, changing before a deep, impersonal force, a force that Labyrinth could neither see nor understand. And it made him afraid."[1]

The musical animals became increasingly brutal and Doc Labyrinth, more responsible than his prototype, Dr. Frankenstein, attempts to reverse his act of creation. He catches a bach bug (formerly a fugue) and returns it to the Machine. It is transformed back into a musical score. Doc Labyrinth plays the score on his grand piano, but the sounds are diabolical, hideous. The order of the Bach fugue has been lost. Return is impossible.

Dick is himself a literary Doc Labyrinth whose wild imagination transforms the artifacts of our contemporary culture into new and unexpected forms. To follow the evolution of his electronic constructs through the maze of his large body of fiction is no easy journey. We often become confused, lost, or disoriented. For every path we select, we uneasily suspect that we have neglected another, more fruitful route. But occasionally he lifts us out of the labyrinth, and from this broader perspective we are given fleeting glimpses of hidden patterns and possible meanings.

One such pattern is the evolving reciprocal relationship between man and the artificial constructs (machines) which he builds. From the earliest to the most recent of Dick's fiction, his presentation of machines undergoes a series of transformations. At first he presents electronic constructs as merely automatons; then they become will-less robot-agents of enemy or alien forces, while masquerading as humans. Next, robots become increasingly more like humans, with a sense of personal identity and a concomitant will to survive; and finally robots actually become superior to humans. At the same time, humans follow a reverse process of devolution. They first fight automated machines; next they become more vitalized and machinelike themselves; then they withdraw into schizophrenia as they reject exploitation by economic and political machinery; and finally schizoid humans become like androids, with mechanical programmed personalities.

Electronic devices animate the devastated settings of almost all of Dick's novels. Typically, few animals have survived the radiation fallout, but objects have become animated. In their smallest forms, they may be metallic "insects" spouting forth shrill commercials or attacking humans. Other small homeostatic devices include whirling spheres with knife-sharp claws, lazy brown-dog reject carts, or electronic animal traps. There are friendly automatic automobiles, homeopapes (electronic newspapers), talking suitcases and vending machines, and a gallery of electronic simulacra of animals and famous people—from squirrels and sheep to presidents, soldiers, and world leaders. Computers advise presidents, teach children, serve as oracles, and perform as psychiatrists. Satellites create communication links encapsulating the globe. Pierre Teilhard de Chardin's "noosphere" is distorted by Dick's imagination into an "electronosphere" where the artificial becomes animate.

In a number of works, the electronic constructs shift from the background setting to the foreground and become major participants, central characters, in the narrative. The fiction of Dick's first period, the 1950s, is primarily short fiction; its tone is dystopian as it explores the horrors of paranoid militarism, totalitarianism, and the manipulation of people through the mass media. Robots and electronic constructs threaten or actually annihilate humanity in a number of these stories.[2] Three stories written in 1953 ("Imposter," "Second Variety," and "The Defenders") and another written in 1955 ("Autofac") are among the most powerful of Dick's short stories. In "Imposter," Earth is attacked by the Outspacers, aliens from Alpha Centauri. Spence Olham, working on a military research project, is accused of being a humanoid robot landed by the Outspacers, who have replaced the real Olham. The alien robot is an immensely powerful bomb, programmed to explode and destroy. Olham's problem is to prove he is not a robot. In the surprise ending, Olham discovers—just before he (and much of Earth) blows up—that he really *is* the robot. This story is a paradigm for much of Dick's fiction exploring artificial intelligence. It details the invasion of the alien into the human realm, the problem of differentiating between the masquerading robot and the authentic man and the accompanying paranoid suspicion, the threat of imminent destruction that will be released if the wrong choice is made, and finally, the unexpected outcome.

In "Second Variety" the enemy invasion involves Russian robots and soldiers rather than an alien robot from outer space. Warfare has reduced Earth to a slagheap of ashes, dust, and radiation. A few surviving UN soldiers stare across the battlefield at a few surviving Russians, while robots and other machines—now become "living things, spinning, creeping, shaking themselves up suddenly from the gray ash"—fight on. The surviving humans agree to a truce, but the robots, mechanically programmed to kill, cannot be halted. Nor can they be definitely identified as robots, since they masquerade as humans—as a wounded soldier, a woman, and a little boy. They "look like people, but they're machines," and the protagonist (Major Hendricks) notes that they just may be "the beginning of a new species. *The* new species. Evolution. The race to come after man." What end, he wonders, awaits man when he designs machines to hunt out and destroy human life wherever they find it? [3]

Whereas "Second Variety" is told entirely from the point of view of the humans involved, "The Defenders" is told in part from the viewpoint of machines, in part from the viewpoint of human beings—a common Dickian technique. In this story humans have lived underground for eight years after decimating Earth's surface with nuclear bombs. They now attempt to continue the war above ground with electronic constructs called "leady." It turns out, however, that the leady quit fighting as soon as the humans went underground; they have since restored the cities, villages, and countryside, and now send down false messages about the progress of nonexistent war while they live in peace above ground. Here Dick first used a dichotomy that is often found in his subsequent fiction—that of the upper and under worlds, and our shifting perspective as we move from one realm to the other. *The Penultimate Truth* (1964), a complex expansion of "The Defenders," also employs this pattern.

"Autofac" is one of the earliest and best stories warning of the ecological disaster likely to be precipitated by uncontrolled, automated production. The setting is a fire-drenched landscape cauterized by H-bomb blasts, where "a sluggish trickle of water made its way among slag and weeds, dripping thickly into what had once been an elaborate labyrinth of sewer mains" ("Autofac," 3). Under the ruined plain of black metallic ash, an automated factory still produces goods for consumers who are now mostly dead. How does one stop automation when it is no longer required? Not easily, answers Dick, who says the story germinated from the thought that "if factories became fully automated, they might begin to show the instinct for survival which organized living entities have . . . and perhaps develop similar solutions."[4] In the story's conclusion, the factory—when it has almost been destroyed—shoots out a torrent of metal seeds that germinate into miniature factories. Dick's technique here is first to create a metaphor—automated factories behave as if they were alive—and then to create a fictional world where the metaphor is *literally* true.

The last major work of interest to our study in Dick's first period is *Vulcan's Hammer* (1960). This novel is preparatory exercise for Dick's subsequent works exploring the theme of totalitarian control, the most notable of which is *The Man in the High Castle* (1962). In *Vulcan's Hammer* a sophisticated computer, Vulcan 3, is used to help run the world government after a devastating war. The totalitarian rule of this machine provokes the hostility of the population, especially that of a fanatical group called The Healers. The killer robots of Dick's earlier short stories have now become killer computers. Vulcan 3 is the third in a series of increasingly sophisticated master computers and is directly linked to its predecessor Vulcan 2. The cumulative effect of this linkage and increased sophistication is the generation of a will to survive so powerful that Vulcan 3 does seemingly paranoid or irrational things. Everyone surrounding the computer is regarded as an enemy to be destroyed. North American Director William Barris, the primary narrator of the novel, wonders whether we have merely anthropomorphized the mechanical construct or whether it really possesses the characteristics of intelligent life. How, he ponders, are we to relate to rulers who are willing to murder anyone as needed, "whoever they are. Man or computer. Alive or only metaphorically alive—it makes no difference."[5] The two political organizations, Unity and The Healers, struggling against each other for domination, are no more than pawns for two machines. At the end of the novel, Father Fields, leader of the revolutionary Healers, says:

> "We humans—god damn it, Barris; we were pawns of those two things. They played us off against one another, like inanimate pieces. The things became alive and the living organisms were reduced to things. Everything was turned inside out, like some terrible morbid view of reality." (VH, 14)

The military machine, the political machine, the economic machine: these are important concerns for Dick. *Vulcan's Hammer* is his first lengthy study of humans who have become so tightly locked into a rigid structure that their roles as members of the organization form the totality of their lives. He suggests the irrational darkness of the mechanical drive to dominate by killing in his description of Vulcan 3, as "buried at the bottom level of the hidden underground fortress. But it was its voice they were hearing" (VH, 11).

In this quotation the computer functions simultaneously and equally on a literal and metaphorical level. The unique richness and depth of Dick's writing may be attributed to the way he fuses the literal and metaphorical so tightly that his images and concepts reverberate in our minds in an almost "stereoscopic" manner. His technique, best described as a complementary process, is to create a fictional world where metaphors from our mundane or everyday world become real: "Computers seem like intelligent beings" becomes "Computers *are* humans." A shift of mental perspective is required to go beneath the surface of the plot and catch the meaning. The fictional image is consciously and deliberately a literal metaphor. Beyond that, in reversal it tells us: Men, driven by unrecognized impulses deeply hidden in the substrata of their minds, become machines who kill.

Dick's next novel, *The Man in the High Castle*, deals further with the theme of the totalitarian state as a machine of domination and destruction. Vulcan 3 now becomes the Nazis, whose paranoid suspicions lead them to plot a sneak nuclear attack on their Japanese allies, whose world view is in many ways the polar opposite of that of the Nazis. This juxtaposition of opposing viewpoints is at this point the essence of the Dickian creative process. Reality is for him a bipolar construction; the closest we can come to grasping it is to mirror in fiction the polarities. (And finally, to fully understand his fiction, certain groups of short and long fiction must be read as single units.)

At this early stage in his creative development, Dick looks at one world view from the perspective of its opposite, and then in a separate work reverses the process. Thus *Vulcan's Hammer* is a metaphor for machines as destructive humans; *The Man in the High Castle* is a metaphor for humans become destructive machines. In the novels that follow—for example, *The Penultimate Truth* and *Do Androids Dream of Electric Sheep?*—both views are present in a single work. The skilled reader who has become used to these contradictions "sees" from opposite directions simultaneously. He is rewarded with a fleeting epiphany— Dick's vision of reality as process. Ultimately, however, one intuits rather than analyzes Dick's meaning. The totality of his complex fictional gestalt cannot be grasped by a mere part-by-part discussion. But perhaps something of the significance of Dick's work can be revealed by literary analysis. However, we must temper our analysis with a more or less intuitive groping if we are to find our way to the power and insight of the fiction.

In his prodigiously productive middle period, Dick published a half dozen very-good-to-excellent novels, three of which— *Martian Time-Slip* (1964), *The Three Stigmata of Palmer Eldritch* (1964), and *Dr. Bloodmoney* (1965)—are generally considered his finest works to date. Two of the other novels, *The Penultimate Truth* and *The Simulacra* (both 1964), are competent but unexceptional novels of interest because automata figure significantly in their plots. In this middle period, Dick's attention shifts from the military, his primary subject in the 1950s, to economic and political matters. His use of point of view also alters, as does his view of reality. He no longer uses a third person point of view, but rather multiple narrative foci, as Darko Suvin so effectively describes in his chapter in this book.[6] The relatively fixed reality of his earlier works now begins to distort and oscillate in uncertain hallucinations, suggesting that our illusions of stable appearances are very fragile fictions.

Dick, exploring the difference between the short story and the novel, suggests:

> If the essence of sf is the idea . . . if indeed the idea is the true "hero," then the sf story probably remains the sf form par excellence, with the sf novel a fanning out, an expansion into all ramifications. Most of my own novels are expansions of earlier stories, or fusions of several stories—superimpositions. The germ lay in the story; in a very real sense, that was its true distillate.[7]

The complexity in meanings of the middle-period novels can often be penetrated by first examining some of the ideas incisively dramatized in his short stories. Two such tales, "Oh, To Be a Blobel!" (1964) and "If There Were No Benny Cemoli" (1963), illuminate the evolution of Dick's ideas about mechanical intelligence—ideas which are transformed in the novels in a myriad of bizarre forms by Dick's prodigious metaphorical inventiveness. These two stories describe the aftereffects of a war and suggest that these aftereffects, powerful and prolonged, are experienced equally by the winner and the loser, thus making military victory meaningless. In war, human creativity—impassioned by the drive to dominate and destroy—couples with technology, and monstrous opportunities to demean and displace commonplace reality arises. The common man, naively trusting and uninstructed in this perverted form of gamesmanship, is the victim. Dick's brilliance lies in his ability to dramatize a concept—such as the one we have just discussed—in a powerful and unexpected metaphor: a metaphor that works by reversal. "Oh, To Be a Blobel!" presents such an ironic metaphor. Here, a decade after a war on Mars between Terran settlers and Blobels (amoeba-like natives of Mars and Titan, George Munster still suffers the aftereffects of the war. As a Terran spy, he had been required to assume Blobel shape to conduct his espionage activities. The government promised to eliminate this alteration and return George to his normal human condition. But they did not keep their promise. For eight hours every day George still turns into a Blobel. This transformation is emotionally traumatic, so he goes to Dr. Jones, a robot analyst, for psychiatric help. The homeostatic analyst, who functions when activated by a $20 platinum coin dropped into a slot, arranges for George to meet with Vivian Arrasmith, a Blobel spy during the war who had assumed human form for her work behind the Terran lines. In a reversal of George's problem, she keeps reverting from Blobel to human form. Each of them at first finds the "alien" form of the other disgusting. But in an ironic climax full of black humor, each finally turns permanently and completely into the form of the respective enemy. Thus, for Dick, the outcome of any war— whether military or economic—is not victory or defeat, but a transformation of the participants into the opposite. We become the goal we pursue, the enemy we fight. This metaphor of ironic transformation is Dick's paradigm for the process of the mechanical. We become what we do. The activities of the body transform the patterns of the intellect. Obsessed with building ever more sophisticated homeostatic machines, we in turn become human machines.

"If There Were No Benny Cemoli," one of the great political short stories in the science-fiction canon, dramatizes the power of electronic media to manipulate reality. The story is set a decade after a nuclear holocaust in an American culture attempting to rebuild. A political group uses a computerized newspaper, a "homeopape," to create an imaginary political revolutionary, "Benny Cemoli," when they need a charismatic figure to distract the attention of the authorities from the group's activities. The homeopape, a reactivated version of the *New York Times,* prints daily editions describing the revolutionary activities of the nonexistent Cemoli. Anyone in a position to look at the real situation is aware that "the newspaper had lost contact with actual events. The reality of the situation did not coincide with the *Times* articles in any way; that was obvious. And yet—the homeostatic system continued on."[8] The reality experienced by Peter Hood, one of the authorities, becomes a discontinuous track of incongruity. There are the events he sees happening around him as compared with the account of those same events printed in the homeopape. The two bear no resemblance. He is disturbed that the fictional account of the nonexistent Benny Cemoli's activities begins to assume more reality than the actual political events. He realizes "we are real only so long as the *Times* writes about us . . . as if we were dependent for our existence on it." The news media no longer describe the real world; they create it. The media images replace the actual in the minds of people everywhere.

These two short stories, then, present related ideas underlying many of Dick's novels. Technologies spawned by war transform man into new, unexpected, and often ironic forms; and technologies through communications media create fictional realities more powerful than the "real." Now let us consider the novels of Dick's middle period.

The Martian desert of *Martian Time-Slip* and *The Three Stigmata of Palmer Eldritch,* peopled with colonists from Earth, functions more as a metaphor for our twentieth-century wasteland culture than as a literal landscape of Mars. The settlers have either been conscripted to live on Mars by the government bureaucracy or lured there by the persuasion of economic interests on Earth. The greatest evil, Dick states in "The Android and the Human," is placing restrictions on a man that force him to fulfill an aim outside his own destiny. The Martian settlers, victims of this evil, consume an illusion of existence supplied by the industrialists who control the world. In *Martian Time-Slip,* children are given the Establishment view of reality through the technology of the Teaching Machines. In *Palmer Eldritch,* the inauthentic reality is patently hallucinatory, induced by Can-D and Chew-Z, the drugs marketed by competing economic complexes. Even though they are aware of the falseness of the world created by Perky-Pat dolls and drugs, the colonists choose this easy escape to the barren existence possible in the lifeless Martian dust. Metaphorically, the drugs and the Teaching Machines mirror all the technology of persuasion—television, radio, schools, newspapers—sustaining the distorted brand of reality which the bureaucracy feeds the masses.

Two characters in *Martian Time-Slip* are of particular interest: Jack Bohlen, the electronics repairman, and Manfred Steiner, the autistic child Jack hopes to cure. Jack's struggle against attacks of schizophrenia succeeds, but Manfred's tomb world lies beyond struggle. Together they dramatize Dick's view of schizophrenia—a view, as critics have noted, similar to R. D. Laing's, for whom a withdrawal into the self may sometimes be the wisest choice in an inhuman environment.[9] The schizoid, defined by Dick as an androidlike personality unable to respond with feelings, appears in later fiction—*Do Androids Dream of Electric Sheep?* (1968) and *We Can Build You* (1969). Dick explains:

> I draw a sharp line between the schizoid personality and actual schizophrenia, which I have the utmost respect for, and for the people who do it—or have it, whatever. I see it this way: the schizoid personality overuses his thinking function at the expense of his feeling function (in Jungian terms) and so has inappropriate or flattened affect; *he* is android-like. But in schizophrenia, the denied feeling function breaks through from the unconscious in an effort to establish balance and parity between the functions. Therefore it can be said that in essence I regard what is called "schizophrenia" as an attempt by a one-sided mind to compensate and achieve wholeness: schizophrenia is a brave journey into the realm of the archetypes, and those who take it—who will no longer settle for the cold schizoid personality—are to be honored. Many never survive this journey, and so trade imbalance for total chaos, which is tragic. Others, however, return from the journey in a state of wholeness; they are the fortunate ones, the truly sane. Thus I see schizophrenia as closer to sanity (whatever that may mean) than the schizoid is. The terrible danger about the schizoid is that he can function; he can even get hold of a position of power over others, whereas the lurid schizophrenic wears a palpable tag saying, "I am nuts, pay no attention to me."[10]

Jack first "falls through the floor of reality"—to use Dick's language in describing one of his favorite techniques—in a schizophrenic attack. Viewing his personnel manager in an electronics firm, he sees through the skin to the bones. He discovers that the bones are wired together, the organs replaced with a plastic and stainless-steel heart, lungs, and kidneys. The voice comes from a tape. Everything about the man is lifeless and mechanical. Later, in a similar attack, he watches the psychiatrist, Dr. Glaub, transform into a thing of cold wires and switches—a mechanical device with a programmed view of reality which he *spiels* to Jack.

Along with these mechanical, shadowy humans who reveal their true nature only in the absolute reality of his recurrent insanity, Jack encounters an array of actual mechanical constructs or simulacra when somewhat against his will he is called to repair the Teaching Machines at his son's school. The Angry Janitor, Thomas Edison, Abraham Lincoln, Kindly Dad, Mark Twain, the

Emperor Tiberius—all the right personnel and historical characters for a school setting, except that they are lifeless, mere programmed machines unable to give genuine responses to human students, used ineffectually to indoctrinate students into the most rigidly conventional of thought patterns.

Manfred's autistic withdrawal into silence is as much an act of self-destruction as the literal suicide of his father, Norbert Steiner. Manfred's nightmare vision of an entropic future (the world of *gubbish*) pushes him to a psychic death; Norbert's exhausted awareness of his failed life in a desert world drives him to a physical death, a suicide, under the wheels of a bus.

The vision of Richard Hnatt, a minor character in *Palmer Eldritch* who is undergoing treatment to accelerate the natural evolutionary process, provides a key to the structure of *Martian Time-Slip*. In Hnatt's vision he sees that:

> Below lay the tomb world, the immutable cause-and-effect world of the demonic. At median extended the layer of the human, but at any instant a man could plunge—descend as if sinking—into the hell-layer beneath. Or: he could ascend to the ethereal world above, which constituted the third of the trinary layers. Always, in his middle level of the human, a man risked the sinking. And yet the possibility of ascent lay before him; any aspect or sequence of reality *could become either*, at any instant. Hell and heaven, not after death but now! Depression, all mental illness, was the sinking. And the other . . . how was it achieved?
>
> Through empathy. Grasping another, not from outside but from the inner.[11] (*3SPE*, 5).

In *Martian Time-Slip*, Jack Bohlen leads a rather ordinary life as an electronics repairman. However, in his schizophrenic visions, he breaks through to the upper and lower realms. Heliogabalus sympolizes the upper realm. A Bleekman (native Martian) and in a deep sense an *authentic* human, he lives with but remains impervious to Arnie Kott's exploitative empire, and his empathy establishes an immediate communication, lying beyond words, with Manfred. Manfred, trapped in the lower realm, a hellish tomb-world of death and entropy, finally drags Arnie Kott down to death when Manfred's hallucinatory world becomes reality for Arnie.

Dick delights in using a technique of sudden reversal, providing a climactic episode or revelation totally violating our expectation. One such ironic reversal full of impish horror is the scene when Jack brings Manfred to school to meet with the Teaching Machines. The reader shares Jack's expectation that the machines will affect Manfred, hopefully breaking into his prison of frozen silence and freeing him to respond. But in fact quite the opposite occurs. Manfred remains voiceless: the machines, electronically keyed to predetermined messages, are decimated by his presence into a chaos permitting only one word of response, repeated in a metallic voice: *gubble, gubble . . .*

Arnie Kott, the union leader who dreams of Martian economic domination in *Martian Time-Slip,* devolves into Palmer Eldritch in Dick's next novel, *The Three Stigmata of Palmer Eldritch.* Eldritch, having succeeded as an interplanetary industrialist by producing an overabundance of consumer goods and distributing them to the wrong places, aspires to extend his power to stellar dimensions. He sets out to the "Prox" (*Proxima Centauri*) system to modernize autofacs along Terran lines. What returns ten years later is a devil with a metal face bearing an "evil, negative trinity of alienation, blurred reality, and despair" (*3SPE,* 13). The three stigmata signal the transformation of the formerly human into the demonic: a mechanical arm, stainless-steel teeth, and artificial stainless-steel eyes in his gaunt, hollowed-out, gray face.[12] A mechanical Red Riding Hood wolf,[13] Eldritch is equipped to function as a machine of destruction: to see, manipulate, and devour the unsophisticated masses of common people.

Eldritch's transforming shapes, as he gradually reveals himself to businessmen Leo Bulero and Barney Mayerson, form a map of Dick's evolving vision of reality manipulators. Eldritch first appears as a voice emanating from an "electronic contraption." The electronic contraption sprouts a handlike extension offering a smoking cigar filled with the drug brought back from Prox. Next, colored slides of the Prox system are offered. Eldritch does not appear in his real shape until two-thirds of the way into the novel, and even then he is first seen as a simulacrum.

Whatever Eldritch may be, he is no longer human. His human eyes, mouth, and hands have all been replaced with mechanical devices that enable him to see, speak and touch. His mask, as Mayerson realizes, infiltrates the lives of all who see him. His power of manipulation creates a hallucination which the settlers accept as reality or as an adequate substitute for reality. By the end of the novel, the outer appearances and inner awarenesses of the characters are transformed into a writhing, multiplying chaos of mechanical eyes and metallic hands. The grinning metal devil is ubiquitous.

The Simulacra and *The Penultimate Truth* return to Earth to study military dictatorship, economic exploitation, and bureaucratic manipulation. In both of these novels, a simulacrum serves as a figurehead-president. The masses of common people, seeing them from a distance, mistakenly assume they are real. *The Simulacra* creates doubly inauthentic leaders: Nicole Thibodeaux, latest in a line of actresses trained to play the role of the First Lady, and her husband, *der Alte*, a simulacrum (thought to be human by the populace) who is replaced every four years. Typical Dickian complexity of meaning abounds here. The hidden rulers, a council of nine, controlling from behind the scene, provide the public with a figurehead ruler who mouths the words of the scripts they write. The public is given the illusion of a democratic process by being allowed to elect the ruler's husband every four years; but, unknown to the public, he is in reality a mere machine. Electronic technology makes possible all these manipulations of reality whereby the artificial and the fake substitute for the authentic. In *The Penultimate Truth,* Stanton Brose, the hidden economic dictator, controls both the military and the government. President Talbot Yancy, a simulacrum programmed to send phoney video messages of hope to the mass of underground factory workers, is a metaphor for the fantasy of honest government and earnest leaders. Script writers create presidents and manipulate massess.

In *Dr. Bloodmoney,* Dick has mastered the complex narrative structure often obscuring the meaning in *Simulacra* and *Penultimate Truth.* The finest of his dystopian novels set in a post-holocaust world, it ends with the hope offered by the mutant homunculus, Bill. Dr. Bluthgeld (*Bloodmoney*), the mad scientist who created the bomb, and Hoppy Harrington, the mad technologist and mutant life form spawned by radiation, struggle for the power of world domination. Hoppy, by the time he destroys Bluthgeld, has become very nearly as paranoid and power-mad as the scientist. Dangerfield, a modern Everyman encapsulated in his artificial mechanical environment, is first deflected from his course into an endlessly circular orbit by Bluthgeld's bombs, then nearly killed by Hoppy's jamming of his broadcasts. In *Palmer Eldritch*, an evil god with a metal face penetrates the planetary system from outside and threatens every man. Here in *Dr. Bloodmoney*, a reversal of this pattern occurs:

> The killing, the slow destruction of Dangerfield, Bonny thought, was deliberate, and it came—not from space, not from beyond—but from below, from the familiar landscape. Dangerfield had not died from the years of isolation; he had been stricken by careful instruments issuing up from the very world which he struggled to contact. If he could have cut himself off from us, she thought, he would be alive now. At the very moment he listened to us, received us, he was being killed—and did not guess.[15]

Man's alienation and despair, Dick now suggests, grow out of the new settings and the new forms his technology has spawned and out of the power to manipulate which they provide. Hoppy *metaphors*[16] the merging of the animate and the inanimate, a new life form resulting from the cross-fertilization of science and technology. Dick explains:

> The greatest change growing across our world these days is probably the momentum of the living towards reflection, and at the same time a reciprocal entry into animation by the mechanical. We hold now no pure categories of the living versus the non-living; this is going to be our paradigm: My character, Hoppy.[17]

Dick's early robots were machines sent by alien enemy forces to attack man. In his middle period, the actual man-made robot or simulacrum became the paradigm for the capitalist-fascist-bureaucratic structures locking the individual in a prisonhouse of false illusions created through electronic constructs. The technologist became a demonic artificer serving the devil of economic greed. In the fiction of the late 1960s, another shift in the evolution of Dick's imagination occurs, as evidenced by a shift in emphasis from the outer space of the social realm to the inner world of the mind. The robot no longer walks wasteland streets or peers from vidscreens via electronic images; rather he haunts the human consciousness and stares out through a mask of flesh.[18] Dick has become aware, he tells us now, that "the greatest pain does not come down from a distant planet, but up from the depth of the human heart."[19] His attention moves to the human as a machine or android.

Dick's Vancouver speech defines these characteristics of the "android" mind that separate it from the authentic ally human: a paucity of feeling, predictability, obedience, inability to make exceptions, and an inability to alter with circumstances to become something new.[20] In his recent fiction exploring the mechanical, his earlier view of androids as artificial constructs masquerading as humans gives way to a view of androids as humans who have become machines. Now robots and men have reserved roles. *Do Androids Dream of Electric Sheep?* (1968) creates a metaphor for this process. In *We Can Build You* (serialized in magazine form in 1969), automata assume the compassion and concern of the authentic human: the Abraham Lincoln simulacrum, although a schizophrenic character, is superior in his insight and humanity to the humans in the novel.

Read as a dramatization of inner space, *Do Androids Dream?* merits recognition as one of Dick's finest novels, a view contrary to most of the current critical judgment. Stanislaw Lem in "Science Fiction; A Hopeless Case—With Exceptions" recognizes the novel as "not important," but then dismisses it as disappointing because it does not offer unequivocal answers to the questions of internal logic that it raises.[21] But the point is, Dick is picturing an inner world that is *without* the logical consistency Lem demands. For Dick, the clear line between hallucination and reality has itself become a kind of hallucination. We have a bimodal brain, or, more precisely according to Dick, two brains housed within the same skull. He recently applauded the research done in this area by Robert E. Ornstein at Stanford University, but indicates he had not been aware of it when he wrote *Do Androids Dream?*[22]

Given its task of inner exploration, the novel discards the multiple foci narrative technique of his previous novels and uses a single point of view. Superficially, *Do Androids Dream?* traces the adventures of policeman Rick Deckard, a bounty hunter who receives $1,000 for each android he kills. The androids, now so sophisticated they can scarcely be differentiated from humans, have been developed to serve as slave labor to the Lunar colonists. Occasionally a few rebel and flee to Earth, where they masquerade as humans and are hunted down and killed by men like Rick. Much of the human population has gone into space to escape a radiation-polluted Earth where almost no forms of life survive. Owning an animal that is really alive is a mark of status on Earth because real animals have become so expensive; many people must settle for cheaper electronic simulations, as does Rick. His dream is to accumulate enough money to buy a real sheep, instead of an electric one. He hopes to achieve this by killing androids.

This gestalt of action is a parable for Rick's inner journey as he discovers that he possesses both a rational and an intuitive self. Two plot lines are metaphoric representations of the two selves: Rick, one protagonist, is the intellectual, unfeeling self; he is the left hemisphere of the brain. John Isidore, the mutant with subnormal I.Q., is the intuitive self who empathizes with all forms; he is the right brain lobe. The novel sets up a series of opposing ideas: people–things; subject–object; animate–inanimate; loving–killing; intuition–logic; human–machine. Double character sets abound; Rick Deckard and Phil Resch; Rachael Rosen and Pris Stratton, John Isidore and Wilbur Mercer. We can only know the penultimate truth; we are always one reflection away from reality, and we see it as in a mirror. Thus the sets of characters mirror truths to each other. For Dick this encounter—not an encounter of truth, but only a reflection of the truth—is caught best in an image used by Saint Paul, who speaks of our seeing "as if by the reflection on the bottom of a polished metal pan."[23]

The complexity of structure and ideas in this rich novel point up the evolutionary process of the Dickian imagination in the fifteen years since those first short stories about robot warfare. But the question for which Dick invents his array of answers is the same as it was then: What happens when man builds machines programmed to kill? The answer Dick fears, is that man will become the machines that kill. This is what Rich Deckard learns about himself: in pursuing the enemy android with a view to kill or be killed, he takes on the characteristics of the enemy and becomes himself an android. In one of the most powerful chapters of the novel (Chapter 12), Rick encounters his double, the android bounty hunter, Phil Resch, who enjoys killing. This mirror episode provides Rich with the insight that he has been transformed into an android-killing machine.

The female androids, Pris and Rachael, both attract and repel Rick. These two simulacra foreshadow the cold, unresponsive female of *We Can Build You,* Pris Frauenzimmer (her name, translated, means "womankind," or does it mean "streetwalker?" The text suggests both—another example of Dickian ambiguity and irony). The android Rachael is "the belle dame sans merci"[24] who fascinates to the point of near destruction. She makes love to Rick without loving him because she, a mere machine, lacks emotional awareness and so is unable to empathize with others. She is, she realizes, not much different from an ant. She and her double, Pris, are mere "chitinous reflexmachines who aren't really alive" (*DAD,* 16).

The secondary plot of the novel records the encounter of John Isidore, a subnormal "chickenhead," with the androids. Contrary to Rick, who hunts androids to kill them, John empathizes with them. He is a follower of Mercerism and is easily able to identify with every other living thing. Wilbur Mercer is a mysterious old man whose image on the black empathy box serves as a focus for the theological and moral system called Mercerism. Its followers unite through empathy, the energy capable of transporting the human mind through the mirror so that it unites with the opposite and sees from the reverse direction. Mercer, in a gentle test of endurance which transcends suffering as he endlessly toils up a barren hill, is reminiscent of Albert Camus' Sisyphus. John Isidore, grasping the handles of the black empathy box, undergoes a "crossing-over," a physical merging with others accompanied by mental and spiritual identification, as follows:

for everyone who at this moment clutched the handles, either here on Earth or on one of the colony planets. He experienced them, the others, incorporated the babble of their thoughts, heard in his own brain the noise of their many individual existences. They—and he— cared about one thing; this fusion of their mentalities oriented their attention on the hill, the climb, the need to ascend. Step by step it evolved, so slowly as to be nearly imperceptible. But it was there. Higher, he thought as stones rattled downward under his feet. Today

we are higher than yesterday, and tomorrow—he, the compound figure of Wilbur Mercer, glanced up to view the ascent ahead. Impossible
to make out the end. Too far. But it will come. (*DAD*, 2)

The novel is full of a pyrotechnic display of self-negating inven-
tions. Rick's love-making with the android, Rachael Rosen—an
act of identification with the other—explodes his will to kill into
nauseated rejection of his work. But threatened by Rachael's
double, Pris, while he is carrying a laser gun, he kills—thus violating his newly found sense of identity. He is instructed by Wilbur Mercer about this curse of man:

"You will be required to do wrong no matter where you go. It is the
basic condition of life, to be required to violate your own identity. At
some time, every creature which lives must do so. It is the ultimate
shadow, the defeat of creation; this is the curse at work, the curse that
feeds on all life. Everywhere in the universe." (DAD, 15)

Reversals and negations like Rick's in loving and killing, are
compounded throughout the novel. Mercer, the mystic, turns out
to be a fake—not a religious leader but an alcoholic has-been
actor. The allegedly real toad Rick discovers on his desert journey and cherishes as an omen of spiritual rebirth turns out to be
an electric one. What does it all mean? Rick's final insight answers the question: "Everything is true, everything anybody has
ever thought" (*DAD*, 20). He could just as well have said that
everything is false. It all depends on the perspective from which
you view "reality." Language limits because a given statement
can only encompass one view at a time. Thus irony provides the
only escape from language through language, for irony contains a
negation of the assertion. Given Dick's view of a puzzling, unde-
fined, metamorphosing cosmos, irony is essential to him in creating his fictional worlds mirroring that view.

How does one survive in this universe of uncertainty where
everything is both true and false? Like John Isidore, one empathizes with and responds to the needs of all forms, blinding
one's eyes to the inauthentic division between the living and non-
living, between the machine and man. Like the shadowy Wilbur
Mercer, one endlessly climbs up, suffering the wounds of rocks
mysteriously thrown, but never reaching a destination. Mercer's

hill mirrors Sisyphus' fate, his rocks the stones of martyred Stephen, his empathy the forgiving, uniting love of Christ.

Only when the divisions Dick has mirrored in the novel are healed by an inner unity growing from an acceptance of all things will artificiality be replaced by authentic existence. If you hold the nineteenth-century view of yourself as a unique, concrete thing, says Dick, you can never merge with the noosphere. The left-hemisphere brain, the isolating android intellect, must merge with the right-hemisphere brain, the collective intuition that we all share. These dream images, if we will listen, partake of the creative power that can transform us from mere machines into authentic humans.[25]

We Can Build You cannot be ignored in a study of Dick's androids because it proposes new pathways in the labyrinthian possibilities of machine intelligence: but it cannot be applauded because it creeps along in a dramatic near-paralysis uncommon to Dick's fiction. The failure is twofold. First, the novel relies on exposition, not metaphor, to make many of its statements. Additionally, it concerns itself with two themes which are not closely related. When, as he can, Dick yokes the unlikely in grotesque marriage, he is brilliant. In this novel, however, the two themes fail to resonate; we are left with a sense of dispassionate incongruity. The first theme concerns the creation of simulacra whose intelligence has all the attributes of human intelligence. How are such forms to be regarded—ethically, legally, and philosophically? What are the implications of destroying such high-level intelligence? Is there a difference between killing an intelligent being and an equally intelligent machine? A writer as different from Dick as Isaac Asimov has successfully dramatized these issues in what is unquestionably his greatest story, "The Bicentennial Man" (1976). Dick plays with the possibilities of this theme in desultory probings, but he actually seems to be more concerned with the second theme: the transformation of the protagonist, Louis Rosen, into an android. This theme makes use of an idea which apparently remained in Dick's mind after he finished the superb *Do Androids Dream?* It can be summarized as: What are we to make of the human who glorifies reason, logic, individual prudence, and self-concern while at the same time he suppresses emotional responses—love, fear, and passion? The answer Dick gives is that we can no longer regard him as human; he has become a logic machine, an android, a schizoid personality.

Both themes—the legal and ethical rights of artificial intelligence and the transformation of a human into an unfeeling machine—are quite substantial and worthy of literary exploration. But, strangely, in this novel Dick's metaphoric inventiveness is often absent. Ideas customarily transformed into unexpected images here become passages of abstract, psychology-text discussion about schizophrenia and encyclopedia excerpts about Abraham Lincoln, Edwin Stanton, and John Wilkes Booth.

We Can Build You is the story of Louis Rosen and Pris Frauenzimmer. She reminds us of the androids, Pris and Rachael, in *Do Androids, Dream?* In *We Can Build You,* she is a teenage schizoid who recovers enough from her mental illness to work in her father's small electronic organ factory. Because sales are poor, the factory turns to manufacturing simulacra, and Pris is the designer of two Civil War robots, Abraham Lincoln and Edwin Stanton, his secretary of war. She becomes obsessed with Sam Barrow, an enterprising and ruthless young millionaire who singlehandedly has opened up the way for housing developments on Luna, Mars, and Venus. Her fascination with his power and grandiose visions leads her to leave her father's small corporation and take her creative talents to Barrow's vast economic empire. The union is a destructive one, driving her eventually to kill a simulacrum.

Pris has the potential for Medealike tragedy as she creates, then destroys her electronic children. That potential must, however, remain undeveloped because of the role she is required to play in the second plot, which records Louis Rosen's mental illness. Louis, the narrator of the story, descends into a schizoid underworld whose final destination is a mental institute. His deterioration is marked by his increasing fascination with Pris, who is like a machine driven by logic and purpose. She has "an ironclad rigid schematic view—a blueprint, an abstraction of mankind. And she lived on it"[26] (*WCBY*, 14). Louis first jokes that he is one of Pris's simulacra. Then he realizes he has fallen in love with her, "a woman with eyes of ice, a calculating, ambitious schizoid type" (*WCBY*, 12). She is indifferent to his love and unable to respond with feelings. Louis is, he senses with foreboding, "doomed to loving something beyond life itself, a cruel, cold, and sterile thing . . ." (WCBY, 14). Pris reminds us of Diana, goddess of the hunt, who is chaste and cold.

So it is not surprising to discover Dick has read sixteenth-century poetry extensively and in creating Pris had particularly in mind a Sir Thomas Wyatt sonnet whose final lines read:

> Who list her hunt, I put him out of doubt,
> As well as I, may spend his time in vain.
> And graven in diamonds in letters plain
> There is written, her fair neck round about:
> *Noli me tangere*, for Caesar's I am,
> And wild for to hold, though I seem tame.[27]

Pris is an inverted, technological Diana of the Wood, ruling not in a natural but a man-made world. The goddess described in Frazer's *The Golden Bough* blesses mankind with fertility; Pris condemns Louis with near-destructive madness.

Countering the schizoid Pris is the schizophrenic simulacrum, A. Lincoln, whose personality is reminiscent of Jack Bohlen's in *Martian Time-Slip*. While Lincoln is emotionally unstable, he is not cold and indifferent to the life around him.

> He might have been remote, but he was not dead emotionally; quite the contrary. So he was the opposite of Pris, of the cold schizoid type. Grief, emotional empathy, were written on his face. He fully felt the sorrows of the war, every single death. (WCBY, 14)

We have here a dramatization of Dick's view of the individual suffering from schizophrenia as contrasted with the schizoid personality.

Dick's view of the machine had evolved by the time he wrote this novel to the point where he could no longer find ground for differentiating between the animate and the inanimate. The simulacrum A. Lincoln proposes this position in a dialogue with the industrialist, Sam Barrow, where they debate the differences between man and machine. They recapitulate the eighteenth- and nineteenth-century argument about the existence of a "vital spirit" in living matter which differentiates it from inanimate matter. Barrow concedes that a machine now can talk, think, move —can in fact do anything a man can.

What then, asks Lincoln, is the difference? Spinoza held that animals were clever machines; the critical difference between man and animal is the presence in man of a soul.

"There is no soul," Barrow said. "That's pap."
"Then," the simulacrum said, "a machine is the same as an animal." It went on slowly in its dry, patient way, "And an animal is the same as a man. Is that not correct?" (WCBY, 9)

We Can Build You, as we noted, must be considered in tracing the evolution of Dick's thinking about artificial intelligence because it documents important developments, but it cannot be admired artistically because it falters in converting idea to metaphor.

Interestingly, in the same year, as he was writing this somewhat disappointing novel (1969), Dick created one of the greatest short stories in all literature exploring man's perception of himself as a machine, "The Electric Ant." This story contains all the lightning inventiveness, and the abrupt yoking of the impossible in calm, ironic understatement that shocks us into a new way of seeing things. This is Dick's literary genius: his metaphorical brilliance, a gift lying closer to the art of the poet than that of the traditional novelist.

"The Electric Ant" is an example of the qualities in Dick's writing that remind his critics of Franz Kafka. We think immediately of "The Metamorphosis," where the first sentence matter-of-factly announces that Gregor Samsa awoke one morning from uneasy dreams to find himself transformed into a gigantic insect. Similarly, in "The Electric Ant," Garson Poole awakens in his hospital bed after an accident which amputated his right hand and discovers that he is not a man but a robot. His skin covers not flesh and blood, but wires, circuits, and miniature components. The objective, restrained prose describing the metamorphosis of Poole's self-image from that of a free human agent to a programmed machine lies in awful tension with the emotional intensity of the event and gives the story its terrible and unique power. All the issues raised by the philosophy of mechanism are explored here in metaphoric form. Are we only bits of matter, controlled by the laws of physics governing inanimate matter? If so, then man's cherished free will is nothing but an illusion. How can we ever know true reality if our perceptions of ourselves and the world around us turn out to be unreliable? My summary comments are the language of philosophical abstraction: Dick's language makes use of the metaphor of the particular. Listen to Garson Poole after his discovery that he is a mere robot utilized by Tri-Plan Electronics Corporation.

> Christ, he thought, it undermines you, knowing this. I'm a freak, he realized. An inanimate object mimicking an animate one. But—he felt alive. Yet . . . he felt differently, now. About himself.

> Programmed. In me somewhere, he thought, there is a matrix fitted in place, a grid screen that cuts me off from certain thoughts, certain actions. And forces me into others. I am not free. I never was, but now I know it; that makes it different. ("The Electric Ant")[28]

Having discovered he is a machine with a programmed "reality" tape, Poole next realizes that this insight gives him the option of altering his tape. He thinks,

> if I control my reality tape, I control reality. At least so far as I am concerned. My subjective reality . . . but that's all there is. Objective reality is a synthetic construct, dealing with a hypothetical universalization of a multitude of subjective realities. ("The Electric Ant")

Is reality only a fiction; or must man make up fictions because reality is unknowable? Are space and time uncertain in their order because man has not yet learned to understand them; or does the universe of space and time eternally move with the mystery beyond human probing? Is the authentic human mind with its high intelligence unique and irreplaceable; or will machines become more intelligent than man? Can they explore new worlds from which man is barred? Dick in his fiction is a seeker who searches not for definitive answers to these puzzles, but for possibilities. His early short stories are straightforward metaphors, simple mirrors, presenting to us the bizarre possibilities his imagination sees. His later metaphors move into realms of increasing complexity and his mirroring device becomes a doubly ironic metaphor composed of opposites facing each other. In order to comprehend this type of metaphor, we have to see in several directions at the same time, to let our awareness slip simultaneously in both directions through the mirror, viewing the polarities of possibility from each direction in the same instant. Thus, for Dick, the enlightened human consciousness is not a *state* of being but an *event* or process of eternal passage between contraries.

We cease our labyrinthian journey through Dick's phantasmagoric worlds of evolving intelligence, human and artificial. It brings us to no conclusion, but perhaps to a peaceful, exhilarating delight at being lost in the metaphorical maze of his and our own imagination. We reach no goal, but share our guide's awareness that nothing can be preserved, either by machines or man. Dick's most recent words interrupt but do not conclude the process of his awareness:

> We humans, the warm-faced and tender, with thoughtful eyes—we are perhaps the true machines. And those objective constructs, the natural objects around us and especially the electronic hardware we build, the transmitters and microwave relay stations, the satellites, they may be cloaks for authentic living reality inasmuch as they may participate more fully and in a way obscured to us in the ultimate Mind. Perhaps we see not only a deforming veil, but backwards. Perhaps the closest approximation to truth would be to say: "Everything is equally alive, equally free, equally sentient, because everything is not alive or half-alive or dead, but rather *lived through*.[29]

What future will unfold for artificial intelligence? Will it increasingly assume and perhaps eventually subsume human intelligence? What of the human brain's capacity to dream, to throw up fireworks of possibility lying outside mundane reality? Will machine intelligence achieve that gift, too? What is the answer to the question Dick's title asks: *Do* androids dream of electric sheep? We know that Dick, according to his own philosophy, would want us to accept only the answer we discover as we look in the mirror of his fiction and see our own awareness reflected back to us. But we can also be certain of his answer. Yes, as each form contains within itself the shadow-image of the potential forms that seed its inevitable transformation, so do androids also dream.

II. Now Wait for This Year*

PHILIP K. DICK

WHEN I LOOK at my stories, written over three decades, I think of the Lucky Dog Pet Store. There's a good reason for that. It has to do with an aspect of not just my life but of the lives of most freelance writers. It's called poverty.

I laugh about it now, and even feel a little nostalgia, because in many ways those were the happiest goddam days of my life, especially back in the early fifties when my writing career began. But we were poor; in fact we—my wife Kleo and I—were *poor* poor. We didn't enjoy it a bit. Poverty does not build good character: that is a myth. But it does make you into a good bookkeeper; you count accurately and you count money, little money, again and again. Before you leave the house to grocery shop you know exactly what you can spend, and you know exactly what you are going to buy, because if you screw up you will not eat the next day and maybe not the day after that.

So anyhow there I am at the Lucky Dog Pet Store on San Pablo

---

*This chapter appeared in slightly different form as the introduction to *The Golden Man*, a collection of Dick's short stories (New York: Berkley, 1980). "Introduction" copyright © 1979 by Philip K. Dick. Reprinted by permission of the author and his agent, Scott Meredith Literary Agency, 845 Third Avenue, New York, NY 10022.

Avenue, in Berkeley, California in the fifties, buying a pound of ground horsemeat. The reason why I'm a freelance writer and living in poverty is (and I'm admitting this for the first time) that I am terrified of Authority Figures like bosses and cops and teachers; I want to be a freelance writer so I can be my own boss. It makes sense. I had quit my job managing a record department at a music store; all night every night I was writing short stories, both science fiction and mainstream . . . and selling the science fiction. I don't really enjoy the taste or texture of horsemeat; it's too sweet . . . but I also do enjoy not having to be behind a counter at exactly nine a.m., wearing a suit and tie and saying, "Yes ma'am, can I help you?" and so forth . . . I enjoyed being thrown out of the University of California at Berkeley because I would not take ROTC—boy, an Authority Figure in a uniform is *the* Authority Figure!—and all of a sudden, as I hand over the 35¢ to the Lucky Dog Pet Store man, I find myself once more facing my personal nemesis. Out of the blue, I am once again confronted by an Authority Figure. There is no escape from your nemesis; I had forgotten that.

The man says, "You're buying this horsemeat and you are eating it yourselves."

He now stands nine feet tall and weighs three hundred pounds. He is glaring down at me. I am, in my mind, five years old again, and I have spilled glue on the floor in kindergarten.

"Yes sir," I admit. I want to tell him, Look: I stay up all night writing science-fiction stories and I'm real poor, but I know things will get better, and I have a wife I love, and a cat named Magnificat, and a little old house I'm buying at the rate of $25 a month payments which is all I can afford—but this man is interested in only one aspect of my desperate (but hopeful) life. I know what he is going to tell me. I have always known. The horsemeat they sell at the Lucky Dog Pet Store is only for animal consumption. But Kleo and I are eating it ourselves, and now we are before the judge; the Great Assize has come; I am caught in another Wrong Act.

I half expect the man to say, "You have a bad attitude."

That was my problem then and it's my problem now: I have a bad attitude. In a nutshell, I fear authority but at the same time I resent it— the authority *and* my own fear—so I rebel. And writing science fiction is a way to rebel. I rebelled against ROTC at U. C. Berkeley and got expelled; in fact was told never to come back. I walked off my job at the record store one day and never came back. Later on I was to oppose the Vietnam War and get my files blown open and my papers gone through and stolen, as was written about in *Rolling Stone*. Everything I do is generated by my bad attitude, from riding the bus to fighting for my country. I even have a bad attitude toward publishers; I am always behind in meeting deadlines (I'm behind in this one, for instance).

Yet, science fiction is a rebellious art form and it needs writers and readers with bad attitudes—an attitude of, "Why?" Or, "How come?" Or, "Who says?" This gets sublimated into such themes as appear in my writing as, "Is the universe real?" Or, "Are we all really human or are some of us just reflex machines?" I have a lot of anger in me. I always have had. Last week my doctor told me that my blood pressure is elevated again and there now seems to be a cardiac complication. I got mad. Death makes me mad. Human and animal suffering makes me mad; whenever one of my cats dies, I curse God and I mean it; I feel fury at him. I'd like to get him here where I could interrogate him, tell him that I think the world is screwed up, that man didn't sin and fall but was pushed—which is bad enough—but was then sold the lie that he is basically sinful, which I know he is not.

I have known all kinds of people (I'm turning fifty in a month and I'm angry about that; I've lived a long time) and those were by and large good people. I model the characters in my novels and stories on them. Now and again one of these people dies, and that makes me mad—really mad, as mad as I can get. "You took my cat," I want to say to God, "and then you took my girlfriend. What are you doing? Listen to me; listen! It's wrong what you're doing."

Basically, I am not serene. I grew up in Berkeley and inherited from it the social consciousness which spread out over this country in the sixties and got rid of Nixon and ended the Vietnam War, plus a lot of other good things, such as the whole civil rights movement. Everyone in Berkeley gets mad at the drop of a hat. I used to get mad at the FBI agents who dropped by to visit with me week after week (Mr. George Smith and Mr. George Scruggs of the Red Squad), and I got mad at friends of mine who were members of the Communist Party; I got thrown out of the only meeting of the U. S. Communist Party I ever attended because I leaped to my feet and vigorously (i.e., angrily) argued against what they were saying.

That was in the early fifties, and now here we are in the very late seventies and I am still mad. Right now I am furious because of my best friend, a girl named Doris, 24 years old. She has cancer. I am in love with someone who could die any time, and it makes fury against God and the world race through me, elevating my blood pressure and stepping up my heartbeat. And so I write. I want to write about people I love, and put them into a fictional world spun out of my own mind, not the world we actually have, because the world we actually have does not meet my standards. Okay, so I should revise my standards, I'm out of step. I should yield to reality. I have *never* yielded to reality. That's what science fiction is all about. If you wish to yield to reality, go read Philip Roth; read the New York literary establishment mainstream best-selling writers. But you are reading science fiction and I am writing it for you. I want to show you, in my writing, what I love (my friends) and what I savagely hate (what happens to them).

I have watched Doris suffer unspeakably, undergo torment in her fight against cancer to a degree that I cannot believe. One time I ran out of the apartment and up to a friend's place, literally ran. My doctor had told me that Doris wouldn't live much longer and I should say good-bye to her and tell her it was because she was dying. I tried to and couldn't, and then I panicked and ran. At my friend's house we sat around and listened to weird records (I'm into weird music in general, both in classical and in rock; it's a comfort). He is a writer, too, a young science-fiction writer named K. W. Jeter—a good one. We just sat there and then I said aloud, really just pondering aloud, "The worst part of it is I'm beginning to lose my sense of humor about cancer." Then I realized what I'd said, and he realized, and we both collapsed into laughter.

So I do get to laugh. Our situation, the human situation, is in the final analysis neither grim nor meaningful, but funny. What else can you call it? The wisest people are the clowns, like Harpo Marx, who would not speak. If I could have anything I want, I would like God to listen to what Harpo was not saying, and understand why Harpo would not talk. Remember, Harpo *could* talk; he just wouldn't. Maybe there was nothing to say; everything has been said. Or maybe, had he spoken, he would have pointed out something too terrible, something we should not be aware of. I don't know. Maybe you can tell me.

Writing is a lonely way of life. You shut yourself up in your study and work and work. For instance, I have had the same agent for twenty-seven years and I've never met him because he is in New York and I'm in California. (I saw him once on TV, on the Tom Snyder "Tomorrow Show," and my agent is one mean dude. He really plays hardball—which an agent is supposed to do.) I've met many other science-fiction writers and become close friends with a number of them. For instance, I've known Harlan Ellison since 1954. Harlan hates my guts. When we were at the Metz Second Annual Science Fiction Festival last year, in France, Harlan tore into me; we were in the bar at the hotel, and all kinds of people, mostly French, were standing around. Harlan shredded me. It was fine; I loved it. It was sort of like a bad acid trip; you just have to kick back and enjoy; there is no alternative.

But I love that little bastard. He is a person who really exists. Likewise van Vogt and Ted Sturgeon and Roger Zelazny and, most of all, Norman Spinrad and Tom Disch, my two main men in the world. The loneliness of the writing per se is offset by the fraternity of writers. Last year a dream of mine of almost forty years was realized: I met Robert Heinlein. It was his writing, and A.E. van Vogt's, which got me interested in science fiction, and I consider Heinlein my spiritual father, even though our political ideologies are totally at variance. Several years ago, when I was ill, Heinlein offered his help, anything he could do, and we had never met; he would phone me to cheer me up and see how I was doing. He wanted to buy me an electric typewriter, God bless him—one of the few true gentlemen in this world. I don't agree with any ideas he puts forth in his writing, but that is neither here nor there. One time when I owed the IRS a lot of money and couldn't raise it, Heinlein loaned the money to me. I think a great deal of him and his wife; I dedicated a book to them in appreciation. Robert Heinlein is a fine-looking man, very impressive and very military in stance; you can tell he has a military background, even to the haircut. He knows I'm a flipped-out freak, and still he helped me and my wife when we were in trouble. That is the best in humanity, there; that is who and what I love.

My friend Doris who has cancer used to be Norman Spinrad's girlfriend. Norman and I have been close for years; we've done a lot of insane things together. Norman and I both get hysterical and start raving. Norman has the worst temper of any living mortal. He knows it. Beethoven was the same way. I now have no temper at all, which is probably why my blood pressure is so high; I can't get any of my anger out of my system. I don't really know—in the final analysis—who I'm mad at. I really envy Norman his ability to get it out of his system. He is an excellent writer and an excellent friend. This is what I get from being a science-fiction writer: not fame and fortune, but good friends. That's what makes it worth it to me. Wives come and girlfriends come and go; we science-fiction writers stay together until we literally die . . . which I may do at any time (probably to my own secret relief). Meanwhile I am writing this article, rereading stories that span a thirty-year period of writing, thinking back, remembering the Lucky Dog Pet Store, my days in Berkeley, my political involvement and how The Man got on my ass because of it . . . I still have a residual fear in me, but I do believe that the reign of police intrigue and terror is over in this country (for a time, anyhow). I now sleep okay. But there was a time when I sat up all night in fear, waiting for the knock on the door. I was finally asked to "come down-town," as they call it, and for hours the police interrogated me. I was even called in by OSI (Air Force Intelligence) and questioned by them; it had to do with terrorist activities in Marin County—not terrorist activities by the authorities this time, but by black ex-cons from San Quentin. It turned out that the house behind mine was owned by a group of them. The police thought we were in league; they kept showing me photos of black guys and asking did I know them? At that point I wouldn't have been able to answer. That was a really scary day for little Phil.

So if you thought writers live a bookish, cloistered life you are wrong, at least in my case. I was even in the street for a couple of years: the dope scene. Parts of that scene were funny and wonderful, and other parts were hideous. I wrote about it in *A Scanner Darkly*, so I won't write about it here. The one good thing about my being in the street was that the people didn't know I was a well-known science-fiction writer—or if they did, they didn't care. They just wanted to know what I had that they could rip off and sell. At the end of the two years everything I owned was gone —literally, including my house. I flew to Canada as Guest of Honor at the Vancouver Science Fiction Convention, lectured at the University of British Columbia, and decided to stay there. The hell with the dope scene! I had temporarily stopped writing; it was a bad time for me. I had fallen in love with several unscrupulous street girls . . . I drove an old Pontiac convertible modified with a four-barrel carburetor and wide tires, and no brakes, and we were always in trouble, always facing problems we couldn't handle. It wasn't until I left Canada and flew down here to Orange County that I got my head together and back to writing. I met a very straight girl and married her, and we had a little baby we called Christopher. He is now five. They left me a couple of years ago. Well, as Vonnegut says, so it goes. What else can you say? It's like the whole of reality: you either laugh or—I guess fold and die.

One thing I've found that I can do that I really enjoy is rereading my own writing, earlier stories and novels especially. It induces mental time travel, the same way certain songs you hear on the radio do (for instance, when I hear Don McLean sing "Vincent," I at once see a girl named Linda wearing a miniskirt and driving her yellow Camaro; we're on our way to an expensive restaurant and I am worrying if I'll be able to pay the bill and Linda is talking about how she is in love with an older science-fiction writer and I imagine—oh vain folly!—that she means me, but it turns out she means Norman Spinrad who I introduced her to); the whole thing returns, an eerie feeling which I'm sure you've experienced. People have told me that everything about me, every facet of my life, psyche, experiences, dreams and fears, are laid out explicitly in my writing, that from the corpus of my work I can be absolutely and precisely inferred. This is true. So when I read my writing, I take a trip through my own head and life, only it is my earlier head and my earlier life. I abreact, as the psychiatrists say. There's the dope theme. There's the philosophical theme, especially the vast epistemological doubts that began when I was briefly attending U.C. Berkeley. Friends who are dead are in my stories and novels. Names of streets! I even put my agent's address in one, as a character's address (Harlan once put his own phone number in a story, which he was to regret later). And of course, in my writing, there is the constant theme of music, love of, preoccupation with, music. Music is the single thread making my life into a coherency.

You see, had I not become a writer I'd be somewhere in the music industry now, almost certainly the record industry. I remember back in the mid sixties when I first heard Linda Ronstadt; she was a guest on Glen Campbell's TV show, and no one had ever heard of her. I went nuts listening to her and looking at her. I had been a buyer in retail records and it had been my job to spot new talent that was hot property, and, seeing and hearing Ronstadt, I knew I was hearing one of the great people in the business; I could see down the pipe of time into the future. Later, when she'd recorded a few records, none of them hits, all of which I faithfully bought, I calculated to the exact *month* when she'd make it big. I even wrote Capitol Records and told them; I said the next record Ronstadt cuts will be the beginning of a career unparalleled in the record industry. Her next record was "Heart Like a Wheel." Capitol didn't answer my letter, but what the hell; I was right, and happy to be right. And that's what I'd be into now, had I not gone into writing science fiction. My fantasy number which I run in my head is that I discover Linda Ronstadt, and am remembered as the scout for Capitol who signed her. I would have wanted that on my gravestone:

HE DISCOVERED LINDA RONSTADT
AND SIGNED HER UP!

My friends are caustically and disdainfully amused by my fantasy life about discovering Ronstadt and Grace Slick and Streisand and so forth. I have a good stereo system (at least my cartridge and speakers are good) and I own a huge record collection, and every night from eleven p.m. to five a.m. I write while wearing my Stax electrostatic top-of-the-line headphones. It's my job and my vice mixed together. You can't hope for better than that: having your job and your sin commingled. There I am, writing away, and into my ears is pouring Bonnie Koloc and no one can hear it but me. The joker is, though, that there's no one but me here anyhow, all the wives and girlfriends having long since left. That's another of the ills of writing; because it is such a solitary occupation, and requires such long-term concentrated attention, it tends to drive your wife or girlfriend away, whoever you're living with. It's probably the most painful price the writer pays. All I have to keep me company are two cats. Like my doper friends (ex-doper friends, since most of them are dead now) my cats don't know I'm a well-known writer, and, as with my doper friends, I prefer it that way.

When I was in France, I had the interesting experience of being famous. I am the best-liked science fiction writer there, best of all in the entire whole complete world! (I tell you that for what it's worth.) I was Guest of Honor at the Metz Festival, which I mentioned, and I delivered a speech which, typically, made no sense whatever. Even the French couldn't understand it, despite a translation. Something goes haywire in my brain when I write speeches; I think I imagine I'm a reincarnation of Zoroaster bringing news of God. So I try to make as few speeches as possible. Call me up, offer me a lot of money to deliver a speech, and I'll give a tacky pretext to get out of doing it; I'll say anything palpably a lie. But it was fantastic (in the sense of not real) to be in France and see all my books in beautiful, expensive editions instead of little paperbacks with what Spinrad calls "peeled eyeball" covers. Owners of bookstores came to shake my hand. The Metz City Council had a dinner and a reception for us writers. Harlan was there, as I mentioned; so was Roger Zelazny and John Brunner and Harry Harrison and Robert Sheckley. I had never met Sheckley before; he is a gentle man. Brunner, like me, has gotten stout. We all had endless meals together; Brunner made sure everyone knew he spoke French. Harry Harrison sang the Fascist national anthem in Italian in a loud voice, which showed what he thought of prestige (Harry is the iconoclast of the known universe). Editors and publishers skulked everywhere, as well as the media. I got interviewed from eight in the morning until three-thirty the next morning; and, as always, I said things which will come back to haunt me. It was the best week of my life. I think that there at Metz I was really happy for the first time—not because I was famous but because there was so much excitement in those people. The French get wildly excited about ordering from a menu; it's like the old political discussions we used to have back in Berkeley, only it's simply food that's involved. Deciding which street to walk up involves ten French people gesticulating and yelling, and then running off in different directions. The French, like myself and Spinrad, see the most improbable possibility in every situation, which is certainly why I am popular there. Take a number of possibilities, and the French and I will select the wildest. So I had come home at last. I could get hysterical among people acculturated to hysteria, people never able to make decisions or execute actions because of the drama in the very process of choosing. That's me: paralyzed by imagination. For me a flat tire on my car is (*a*) The End of the World; and (*b*) An Indication of Monsters (although I forget why).

This is why I love science fiction. I love to read it; I love to write it. The science-fiction writer sees not just possibilities but *wild* possibilities. It's not just "What if—." It's "My God; what if—." In frenzy and hysteria. The Martians are always coming. Mr. Spock is the only one calm. This is why Spock has become a cult god to us; he calms our normal hysteria. He balances the proctivity of science-fiction people to imagine the impossible.

KIRK (*frantically*): Spock, the *Enterprise* is about to blow up!
SPOCK (*calmly*): Negative, Captain; it's merely a faulty fuse.

Spock is always right, even when he's wrong. It's the tone of voice, the supernatural reasonability; this is not a man like us; this is a god. God talks this way; every one of us senses it instinctively. That's why they have Leonard Nimoy narrating pseudo-science TV programs. Nimoy can make anything sound plausible. They can be in search of a lost button or the elephants' graveyard, and Nimoy will calm our doubts and fears. I would like him as a psychotherapist; I would rush in frantically, filled with my usual hysterical fears, and he would banish them.

PHIL (*hysterically*): Leonard, the sky is falling!
NIMOY (*calmly*): Negative, Phil; it's merely a faulty fuse.

And I'd feel okay and my blood pressure would drop and I

could resume work on the novel I'm three years behind on vis-à-vis my deadline.

In reading my stories, you should bear in mind that most were written when science fiction was so looked down upon that it virtually was not there, in the eyes of all America. This was not funny, the derision felt towards science-fiction writers. It made our lives wretched. Even in Berkeley—or especially in Berkeley—people would say, "But are you writing anything serious?" We made no money; few publishers published science fiction (Ace Books was the only regular book publisher of it); and really cruel abuse was inflicted on us. To select science-fiction writing as a career was an act of self-destruction; in fact, most *writers*, let alone other people, could not even conceive of someone considering it. The only non-science-fiction writer who ever treated me with courtesy was Herbert Gold, whom I met at a literary party in San Francisco. He autographed a file card to me this way: "To a colleague, Philip K. Dick." I kept the card until the ink faded and was gone, and I still feel grateful to him for his charity. (Yes, that was what it was, then, to treat a science-fiction writer with courtesy.) To get hold of a copy of my first published novel, *Solar Lottery,* I had to special-order it from the City Lights Bookshop in San Francisco, which specialized in the outré. So in my head I have to collate the experience in 1977 of the mayor of Metz shaking hands with me at an official city function, and the ordeal of the fifties when Kleo and I lived on ninety dollars a month, when we could not even pay the fine on an overdue library book and when I wanted to read a magazine I had to go to the library because I could not afford to buy it, when we were literally living on dog food. But I think you should know this—specifically, in case you are, say, in your twenties and rather poor and perhaps becoming filled with despair, whether you are a science-fiction writer or not, whatever you want to make of your life. There can be a lot of fear, and often it is justified fear. People do starve in America. My financial ordeal did not end in the fifties; as late as the mid-seventies I still could not pay my rent, nor afford to take Christopher to the doctor, nor own a car, nor have a phone. In the month that Christopher and his mother left me I earned nine dollars, and that was just three years ago. Only the kindness of my agent, Scott Meredith, in loaning me money when

I was broke got me through. In 1971 I actually had to beg friends for food. Now look; I don't want sympathy; what I am trying to do is tell you that your crisis, your ordeal, assuming you have one, is not something that is going to be endless, and I want you to know that you will probably survive it through your courage and wits and sheer drive to live. I have seen uneducated street girls survive horrors that beggar description. I have seen the faces of men whose brains had been burned out by drugs, men who still could think enough to be able to realize what happened to them; I watched their clumsy attempts to weather that which cannot be weathered. As in Heine's poem "Atlas," this line: "I carry that which can't be carried." And the next line is, "And in my body my heart would like to break!" But this is not the sole constituent of life, and it is not the sole theme in fiction, mine or anyone else's, except perhaps for the nihilist French existentialists. Kabir, the sixteenth-century Sufi poet, wrote, "If you have not lived through something, it is not true." So live through it; I mean, go all the way to the end. Only then can it be understood, not along the way.

If I had to come forth with an analysis of the anger that lies inside me, which expresses itself in so many sublimations, I would guess that probably what arouses my indignation is seeing the meaningless. That which is disorder, the force of entropy—there is no redemptive value of something that can't be understood, as far as I am concerned. My writing, in toto, is an attempt on my part to take my life and everything I've seen and done, and fashion it into a work which makes sense. I'm not sure I've been successful. First, I cannot falsify what I have seen. I see disorder and sorrow, and so I have to write about it; but I've seen bravery and humor, and so I put that in, too. But what does it all add up to? What is the vast overview which is going to impart sense into the entirety?

What helps for me—if help comes at all—is to find the mustard seed of the funny at the core of the horrible and futile. I've been researching ponderous and solemn theological matters for five years now, for my novel-in-progress, and much of the Wisdom of the World has passed from the printed page and into my brain, there to be processed and secreted in the form of more words: words in, words out, and a brain in the middle wearily trying to determine the meaning of it all. Anyhow, the other night I started on the article on Indian Philosophy in the *Encyclopedia of Philosophy*, an eight-volume learned reference set which I esteem. The time was four a.m.; I was exhausted—I have been working endlessly like this on this novel, doing this kind of research. And there, at the heart of this solemn article, was this:

> The Buddhist idealists used various arguments to show that perception does not yield knowledge of external objects distinct from the percipient . . . The external world supposedly consists of a number of different objects, but they can be known as different only because there are different sorts of experiences "of" them. Yet if the experiences are thus distinguishable, there is no need to hold the superfluous hypothesis of external objects.

In other words, by applying Ockham's razor to the basic epistemological question of "What is reality?" the Buddhist idealists reach the conclusion that belief in an external world is a "superfluous hypothesis"—i.e., it violates the Principle of Parsimony—which is the principle underlying all Western science. Thus the external world is abolished, and we can go about more important business—whatever that might be.

That night I went to bed laughing. I laughed for an hour. I am still laughing. Push philosophy and theology to their ultimate (and Buddhist idealism probably is the ultimate of both) and what do you wind up with? Nothing. Nothing exists (they also proved that the self doesn't exist, either). As I said earlier, there is only one way out: seeing it all as ultimately funny. Kabir, whom I quoted, saw dancing and joy and love as ways out, too; and he wrote about the sound of "the anklets on the feet of an insect as it walks." I would like to hear that sound; perhaps if I could, my anger and fear, and my high blood pressure, would go away.

PHILIP K. DICK

SANTA ANA, CALIFORNIA

NOVEMBER 1978

Notes*

CHAPTER 2: PATRICIA S. WARRICK

1. Bruce Gillespie, "Mad, Mad Worlds: Seven Novels of Philip K. Dick," *SF Commentary* 1 (Jan. 1969). Reprinted in *Philip K. Dick: Electric Shepherd*, ed. Bruce Gillespie (Melbourne, Australia: Norstrilia Press, 1975), p. 16.
2. Darko Suvin, "P.K. Dick's Opus: Artifice as Refuge and World View," *Science-Fiction Studies* 5 (March 1975), p. 10. Reprinted in this volume in slightly revised form.
3. Gillespie, "Mad, Mad Worlds," p. 16.
4. *"Vertex* Interviews Philip K. Dick," *Vertex* (Feb. 1974), p. 97.
5. Gillespie, "Mad, Mad Worlds," p. 11.
6. Dick says that his interest in the Nazis began in World War II when: "I majored in German in high school. Also, I very much loved the music of Beethoven, Schubert, and Wagner, and I wanted to read Goethe and Heine and Schiller in the original German. I collected rare old 78 Wagner records, and even had an excerpt from *Parsifal* conducted by Wagner's son Siegfried Wagner (an experimental electric recording cut in 1927 at Bayreuth)."
7. Philip K. Dick, *The Man in the High Castle* (New York: Putnam, 1962), Chapter 3. Subsequent references will be included in parentheses in the text, with novel abbreviated as *MHC,* followed by chapter number. A similar practice will be used in the other chapters in this volume.

---

*NOTE: There are no notes for Chapters 1, 5, and 11.

8. Angus Taylor in his interesting essay, "The Politics of Space, Time, and Entrophy," *Foundation* 10 (June 1976), p. 40, comments on Dick's treatment of the destructive fascist concept in *The Man in the High Castle*.

9. Jean-Michel Angebert's *The Occult and the Third Reich* (New York: McGraw-Hill, 1975), originally published in France in 1971, suggests that in the Nazis, the German fascination with the ideal moved into an esoteric and demoniacal neo-Pagan faith. The preface to this study claims that "the Nazi cosmology was an intricate synthesis of the historical, philosophic, religious, social, and occult, nurtured by an ancient neo-Paganism whose profile is accurately revealed for the first time in the Cathar heresy of the Middle Ages."

10. Herrlee G. Creel, *What Is Taoism* (Chicago: Univ. of Chicago Press, 1970), p. 5.

11. Lao-tsu, *Tao-te Ching* (New York: Vintage, 1972), p. 1.

12. Philip Rawson and Laszlo Legeza, *Tao* (London: Thames and Hudson, 1973), p. 10.

13. Wing-Tsit Chan, trans., *A Source Book in Chinese Philosophy* (Princeton: Princeton Univ. Press, 1963), p. 177.

14. Fritjof Capra, *The Tao of Physics* (Berkeley, CA.: Shambhala, 1975), pp. 18–19.

15. Wing-Tsit Chan, trans., *A Source Book in Chinese Philosophy*, p. 245.

16. Capra, *The Tao of Physics,* p.160.

17. Joseph Needham, *Science and Civilization in China,* Vol. 2 (Cambridge, Eng.: Cambridge Univ. Press, 1956), pp. 76–77.

18. Chang Chung-yuan, *Tao: A New Way of Thinking* (New York: Harper & Row, 1975), pp. vii–viii.

19. Private letter from Dick dated October 27, 1977.

20. Wing-Tsit Chan, trans., *A Source Book in Chinese Philosophy*, Chapter 13, passim.

21. For further discussion of the *I Ching* see Chapters 3 and 4 of John Blofeld's edition (New York: E. P. Dutton, 1968), and also Chapter 14 of James K. Feibleman's *Understanding Oriental Philosophy* (New York: New American Library, 1967).

22. Suvin, "P. K. Dick's Opus," p. 9. Reprinted in this volume.

23. Brian Aldiss, in "Dick's Maledictory Web: About and Around *Martian Time-Slip,"* *Science-Fiction Studies* 5 (March 1975), pp. 42–47, explores this narrative network in some detail. This article is reprinted elsewhere in this volume.

24. Suvin, "P. K. Dick's Opus," p. 9. Reprinted in this volume.

25. *"Vertex* Interviews Philip K. Dick," p. 37.

26. Creel, *What Is Taoism?* pp. 35–36.

27. Needham, *Science and Civilization in China,* p. 71.

28. Reprinted in *Philip K. Dick: Electric Shepherd,* p. 45.

29. Harlan Ellison, ed., *Dangerous Visions* (Garden City, NY: Doubleday, 1967), p. 215.

30. *Electric Shepherd*, p. 65.
31. Fredric Jameson, "After Armageddon: Character Systems in *Dr. Bloodmoney*," *Science-Fiction Studies* 5 (March 1975), pp. 31–42. This essay discusses Dick's narrative techniques.
32. See Fung Yu-Lan, *A History of Chinese Philosophy*, Vol. 1 (London: George Allen & Unwin, 1937), for an expanded discussion of the superior man. Pages 68–69 and Chapter 14 are helpful.
33. *Electric Shepherd*, p. 32.
34. Ibid.
35. Ibid., p. 45.
36. Dick, "The Android and the Human," in *Electric Shepherd*, p. 55.
37. P. K. Dick, private letter dated Oct. 8, 1977.
38. Angebert's *The Occult and the Third Reich*, pp. 206–11, describes in detail this castle system. Dick would not have had this source available when he wrote *High Castle*, since Angebert's study was not published until later. A private letter from Dick, dated Nov. 18, 1977, does make reference to *The Occult and the Third Reich*.
39. P. K. Dick, private letter dated Oct. 8, 1977.
40. In the Oct. 8 letter, Dick says that "to a certain degree the choice of the title was suggested by rumors of the way Bob Heinlein lives, which is to say, cut off in a virtually fortified castle-like structure with closed-circuit TV to scan whoever shows up at his door."
41. Dick, "The Android and the Human," in *Electric Shepherd*, pp. 62–63.
42. *Electric Shepherd*, p. 45.

CHAPTER 3: N. B. HAYLES

1. Perhaps the most instructive attempt to explain rationally all the details of a Dickian world is Stanislaw Lem's exegesis of *Ubik* in *SF Commentary* 35/36/37 (1972), pp. 7–36. By 1975, however, Lem admits, after repeating his original scheme to explain inconsistencies in the half-lifers' world, that "to make the plot fully consistent along the lines sketched above is impossible." Lem, "Philip K. Dick: A Visionary Among the Charlatans," trans. Robert Abernathy, *Science-Fiction Studies* 5 (March 1975), pp. 58–59.
2. Lao-tzu, *Tao-te Ching*, trans. Ch'u Ta-Kao, quoted in Fritjof Capra, *The Tao of Physics* (New York: Bantam, 1977), p. 95
3. C. G. Jung, *Synchronicity: An Acausal Connecting Principle*, trans. R.F.C. Hull, Bollingen Series (Princeton, NJ: Princeton Univ. Press, 1973).
4. Philip K. Dick, *The Man in the High Castle* (New York: Putnam, 1962), Chapter 1.
5. C. G. Jung, "Foreward," *The I Ching*, trans. Richard Wilhelm, Bollingen Series XIX (Princeton, NJ: Princeton Univ. Press, 1967), p. xxii.
6. Ibid., p. xxiv.

7. Ibid.
8. G. F. Chew, "Bootstrap": A Scientific Idea?" *Science* 161 (May 23, 1968), pp. 762–65; "Hadron Bootstrap: Triumph or Frustration?" *Physics Today* 23 (Oct. 1970), pp. 23–28. Chew's ideas are discussed in Capra, *The Tao of Physics*, pp. 275–92.
9. For a fuller discussion of Dick's use of these techniques, see Darko Suvin, "P. K. Dick's Opus: Artifice as Refuge and World View," *Science-Fiction Studies* 5 (March 1975), pp. 8–22. This essay is reprinted in this volume in a slightly revised form.
10. Personal communication from Keith Rielson (Riverside, CA.), Feb. 24, 1980. Professor Rielson teaches at California State College at Fullerton, where Dick has personal friends and where he appears from time to time for symposia, writing conferences, etc. Professor Rielson's information comes both from Dick's friends and from remarks Dick has made in public appearances.
11. Philip K. Dick, "Man, Android and Machine" in *Science Fiction at Large,* ed. by Peter Nicholls (New York: Harper & Row, 1976), pp. 202–24.
12. Ibid., p. 204.
13. Ibid.
14. In her essay, "The Labyrinthian Process of the Artificial: Dick's Androids and Mechanical Constructs," Patricia Warrick develops this distinction at some length, in *Extrapolation* 20 (1979), pp. 133–53. This essay appears elsewhere in this volume.
15. Dick, "Man, Android and Machine," p. 205.
16. Robert E. Ornstein, *The Nature of Human Consciousness,* cited in "Man, Android and Machine," pp. 211–12.

CHAPTER 4: DARKO SUVIN

1. The chronology of Dick's *publications,* taking into account only his books, looks as follows (S means stories collected or otherwise published in books, with the lead story "The Variable Man" somewhat arbitrarily classifed as a novel; N means novels; the 1967 *Ganymede Takeover,* written in collaboration with Ray Nelson, is counted as one-half of a novel and will not be further considered here):

	1952	1953	1954	1955	1956	1957	1958
S	2	12	13	6	2	—	—
N	—	—	—	1	2	3	—

	1959	1960	1961	1962	1963	1964	1965	1966
S	1	—	—	—	2	2	1	1
N	1	2	—	1	1	5	1	3

	1967	1968	1969	1970	1971	1972	1973	1974
S	1	—	—	—	—	—	—	1
N	2-1/2	1	3	1	—	1	—	1

Though I rather enjoy some of Dick's stories, from "The Preserving Machine" (1953) and "Nanny" (1955) to "Oh, to Be a Blobel!" (1964), they are clearly secondary to his novels, where the themes of the most interesting stories are developed more fully. The novel format allows Dick to develop his peculiar strength of alternate-world creation by means of arresting characters counterposed to each other in cunningly wrought plots. In this chapter I shall concentrate on discussing his novels.

2. Fredric Jameson, "After Armaggedon: Character Systems in *Dr. Bloodmoney,*" *Science-Fiction Studies* 5 (March 1975), pp. 31–42.

3. Stanislaw Lem, "Philip K. Dick: A Visionary Among the Charlatans," trans. Robert Abernathy, *Science-Fiction Studies* 5 (March 1975).

CHAPTER 6: HAZEL PIERCE

1. George Turner, "Philip K. Dick Saying It All Over Again," in *Philip K. Dick: Electric Shepherd*, ed. Bruce Gillispie (Melbourne, Australia: Norstrilia Press, 1975), pp. 47–48. Originally published in *SF Commentary* 17 (Nov. 1970), pp. 33–34.

2. George Turner, "Philip K. Dick by 1975: *Flow My Tears, the Policeman Said,*" in *Philip K. Dick: Electric Shepherd*, p. 94.

3. Robert H. Canary, "Science Fiction as Fictive History," *Extrapolation* 16 (1974), pp. 89ff.

4. Gérard Klein, "Discontent in American Science Fiction," trans. Darko Suvin and Leila Lecorps, *Science-Fiction Studies* 4 (1977), p. 10.

5. Stanislaw Lem, "Philip K. Dick: A Visionary Among the Charlatans," trans. Robert Abernathy, *Science-Fiction Studies* 5 (March 1975), pp. 54–67.

6. Philip K. Dick, "Who Is an SF Writer?" in *Science Fiction: The Academic Awakening*, ed. Willis E. McNelly (Shreveport, LA.: Centenary College of Louisiana, 1974), p. 46. This is a CEA Chapbook published by the College English Association and distributed as a supplement to *The CEA Critic.*

7. Reprinted in *Philip K. Dick: Electric Shepherd*, pp. 49–68.

8. Nicolò Machiavelli, *The Prince*, trans. W. K. Marriott (New York: E. P. Dutton Everyman's Library, 1958), p. 144.

9. In 1964 he published five novels, as well as two short stories.

10. *The Confessions of St. Augustine*, trans. John K. Ryan (New York: Doubleday Image Books, 1960), p. 291.

11. From a letter of comment reprinted in *Philip K. Dick: Electric Shepherd*, p. 45.

12. John Neihardt, *Black Elk Speaks* (Lincoln, NE.: Univ. of Nebraska Press, 1961), p. 43.

CHAPTER 7: MICHAEL BISHOP

1. Brian W. Aldiss, "Dick's Maledictory Web: About and Around *Martian Time-Slip*," *Science-Fiction Studies* 5 (March 1975), pp. 42–47. Reprinted in this volume in slightly different form.
2. Norman Spinrad, "Introduction" to Philip K. Dick's *Dr. Bloodmoney* (Boston: Gregg Press, 1977), pp. v–xiv.
3. Ibid.
4. Stanislaw Lem, "Philip K. Dick: A Visionary Among the Charlatans," trans. Robert Abernathy, *Science-Fiction Studies* 5 (March 1975), pp. 54–67. My principal quarrel with Lem centers on the tone of lofty, Continental condescension he brings to his praise of Dick's work. A telling example of this tone comes through in his contention that Dick's work displays a "tawdriness which is not without a certain charm, being reminiscent of the goods offered at county fairs by primitive craftsmen who are at once clever and naive, possessed of more talent than self-knowledge" (p. 62). Although a novel such as *Ubik* is not without flaws, this appraisal does less to elucidate their origins than to elevate Lem himself to an Olympian pedestal. From this vantage he hurls thunderbolts of rather rarefied psychoanalysis. I suppose I ought to add that, on the whole, I am a devout admirer of Lem's fiction.
5. It's interesting to note that the bomb responsible for plunging Joe Chip and his cohorts into half-life detonates only after it has floated to the ceiling. Compare this happening to Ella Runciter's description of half-life as a kind of disembodied floating.
6. Darko Suvin, "Philip K. Dick's Opus: Artifice as Refuge and World View (Introductory Reflections)," *Science-Fiction Studies* 5 (March 1975), pp. 8–22. Reprinted in this volume in slightly different form.
7. Siegfried Mandel, *Dictionary of Science* (New York: Dell Publishing Co., 1969), p. 159.
8. Dylan Thomas, *Collected Poems* (New York: New Directions, 1957), p. 110.
9. Albert Camus, *The Myth of Sisyphus and Other Essays,* trans. Justin O' Brien (New York: Vintage Books, 1959), pp. 89–90.
10. Peter Fitting, *"Ubik*: The Destruction of Bourgeois SF," *Science-Fiction Studies* 5 (March 1975), pp. 47–54. Reprinted in this volume in slightly different form. As these notes have indicated, the March 1975 issue of *Science-Fiction Studies* is expressly devoted to the work of Philip K. Dick.

CHAPTER 8: PETER FITTING

1. The most recent such study, as of this writing, is David Ketterer's *New Worlds for Old* (1974), which argues science fiction's pedigree by attributing it to a "form of accepted literature" which Ketterer identifies as "apocalyptic" (p. ix): "If more teachers of literature are to be convinced that science fiction is a viable area of study, it must

be demonstrated to them that a novel such as *The Martian Chronicles* can open up to intense critical scrutiny just as *Moby Dick* can'' (p. x). And to accomplish this accreditation, he will employ a "critical strategy [which] involves the comparative, hopefully mutually illuminating consideration of science-fictional and non-science-fictional or 'classic' manifestations of the apocalyptic imagination'' (p. x).

2. See the counterblast of Stanislaw Lem, "Philip K. Dick, czyli fantomatyka mimo woli," in his *Fantastyka i Futurologia* (Krakow, 1973), 1:174–92. A modified version of this study appears in *SF Commentary* 35/36/37 (Sept. 1973) as "Science Fiction: A Hopeless Case—with Exceptions.'' The exception is Dick, of whom Lem writes (pp. 22–23): "The surfaces of his books seem quite coarse and raw to me, connected with the omnipresence of trash. . . . Dick cannot tame trash; rather he lets loose a pandemonium and lets it calm down on its way. His metaphysics often slips in the direction of cheap circus tricks. His prose is threatened by uncontrolled outgrowths, especially when it boils over into a long series of fantastic freaks, and therefore loses all its functions of message.''

3. This discussion is based largely on the critical theories of the Tel Quel group: *Tel Quel: Théorie d'ensemble* (Paris, 1968), in particular the critical and theoretical writings of Roland Barthes, Jacques Derrida, Julia Kristeva, Jean Ricardou, and Philippe Sollers. For a critical appreciation of their work, see Fredric Jameson, *The Prison House of Language* (Princeton, NJ: Princeton Univ. Press, 1972), pp. 172–86.

4. Marx's theory of value is set out in Part I, Vol. I of *Capital*, "Commodities and Money.'' In 1914 Lenin summed that theory up as follows: "A commodity is, in the first place, a thing that satisfies a human want; in the second place, it is a thing that can be exchanged for another thing. The utility of a thing makes it a *use-value*. Exchange value (or simply, value) is first of all the ratio, the proportion, in which a certain number of use-values of one kind can be exchanged for a certain number of use-values of another kind. . . . Their common feature is that they are *products of labor*. . . . The production of commodities is a system of social relations in which the individual producers create diverse products (the social division of labor), and in which all these products are equated to one another in the process of exchange. Consequently, what is common to all commodities is not the concrete labor of a definite branch of production, not labor of one particular kind, but *abstract* human labor—human labor in general. . . . After making a detailed analysis of the twofold character of the labor incorporated in commodities, Marx goes on to analyze the *form of value* and *money*. Here, Marx's main task is to study the *origin of the money form of value, to study the historical process* of the development of exchange, beginning with individual and incidental acts of exchange . . . , passing on to the

universal form of value, in which a number of different commodities are exchanged for one and the same particular commodity, the universal equivalent. As the highest product of the development of exchange and commodity production, money masks, conceals, the social character of all individual labor, the social link between individual producers united by the market" (*Collected Works*, Moscow: 1964, 21:59–61).

The specific parallel between *value* and *meaning* is developed by J.–J. Goux, "Marx et l'inscription du travail" in *Tel Quel*, op. cit.: "The phonic or scriptural materials become simply signs, simple signifiers (of an exterior, transcendent meaning); but their transforming function (as a means of production) and their transformed characteristics (as a product) are denied. The fact that any meaning is but the product of work on and the work of real signs—the result of textual production—is hidden, as is the original use (or merchandise) value of money (gold or silver whose value comes from the work invested in its extraction) in order to reduce it to an arbitrary secondary sign, only a sign" (p. 193).

5. Darko Suvin, "On the Poetics of the Science Fiction Genre," *College English* 34 (1972), p. 375.

6. In Lem's *Solaris* (1961), the narrator describes the theories of the Solarist Grastrom who "set out to demonstrate that the most abstract achievements of science, the most advanced theories and victories of mathematics represented nothing more than a stumbling one- or two-step progression from our rude, prehistoric, anthropomorphic understanding of the universe around us. He pointed out correspondences with the human body—the projection of our senses, the structure of our physical organization, and the physiological limitations of man—in the equations of the theory of relativity, the theorem of magnetic fields and the various unified field theories" (*Solaris*, 11).

The investigation of the metaphysical or ideological presuppositions of science and scientific method as well as the demystification of science's claims for its neutrality and objectivity, have been the subject of a number of interesting and very different studies in recent years, from Boris Eizykman's important *Science Fiction et capitalisme: critique de la position de désir de la science* (Paris, 1974) to Arthur Koestler's *The Sleepwalkers* (1968) and Daniel Greenburg's *The Politics of Pure Science* (1967). For a look at the interrelationships of science, Marxism, and political goals, and the resulting successes and failures in the Soviet Union, see Loren Graham's very valuable *Science and Philosophy in the Soviet Union* (1972).

CHAPTER 9: EUGENE WARREN

1. R. G. Collingwood, *The Idea of Nature* (New York and London: Oxford Univ. Press, 1960), p. 7.

2. Daniel J. Boorstin, *The Image: A Guide to Pseudo-Events* (New York: Harper Colophon Books, 1964).
3. Paul Williams, "The True Stories of Philip K. Dick," *Rolling Stone* (Nov. 6, 1975), p. 45.
4. Philippians 2:6–8.
5. Jacques Ellul, *Propaganda: The Formation of Men's Attitudes,* trans. Konrad Kellen and Jean Lerner (New York: Vintage Books, 1973). p. 173.
6. Ibid., p. 175.
7. Isaiah 29:16, 45:9; Romans 9:21.
8. Gershom Scholem, *Kabbalah* (New York: Quadrangle/The New York Times Book Co., 1974), pp. 128–44.
9. See C. G. Jung, *Psyche and Symbol,* ed. Violet S. De Laszlo (Garden City, NY: Doubleday Anchor Books, 1958), pp. 9ff.
10. Job 38:4–5a.
11. Philip K. Dick, "Afterthoughts by the Author," in *The Best of Philip K. Dick,* ed. John Brunner (New York: Ballantine, 1977), pp. 359–94.
12. Corinthians 15:51–52.
13. Cf. the repeated assertion in *The Penultimate Truth* that "genesis is right, there's a stigma on us."

CHAPTER 10: PATRICIA S. WARRICK

1. Philip K. Dick, "The Preserving Machine," in *The Preserving Machine* (New York: Ace Books, 1968).
2. Other pertinent works not discussed in this chapter are the short novel *The Variable Man,* "The Great C," "Progeny," "War Veteran," and "Service Call."
3. Paul Dickson, in *The Electronic Battlefield* (Bloomington, IN.: Indiana Univ. Press, 1976), describes the conversion of warfare to contests between electronic devices. This process began in the 1960s, a decade after Dick's stories; thus, his imaginary creations have turned out to be amazingly prophetic.
4. Dick, "Afterthoughts by the Author," in *The Best of Philip K. Dick* (New York: Ballantine Books, 1977).
5. Dick, *Vulcan's Hammer* (New York: Ace Books, 1960).
6. Darko Suvin, "P. K. Dick's Opus: Artifice as Refuge and World View," *Science-Fiction Studies* 5 (March 1975), pp. 8–22. Reprinted in slightly different form in this volume.
7. Dick, "Afterthoughts by the Author," *The Best of Philip K. Dick.*
8. Dick, "If There Were No Benny Cemoli," in *The Best of Philip K. Dick.*
9. See Angus Taylor's brief but insightful comments in his *Philip K. Dick and the Umbrella of Light* (Baltimore: T-K Graphics, 1975).
10. Private letter from Philip K. Dick, 1978.
11. Dick, *The Three Stigmata of Palmer Eldritch* (Garden City, NY: Doubleday, 1965.)

12. The source for the Palmer Eldritch face, Dick says in "Man, Android and Machine," is the war-masks of the Attic Greeks. This essay appears in *Science Fiction at Large,* ed. Peter Nicholls (New York: Harper & Row, 1976).
13. Suvin, "P. K. Dick's Opus," p. 14.
14. Fredric Jameson, "After Armageddon: Character Systems in *Dr. Bloodmoney,*" *Science-Fiction Studies* 2 (March 1975), pp. 39–40.
15. Dick, *Dr. Bloodmoney* (New York: Ace Books, 1965), p. 26.
16. I am aware that in using *metaphors* as a verb instead of a noun, I am either violating or augmenting the English language. But because Dick constantly creates images of processes rather than describing states, a verb form seems necessary. I prefer *metaphors* to the more mathematical verb *models.*
17. Dick, "Man, Android and Machine," p. 203.
18. Ibid., p. 204.
19. Dick, "Afterthoughts by the Author," p. 444.
20. Dick's Vancouver speech is published in *Philip K. Dick: Electric Shepherd,* ed. Bruce Gillespie (Melbourne, Australia: Norstrilia Press, 1975), pp. 57, 63.
21. Ibid., p. 86.
22. Dick, "Man, Android and Machine," pp. 211–12.
23. Ibid., p. 206.
24. The story of a man destroyed by his love for a *femme fatale* has been told repeatedly in fairy tales, myths, and poems. One of the best-known treatments is John Keat's poem, "La Belle Dame sans Merci."
25. Dick, "Man, Android and Machine," pp. 214–15.
26. Dick, *We Can Build You* (New York: DAW Books, 1972).
27. The first line of Wyatt's untitled sonnet, which can be found in any collection of Elizabethan poetry, is "Whoso list to hunt, I know where is an hind."
28. Dick, "The Electric Ant," in *The Best of Philip K. Dick.*
29. Dick, "Man, Android and Machine," p. 220.

Philip K. Dick: A Biographical Note

PHILIP KENDRED DICK was born in Chicago, Illinois, on December 16, 1928. He spent most of his youth in California, graduating from Berkeley High School in 1945 and later attending the University of California campus in that city for one year. A man of great intellect, he was largely self-educated. Before becoming a full-time writer, he was employed at a record store and worked as an announcer for a radio program in the San Francisco Bay area. He was married five times, and he had two daughters and a son. For more details concerning his early life, see his stunning essay in this volume.

Dick entered the science-fiction field with a burst of energy, producing a remarkable number of stories in four years beginning with "Beyond Lies the Wub" in the July 1952 issue of *Planet Stories*. His first novel, *Solar Lottery*, appeared in 1955. The publisher of this novel was Ace Books, at that time publishing "Ace Doubles," which consisted of two novels bound back to back. Dick's books for Ace in the 1950s and early 1960s, including such notable works as *The World Jones Made* and *The Simulacra*, were not well known or appreciated during this period, but were later rediscovered by critics and readers.

Perhaps his best-known work was the novel *The Man in the High Castle*, published by Putnam in 1962, an alternate-history story about life in a United States that had lost the Second World War and was occupied by the Germans and the Japanese. The book won the Hugo Award in 1963. Philip Dick also won the John W. Campbell Award for *Flow My Tears, the Policeman Said* (1974; Award 1975).

A prolific and skillful writer, Dick produced more than thirty science-fiction novels in this thirty-year career, including such important works as *Martian Time-Slip* (1964), *Dr. Bloodmoney* and *The Three Stigmata of Palmer Eldritch* (both 1965), *Now Wait for Last Year* (1966), *Do Androids Dream of Electric Sheep?* (1968), *Ubik* (1969), *A Scanner Darkly* (1977), and *Valis* and *The Divine Invasion* (both 1981). His definitive short-story collection is *The Best of Philip K. Dick* (1977).

Do Androids Dream of Electric Sheep? was filmed under the title *Blade Runner* in 1982. Philip K. Dick died tragically of a stroke in March of that year, but he has left a legacy of great works of modern science fiction. Additional unpublished novels are known to exist.

Philip K. Dick: A Bibliography

Compiled by MARSHALL B. TYMN

ALTHOUGH not intended to be definitive, this bibliography is comprehensive in its scope and is representative of Philip K. Dick's total output. All items are listed in alphabetical order. The last section gives a list of important critical articles about his work. I would like to thank Fred Patten for his listing of the magazine fiction in *Philip K. Dick: Electric Shepherd*; this saved me many hours of work with the NESFA indices.

Books and Pamphlets

The Best of Philip K. Dick [story collection]. Ed. John Brunner. New York: Del Rey, 1977 pb.
Blade Runner. See *Do Androids Dream of Electric Sheep?*
The Book of Philip K. Dick [story collection]. New York: DAW, 1973 pb.
Clans of the Alphane Moon [novel]. New York: Ace, 1964 pb.
Confessions of a Crap Artist [novel]. New York: Entwhistle, 1975.
The Cosmic Puppets [novel]. New York: Ace, 1957 pb (bound with *Sargasso of Space* by Andrew North).
Counter-Clock World [novel]. New York: Berkley, 1967 pb; London: Sphere, 1977.
The Crack in Space [novel]. New York: Ace, 1966 pb.
Deus Irae [novel, with Roger Zelazny]. Garden City, NY: Doubleday, 1976; New York: Dell, 1977 pb.
The Divine Invasion [novel]. New York: Timescape Books, 1981 pb.

Do Androids Dream of Electric Sheep? [novel]. Garden City, NY: Doubleday, 1968; New York: Signet, 1969 pb. (Filmed under the title *Blade Runner*.)

Dr. Bloodmoney, or How We Got Along After the Bomb [novel]. New York: Ace, 1965 pb; Boston: Gregg Press, 1977.

Dr. Futurity [novel]. New York: Ace, 1960 pb (bound with *Slavers of Space* by John Brunner).

Eye in the Sky [novel]. New York: Ace, 1957 pb; Boston: Gregg Press, 1979.

Flow My Tears, the Policeman Said [novel]. Garden City, NY: Doubleday, 1974; New York: DAW, 1975 pb.

Galactic Pot-Healer [novel]. New York: Berkley, 1969 pb; Garden City, NY: SFBC, 1970.

The Game-Players of Titan [novel]. New York: Ace, 1963 pb; London: Sphere, 1974.

The Ganymede Takeover [novel, with Ray Nelson]. New York: Ace, 1967 pb.

The Golden Man [story collection]. New York: Berkley, 1980 pb; Garden City, NY: SFBC, 1981.

A Handful of Darkness [story collection]. London: Rich & Cowan, 1955; Panther, 1966 pb.

The Man in the High Castle [novel]. New York: Putnam, 1962; Popular Library, 1964 pb.

The Man Who Japed [novel]. New York: Ace, 1956 pb (bound with *The Space-Born* by E.C. Tubb).

Martian Time-Slip [novel]. New York: Ballantine, 1964 pb; London: New American Library, 1976.

A Maze of Death [novel]. Garden City, NY: Doubleday, 1970; New York: Paperback Library, 1971 pb.

Now Wait for Last Year [novel]. Garden City, NY: Doubleday, 1966; New York: Macfadden, 1968 pb.

Our Friends from Frolix 8 [novel]. New York: Ace, 1970 pb; Garden City, NY: SFBC, 1971.

The Penultimate Truth [novel]. New York: Belmont, 1964 pb; London: Jonathan Cape, 1967.

A Philip K. Dick Omnibus [novel collection]. London: Sidgwick & Jackson, 1970.

The Preserving Machine and Other Stories [story collection]. New York: Ace, 1969 pb; Garden City, NY: SFBC, 1970.

A Scanner Darkly [novel]. Garden City, NY: Doubleday, 1977; New York: Del Rey, 1977 pb.

The Simulacra [novel]. New York: Ace, 1964 pb.

Solar Lottery [novel]. New York: Ace, 1955 pb (bound with *The Big Jump* by Leigh Brackett); London: Rich & Cowan, 1956, heavily edited as *World of Chance*.

The Three Stigmata of Palmer Eldritch [novel]. Garden City, NY: Doubleday, 1965; Garden City, NY: SFBC, 1965.

Time Out of Joint [novel]. Philadelphia: Lippincott, 1959; New York: Belmont 1965 pb.

The Transmigration of Timothy Archer [novel]. New York: Timescape Books, 1982.

Ubik [novel]. Garden City, NY: Doubleday, 1969: New York: Dell, 1970 pb.

The Unteleported Man [novel]. New York: Ace, 1966 pb (bound with *The Mind Monsters* by Howard L. Cory).

Valis [novel]. New York: Bantam, 1981 pb.

The Variable Man and Other Stories [story collection]. New York: Ace, 1957 pb.

Vulcan's Hammer [novel]. New York: Ace, 1960 pb (bound with *The Skynappers* by John Brunner).

We Can Build You [novel]. New York: DAW, 1972 pb.

The World Jones Made [novel]. New York: Ace, 1956 pb (bound with *Agent of the Unknown* by Margaret St. Clair); London: Sidgwick, 1968.

The Zap Gun [novel]. New York: Pyramid, 1967 pb.

Short Fiction

"A. Lincoln, Simulacrum." *Amazing* (Nov. 1969, Jan. 1970).

"Adjustment Team." *Orbit Science Fiction* (Sept.-Oct. 1954).

"The Alien Mind." *F&SF* (Oct. 1981).

"Autofac." *Galaxy* (Nov. 1955). Collected in *The Best of Philip K. Dick.*

"Beyond Lies the Wub." *Planet Stories* (July 1952). Collected in *The Best of Philip K. Dick.*

"Beyond the Door." *Fantastic Universe* (Jan. 1954).

"Breakfast at Twilight." *Amazing* (July 1954). Collected in *The Best of Philip K. Dick.*

"The Builder." *Amazing* (December 1953, Jan. 1954).

"Cantata 140." *F&SF* (July 1964).

"Captive Market." *World of If* (April 1955).

"Chains of Air, Web of Aether." In *Stellar #5*. Ed. Judy-Lynn Del Rey. New York: Ballantine, 1980 pb.

"The Chromium Fence." *Imagination* (July 1955).

"Colony." *Galaxy* (June 1953). Collected in *The Best of Philip K. Dick.*

"The Commuter." *Amazing* (Aug.-Sept. 1953).

"The Cookie Lady." *Fantasy Fiction* (June 1953).

"The Cosmic Poachers." *Imagination* (July 1953).

"The Crawlers." *Imagination* (July 1954).

"The Crystal Gift." *Planet Stories* (Jan. 1954).

"The Days of Perky Pat." *Amazing* (Dec. 1963). Collected in *The Best of Philip K. Dick.*

"The Defenders." *Galaxy* (Jan. 1953).

"The Electric Ant." *F&SF* (Oct. 1969). Collected in *The Best of Philip K. Dick*.

"Exhibit Piece." *Worlds of If* (Aug. 1954).

"The Exit Door Leads In." In *The Best Science Fiction of the Year #9*. Ed. Terry Carr. New York: Ballantine, 1980 pb.

"Expendable." *F&SF* (July 1953). Collected in *The Best of Philip K. Dick*.

"Explorers We." *F&SF* (Jan. 1959).

"The Eyes Have It." *Science Fiction Stories 1* (1953).

"Fair Game." *Worlds of If* (Sept. 1959).

"Faith of Our Fathers." In *Dangerous Visions*. Ed. Harlan Ellison. Garden City, NY: Doubleday, 1967. Collected in *The Best of Philip K. Dick*.

"The Father-thing." *F&SF* (Dec. 1954). Collected in *The Best of Philip K. Dick*.

"Foster, You're Dead." In *Star Science Fiction Stories 3*. Ed. Frederik Pohl. New York: Ballantine, 1955. Collected in *The Best of Philip K. Dick*.

"Frozen Journey." *Playboy* (Dec. 1980).

"A Game of Unchance." *Amazing* (July 1964).

"A Glass of Darkness." *Satellite Science Fiction* (Dec. 1956).

"The Golden Man." *Worlds of If* (April 1954).

"The Great C." *Cosmos* (Sept. 1953).

"The Gun." *Planet Stories* (Sept. 1952).

"The Hanging Stranger." *Science Fiction Adventures* (Dec. 1953).

"Holy Quarrel." *Worlds of Tomorrow* (May 1966).

"The Hood Maker." *Imagination* (June 1955).

"Human Is." *Startling Stories* (Winter 1955). Collected in *The Best of Philip K. Dick*.

"If There Were No Benny Cemoli." *Galaxy* (Dec. 1963). Collected in *The Best of Philip K. Dick*.

"The Impossible Planet." *Imagination* (Oct. 1953).

"Imposter." *Astounding* (June 1953). Collected in *The Best of Philip K. Dick*.

"The Indefatigable Frog." *Fantastic Story Magazine* (July 1953).

"The Infinites." *Planet Stories* (May 1953).

"James P. Crow." *Planet Stories* (May 1954).

"Jon's World." In *Time to Come*. Ed. August Derleth. New York: Farrar, Straus and Giroux, 1954.

"King of the Elves." *Beyond Fantasy Fiction* (Sept. 1953).

"The Last of the Masters." *Orbit Science Fiction* (Nov.-Dec. 1954).

"The Little Black Box." *Worlds of Tomorrow* (Aug. 1964).

"The Little Movement." *F&SF* (Nov. 1952).

"A Little Something for Us Tempunauts." In *Final Stage*. Ed. Edward L. Ferman and Barry N. Malzberg. New York: Charterhouse, 1974. Collected in *The Best of Philip K. Dick*.

"Martians Come in Clouds." *Fantastic Universe* (June-July 1953).

"Meddler." *Future* (Oct. 1954).
"The Minority Report." *Fantastic Universe* (Jan. 1956).
"Misadjustment." *Science Fiction Quarterly* (Feb. 1957).
"The Mold of Yancy." *Worlds of If* (Aug. 1955).
"Mr. Spaceship." *Imagination* (Jan. 1953).
"Nanny." *Startling Stories* (Spring 1955).
"Not by Its Cover." *Famous Science Fiction* (Summer 1968).
"Novelty Act." *Fantastic* (Feb. 1964).
"Null-O." *Worlds of If* (Dec. 1958).
"Of Withered Apples." *Cosmos* (July 1954).
"Oh, to Be a Blobel!" *Galaxy* (Feb. 1964). Collected in *The Best of Philip K. Dick.*
"Out in the Garden." *Fantasy Fiction* (Aug. 1953).
"Pay for the Printer." *Satellite Science Fiction* (Oct. 1956).
"Paycheck." *Imagination* (June 1953). Collected in *The Best of Philip K. Dick.*
"Piper in the Woods." *Imagination* (Feb. 1953).
"Planet for Transients." *Fantastic Universe* (Oct.-Nov. 1953).
"Precious Artifact." *Galaxy* (Oct. 1964).
"The Pre-Persons." *F&SF* (Oct. 1974).
"A Present for Pat." *Startling Stories* (Jan. 1954).
"The Preserving Machine." *F&SF* (June 1953).
"Prize Ship." *Thrilling Wonder Stories* (Winter 1954).
"Progeny." *Worlds of If* (Nov. 1954).
"Project: Earth." *Imagination* (Dec. 1953).
"Prominent Author." *Worlds of If* (May 1954).
"Psi-Man, Heal My Child!" *Imaginative Tales* (Nov. 1955).
"Rautavaara's Case." *Omni* (Oct. 1980).
"Recall Mechanism." *Worlds of If* (July 1959).
"Retreat Syndrome." *Worlds of Tomorrow* (Jan. 1965).
"Return Match." *Galaxy* (Feb. 1967).
"Roog." *F&SF* (Feb. 1963). Collected in *The Best of Philip Dick.*
"Sales Pitch." *Future* (June 1954).
"Second Variety." *Space Science Fiction* (May 1953). Collected in *The Best of Philip K. Dick.*
"Service Call." *Science Fiction Stories* (July 1955). Collected in *The Best of Philip K. Dick.*
"Shell Game." *Galaxy* (Sept. 1954).
"The Short Happy Life of the Brown Oxford." *F&SF* (Jan. 1954).
"The Skull." *Worlds of If* (Sept. 1952).
"Small Town." *Amazing* (May 1954).
"Souvenir." *Fantastic Universe* (Oct. 1954).
"Stand-by." *Amazing* (Oct. 1963).
"Strange Eden." *Imagination* (Dec. 1954).
"A Surface Raid." *Fantastic Universe* (July 1955).
"Survey Team." *Fantastic Universe* (May 1954).
"Time Pawn." *Thrilling Wonder Stories* (Summer 1954).

"To Serve the Master." *Imagination* (Feb. 1956).
"Tony and the Beetles." In *Orbit 2*. Ed. Damon Knight. New York: Putnam, 1967.
"The Trouble with Bubbles." *Worlds of If* (Sept. 1953).
"The Turning Wheel. *Science Fiction Stories 2* (1954).
"The Unreconstructed M." *Science Fiction Stories* (Jan. 1957).
"The Unteleported Man." *Fantastic* (Dec. 1964).
"Upon the Dull Earth." *Beyond Fantasy Fiction 9* (Nov. 1954).
"The Variable Man." *Space Science Fiction* (Sept. 1953).
"Vulcan's Hammer." *Future 29* (1956).
"War Game." *Galaxy* (Dec. 1959).
"War Veteran." *Worlds of If* (March 1955).
"The War with the Fnools." *Galaxy* (Feb. 1969).
"Waterspider." *Worlds of If* (Jan. 1964).
"We Can Remember It For You Wholesale." *F&SF* (April 1966).
"What the Dead Men Say." *Worlds of Tomorrow* (June 1964).
"What'll We Do With Ragland Park?" *Amazing* (Nov. 1963).
"A World of Talent." *Galaxy* (Oct. 1954).
"The World She Wanted." *Science Fiction Quarterly* (May 1953).
"Your Appointment Will Be Yesterday." *Amazing* (Aug. 1966).

Articles and Essays

"The Android and the Human" [speech]. *SF Commentary* (Dec. 1972).
"A Clarification" (on Stanislaw Lem). *Science-Fiction Studies* (March 1978).
"Drugs, Hallucinations, and the Quest for Reality." *Lighthouse* (Nov. 1964).
"Man, Android and Machine." In *Science Fiction at Large*. Ed. Peter Nicholls. London: Gollancz, 1976, and New York: Harper & Row, 1977.
"The Profession of Science Fiction: XVII: The Lucky Dog Pet Store." *Foundation* 17 (1979). Reprinted in slightly different form in this volume as "Now Wait for This Year."
"Who is An SF Writer?" In *Science Fiction: The Academic Awakening*. Ed. Willis E. McNelly. Shreveport, LA.: College English Association, 1974.

General

"Foreword" (unpublished) to *The Preserving Machine*. In *Science-Fiction Studies* (March 1975).
"Anthony Boucher." *F&SF* (Aug. 1968).
"An Open Letter to Joanna Russ." *Vertex* (Oct. 1974).

Selected Criticism

Aldiss, Brian W. "Dick's Maledictory Web: About and Around *Martian Time-Slip.*" *Science-Fiction Studies* 5 (March 1975). Reprinted in slightly different form in this volume.

Bray, Mary Kay. "Mandalic Activism: An Approach to Structure, Theme, and Tone in Four Novels by Philip K. Dick." *Extrapolation* (Summer 1980).

De Prez, Daniel. "An Interview with Philip K. Dick." *Science Fiction Review* (Aug. 1976).

Fitting, Peter. "*Ubik*: The Deconstruction of Bourgeois SF." *Science-Fiction Studies* (March 1975). Reprinted in slightly different form in this volume.

Gillespie, Bruce, ed. *Philip K. Dick: Electric Shepherd.* Melbourne, Australia: Norstrilia Press, 1975.

Green, Terence M. "Philip K. Dick: A Parallax View." *Science Fiction Review* (May 1976).

Hogan, Patrick G., Jr. "Philip K. Dick." In *Twentieth-Century American Science-Fiction Writers.* Ed. David Cowart and Thomas L. Wymer. Detroit: Gale Research, 1981.

Jameson, Fredric. "After Armageddon: Character Systems in *Dr. Bloodmoney.*" *Science-Fiction Studies* (March 1975).

Le Guin, Ursula K. "Science Fiction as Prophesy: Philip K. Dick." *New Republic* (Oct. 30, 1976).

Lem, Stanislaw. "Philip K. Dick: A Visionary Among the Charlatans." Trans. Robert Abernathy. *Science-Fiction Studies* (March 1975).

Levack, Daniel J.H. *PKD: A Philip K. Dick Bibliography.* San Francisco: Underwood/Miller, 1981.

Lupoff, Richard. "The Realities of Philip K. Dick." *Starship* (Summer 1979).

Pagetti, Carlo. "Dick and Meta-SF." *Science-Fiction Studies* (March 1975).

"Philip K. Dick." In *Twentieth-Century Science-Fiction Writers.* Ed. Curtis C. Smith. New York: St. Martin's, 1981.

Platt, Charles. "Philip K. Dick." In *Dream Makers: The Uncommon People Who Write Science Fiction.* New York: Berkley, 1980.

Suvin, Darko. "P. K. Dick's Opus: Artifice as Refuge and World View (Introductory Reflections)." *Science-Fiction Studies* (March 1975). Reprinted in slightly different form in this volume.

Taylor, Angus. *Philip K. Dick & the Umbrella of Light.* Baltimore: T-K Graphics, 1975.

———. "The Politics of Space, Time and Entropy." *Foundation* (June 1976).

Tolley, Michael J. "Beyond the Enigma: Dick's Questors." In *The Stellar Gauge: Essays on Science Fiction Writers.* Ed. Michael J. Tolley and Kirpal Singh. Carlton, Victoria, Australia: Norstrilia Press, 1980.

Warren, F. E. "Philip K. Dick: Exile in Paradox." *Christianity Today* (May 20, 1977).

Warrick, Patricia. "The Encounter of Taoism and Fascism in Philip K. Dick's *The Man in the High Castle.*" *Science-Fiction Studies* (July 1980). Reprinted in this volume in slightly different form.

————. "The Labyrinthian Process of the Artificial: Dick's Androids and Mechanical Constructs." *Extrapolation* (Summer 1979). Reprinted in slightly different form in this volume.

Watson, Ian. "Le Guin's *Lathe of Heaven* and the Role of Dick: The False Reality as Mediator." *Science-Fiction Studies* (March 1975).

Wolk, Anthony. "The Sunstruck Forest: A Guide to the Short Fiction of Philip K. Dick." *Foundation* (Jan. 1980).

Contributors

BRIAN W. ALDISS has won both the Hugo and Nebula Awards for his science fiction, and is widely regarded as one of the major science fiction writers in the world. He is an active member of England's literary scene where he has, among other things, served as a judge on the panel to select the recipient of the Booker Prize, England's most prestigious literary award. As a critic Mr. Aldiss has won the James Blish Award and the 1978 Pilgrim Award from the Science Fiction Research Association. Three of his major critical works are *Science Fiction Art*, *Billion Year Spree: A History of Science Fiction*, and *Hell's Cartographers: Some Personal Histories of Science Fiction Writers*. His many novels include *A Rude Awakening*, *The Dark Light Years*, *Frankenstein Unbound*, and *Hothouse* (or *The Long Afternoon of Earth*).

MICHAEL BISHOP recently received a Nebula Award for "The Quickening," voted the best science fiction novelette of 1981 by the Science Fiction Writers of America. His most recent books are a novel, *No Enemy But Time*, and a collection of short stories, *Blooded on Arachne*. He has published reviews and criticism in several newspapers and journals, including *The Washington Post Book World*, *The Magazine of Fantasy & Science Fiction*, and, in England, *The Libertarian Review* and *Foundation*. Another collection of short stories, *One Winter in Eden*, is scheduled for publication in 1983.

THOMAS M. DISCH is the author of many volumes of fiction and poetry. Among the most recent are his novel *Neighboring Lives* (with co-author Charles Naylor), a collection of stories called *The Man Who Had No Idea*, and two volumes of poetry, *Burn This* and *Orders of the Retina*. His critical writing has appeared in the *Times Literary Supplement* (London), the *New York Times Book Review*, the *Washington Post Book World*, *Foundation*, and *The Magazine of Fantasy & Science Fiction*. He is also Books Editor for *Twilight Zone*.

PETER FITTING is Associate Professor of French at the University of Toronto. A science fiction critic and essayist whose work has appeared in the United States and Canada, Mr. Fitting is presently at work on a major study on Philip K. Dick.

N.B. HAYLES is Assistant Professor in English at Dartmouth College. She has published articles on science fiction, Shakespeare, and various modern authors including D. H. Lawrence and Vladimir Nabokov. She holds degrees in both chemistry and English, and is the author of the forthcoming book *The Cosmic Web: Scientific Models and Literary Strategies in the Twentieth Century*. She is also a contributor to *Ursula K. Le Guin* in the Writers of the 21st Century Series.

BARRY N. MALZBERG received the John W. Campbell Memorial Award for his novel *Beyond Apollo*. Among his many outstanding works are the novels *Guernica Night*, *Chorale*, *Destruction of the Temple*, and a volume of his critical writings, *Engines of the Night*. Some of his finest short fiction is included in *The Best of Barry N. Malzberg*.

HAZEL PIERCE is Professor of English at Kearney State College, Kearney, Nebraska. She has contributed essays to *Isaac Asimov* and *Ray Bradbury* in the Writers of the 21st Century Series as well as to *Survey of Science Fiction Literature* (1979) and *Twentieth Century Science Fiction Writers* (1981). She is the author of *The Starmont Reader's Guide to Philip K. Dick* as well as critical articles on William Blake and Lord Byron.

DARKO SUVIN is a Professor in the English Department at McGill University, Montreal. He is the author of *Metamorphoses of Science Fiction* and *Russian Science Fiction, 1956-1974: A Bibliography* and an editor of *H. G. Wells and Modern Science Fiction* (co-editor Robert M. Philmus). He has also served as one of the editors for the well-known journal *Science-Fiction Studies*, from which he edited two volumes of essays in *Science-Fiction Studies: Selected Articles on Science Fiction, 1973-1975* and *1976-1977* (co-editor R. D. Mullen). His scholarly articles, essays, and critiques have appeared in numerous books and journals in both the United States and Canada.

MARSHALL B. TYMN, an Associate Professor of English at Eastern Michigan University, has taught science fiction there since 1974, and is director of the annual Conference on Teaching Science Fiction, a national workshop. Dr. Tymn is the author of numerous reference works and articles about science fiction and the literature of fantasy. His latest works are *Fantasy Literature: A Core Collection and*

Reference Guide (1979) and *The Science Fiction Reference Book* (1981). His bibliographic articles and essays have appeared in *Extrapolation*, *Choice*, *CEA Critic*, *English Journal*, *Media & Methods*, *Mosaic*, *Handbook of American Popular Culture*, and other sources. Dr. Tymn is editor of a major critical series published by Greenwood Press, *Contributions to the Study of Science Fiction and Fantasy* and is bibliographer for Taplinger's Writers of the 21st Century Series. He is a former officer of the Science Fiction Research Association and an affiliate member of the Science Fiction Writers of America.

EUGENE WARREN is a poet who teaches writing and literature at the University of Missouri, Rolla. His books of poetry include *Christographia*, *Geometries of Light*, and *Fishing at Easter*. He has also published essays in poetics and articles on C. S. Lewis and Charles Williams.

PATRICIA S. WARRICK is a Professor of English at the University of Wisconsin (Fox Valley) and a critic of contemporary literature with a special interest in science fiction. She is the co-editor of a number of anthologies, including *The New Awareness*, *Psychology through Science Fiction*, and *Political Science Fiction*. She has published articles in *Critique*, *Extrapolation*, and *Science-Fiction Studies*, and she is a contributor to *Isaac Asimov* in the Writers of the 21st Century Series. Her most recent book is *The Cybernetic Imagination in Science Fiction*. She is currently completing a book-length study of the fiction of Philip K. Dick.

Index